URBAN ECONOMICS

Edwin S. Mills

Professor of Economics and Public Affairs
Gerald L. Phillippe Professor of Urban Studies
Princeton University

Scott, Foresman and Company
Glenview, Illinois   London

For Susan and Alan

Library of Congress Catalog Card Number: 79–188620

Copyright © 1972 by Scott, Foresman and Company
Glenview, Illinois 60025

Philippines Copyright 1972 by Scott, Foresman and Company

All Rights Reserved

Printed in the United States of America

Regional offices of Scott, Foresman and Company are
located in Dallas, Oakland, N.J., Palo Alto, and
Tucker, Ga.

Preface

The purpose of this book is to introduce the study of urban economics. Part I provides a theoretical and empirical framework for analyzing the urban economy. Part II applies the tools developed in Part I to several of the most urgent urban problems of the 1970s.

In writing the book, I have been conscious of the fact that urban economics is a diffuse subject, and that no one selection of topics or techniques can satisfy everyone. My intention has been to build a unified thread of analysis useful in understanding a variety of urban phenomena and problems. The price paid for this strategy is that several interesting and useful approaches to the subject have been ignored. Thus I have intentionally kept the book short, so that it can be supplemented with reading that presents alternative views. Some possibilities for this reading are listed at the ends of the chapters.

The book is mainly intended as a text in upper-division undergraduate courses in urban economics. It can also be used as a core text with supplementary reading in graduate-level urban economics courses. If desired, it could be used as supplementary reading in intermediate price-theory courses. The central chapters in the book apply to an urban context many of the important topics in the theories of production, consumer behavior, and equilibrium.

Any student who has mastered a modern intermediate price-theory text should be able to follow the argument without difficulty. With help from the instructor, students who have had only a one-year introduction to economics should also be able to use the book. Although high-school algebra and diagrammatic analysis are used freely, calculus is used only in Chapter 5. Most students with at least a semester of calculus can follow that chapter. If necessary, students with no calculus can omit it.

In writing the book, I have of course drawn on the work of many scholars. I trust I have properly acknowledged my debt to them at the appropriate places. I have also learned much from the students to whom I have taught urban economics at Johns Hopkins and Princeton. Most important, Daniel Hamermesh, John Kain, and James Kane read the manuscript in draft and made many valuable suggestions. The index was prepared by Katherine and Paul Courant.

Princeton, N.J.   Edwin S. Mills
January 1972

Contents

PART ONE   THEORETICAL FOUNDATIONS AND HISTORICAL
            TRENDS

Introduction 1

1   The Nature of Urban Areas   7

What is a City? 7
A Note on Statistical Data 10
Why Urban Areas? 11
   Scale Economies 13
   Agglomeration Economies 16
   Comparative Advantage 17
Limits to Urban Size 20
Summary 21
Discussion Questions 22
References and Further Reading 22

2   Urbanization and the Growth of Urban Areas in
    the United States   23

Long-Term Trends 23
Recent Trends 27
   SMSA Population 27
   SMSA Employment 28
   SMSA Manufacturing Employment 31
Summary 35
Discussion Questions 36
References and Further Reading 36

3 Theory of Land Rent and Land Use 37

Some Terms 38
Theory of Land Rent and Land Use 39
  Ricardo's Theory 40
  Neoclassical Theory 43
  Synthesis 46
Welfare and Ethical Aspects of Land Rent 48
Conclusion and Summary 51
Discussion Questions 51
References and Further Reading 52

4 Theoretical Analysis of Urban Structure 53

An Urban Area with a Single Industry 54
  Production Conditions 54
  Market Equilibrium Conditions 57
Households in a Spatial Context 59
  Assumptions of the Model 60
  Implications of the Model 62
Several Urban Sectors 65
  Two Industries 66
  Households and Industries 69
Realistic Urban Location Patterns 72
Some Qualifications 75
Summary 76
Discussion Questions 77
References and Further Reading 77

5 A Simplified Mathematical Model of Urban Structure 78

A Model of Urban Structure 78
  Housing Supply and Demand 79
  Other Equilibrium Conditions 81
Solution of the Model 82
Two Household Sectors 85
Summary 88
Discussion Questions 89
References and Further Reading 89

6   Trends in Suburbanization of Urban Areas in
    the United States   90

    Measures of Suburbanization 91
    Population and Employment Suburbanization since World War II 93
    Density Functions 95
    Prewar Suburbanization 99
    Summary 102
    Discussion Questions 102
    References and Further Reading 102

7   The Size Distributions of Urban Areas   103

    The Nature of Urban Area Size Distributions 104
    The Evidence 105
    Theories of Urban Area Size Distribution 108
        The Beckmann Model 108
        The Simon Model 112
    Evaluation 115
    Summary 116
    Discussion Questions 116
    References and Further Reading 117

8   Welfare Economics and Urban Problems   118

    What is Welfare Economics? 118
    Criteria of Economic Performance 120
    Conditions for Economic Efficiency 121
        A Pure Consumption Model 121
        A Production-Consumption Model 124
        A Variable Input/Output Model 127
    Some Causes of Resource Misallocation 130
        Monopoly and Monopsony 130
        External Economies and Diseconomies 130
        Taxes 133
    Summary 135
    Discussion Questions 136
    References and Further Reading 136

PART TWO   URBAN PROBLEMS AND THE PUBLIC SECTOR

9 The Problem of Poverty   139

The Culture of Poverty 139
Measures of Poverty 140
The Demography of Poverty 142
Race and Poverty 146
Public Policies for Reducing Poverty 149
    Macroeconomic Policies 149
    Income Maintenance Policies 150
Further Possible Steps for Reducing Poverty 155
    Reform of Income Maintenance Policies 155
    Negative Income Taxes 158
Summary 160
Discussion Questions 160 .
References and Further Reading 161

10 Housing, Slums, and Urban Renewal   162

Structure of the Housing Industry 163
    Supply 163
    Demand 164
Trends in Slum Housing 165
Causes of Slums 167
    Demand for Housing 168
    Racial Discrimination 169
    The Neighborhood Effect 173
    Flattening of Rent-Distance Functions 175
    Supply of Housing 176
The Consequences of Slums 178
A Catalog of Public Policies 179
    Real-Estate Taxation 179
    Income Taxes on Owner-Occupied Housing 180
    Accelerated Depreciation 181
    Zoning 182
    Mortgage Guarantees 183
    Building Codes 183
    Rent Control 185
    Public Housing and Rent Supplements 186

Urban Renewal 186
Summary 190
Discussion Questions 190
References and Further Reading 191

11 Urban Transportation   192

Trends in Urban Transportation 194
Pricing and Demand for Urban Transportation 198
   The Abstract-Mode Approach to Transportation Demand 199
   Congestion 201
   Pricing Policy 205
   Cost and Supply of Alternate Urban Transportation Systems 207
   Mass Transit Systems 209
The Effects of Transportation on Urban Structure 212
Transportation and Urban Poverty 214
Summary 215
Discussion Questions 216
References and Further Reading 217

12 Financing Local Government   218

The System of State and Local Governments 219
Trends in State and Local Government Finance 220
   Revenue 221
   Expenditure 222
The Plight of SMSA Central-City Governments 224
Reasons for Financial Problems in State and Local Governments 227
   Rising Relative Prices of Services 227
   Rapidly Rising Demand for Public Services 228
   Regressiveness of State and Local Taxes 228
   Special Problems of Central Cities 229
   Waste and Corruption 229
Some Basic Issues in the Provision of Local Public Services 230
   Scale Economies 230
   Consensus 232
   Spillovers 234
   Income Redistribution 236
Local Government Tax Reforms 237
   Property Taxes 237

Local Income Taxes 239
Summary 241
Discussion Questions 241
References and Further Reading 242

13 Pollution and Environmental Quality   243

What is Pollution? 244
Materials Balance 245
    Ways to Affect Discharges 246
    Form of Discharges 247
    Absorptive Capacity of the Environment 248
Amounts and Effects of Pollutants 249
    Air Pollution 249
    Water Pollution 251
    Solid Waste Pollution 255
Alternative Public Policies 256
    Public Collection and Disposal 257
    Regulation and Enforcement 257
    Subsidization 258
    Charges 259
Current Public Policy: A Brief Summary 260
    Water Pollution 260
    Air Pollution 261
    Solid Waste Pollution 262
Directions for Public Policy 262
Summary 263
Discussion Questions 263
References and Further Reading 264

14 The Public Sector and Urban-Area Prospects   265

Index 269

Introduction

What is urban economics, and why should college students study it in the 1970s? The first part of the question is easy to answer; the second, a bit more difficult.

Urban economics is a specialty within economics in which economists use their tools of analysis to understand and evaluate urban economic phenomena. Like international trade, money and banking, labor economics, or any other specialty, urban economics has developed because economists have found it desirable to undertake specialized theoretical and empirical studies in order to understand certain aspects of economic life. But urban economics is a newer and somewhat more diffuse specialty than most in economics. Although individual economists as well as other social scientists have studied specific urban phenomena and problems for decades, only since World War II have economists begun systematically to apply the tools of their trade to studies of the urban economy. And only since the war has urban economics become a recognized specialty in the discipline. Even today, many more economists specialize in international trade than in urban economics. And there are many times more agricultural economists than urban economists.

When students are asked why they want to study urban economics, they usually answer that they want to gain insight into urban problems such as poverty, slums, pollution, segregation, suburban sprawl, and the financing of local public services. Every newspaper reader knows that urban areas are the scene of most of our urgent and serious domestic problems. The desire to contribute to their solution certainly justifies the study of urban economics, and it is the reason that many economists and other social scientists have become interested in the subject.

But it is only half the story. The study of public and private measures to improve the economic welfare of urban residents is called "normative" urban economics. The term is used in the same sense as in microeconomic theory, where it is contrasted with "positive" economics: the study of economic activity for the purely scientific purpose of understanding certain aspects of the world we live in, without regard to the worthy desire to improve it.

1

Both positive and normative urban economics are included in this book. Part I is positive, and presents a theoretical and empirical framework within which to analyze urban processes and problems. Part II is normative, and the tools of analysis are elaborated and applied to several of the most prominent contemporary urban problems. The terms "normative" and "positive" as applied to economics are discussed at somewhat greater length in Chapter 8.

The point here is that there are important reasons to study urban economics as a branch of positive economics. The most obvious reason is as a foundation for normative urban economics. It is the reason that a medical student studies physiology or anatomy, and that an economics student interested in antitrust policy studies microeconomic theory. It is important to understand how a system works if you want to change it to improve its performance, whether the system is the human body or the urban economy. An urban economy is a complex and interdependent mechanism, and examples are legion in which public policies have been ineffective or harmful in solving problems they were intended to solve. (Several prominent examples are discussed in Part II of this book.) The desirability of almost every public policy depends on qualitative and quantitative effects which can only be predicted on the basis of considerable understanding of the way the system works.

A second reason for the study of positive urban economics is that cities are among man's most important social inventions, and it is a fundamental intellectual challenge to understand their functions and their mechanisms. Some people have lived in cities since before the beginning of recorded history. Since the industrial revolution, urbanization has been massive in industrializing countries and, as Kingsley Davis has shown in his masterful essay, the trend has become worldwide in the twentieth century. Cities have always been focal points in man's struggle to achieve a decent standard of living and a government that will respect his rights and respond to his needs. And they have been the locus of the revolutionary social and economic changes that have occurred during recent centuries. Meadows and Mizruchi have collected together many interesting essays by social scientists on the political, sociological, and economic aspects of urbanization.

What are the economic purposes of cities and why have they grown so rapidly during the last century or two? What are the reasons for the spatial patterns in which markets organize economic activities in urban areas? What effects do improvements in transportation systems have on suburbanization and population density in urban areas? These are important intellectual issues and should be of interest to those who want to understand the world in which they live.

REFERENCES

Kingsley Davis, "The Urbanization of Human Populations," *Scientific American*, Vol. 213, No. 3 (September 1965), 41–53.
Paul Meadows and Ephraim Mizruchi (editors), *Urbanism, Urbanization and Change: Comparative Perspectives*, 1969.

Part One
Theoretical Foundations and Historical Trends

Chapter 1

The Nature
of Urban Areas

"What are cities and why do they exist?" This is certainly the most fundamental question the urban specialist can ask. In a sense, we all know what a city is. Nevertheless, to avoid confusion, it is worthwhile to start with some careful definitions. The reasons for the existence of cities are somewhat more difficult to specify, and are much more controversial. But ideas about the reasons for cities color all thoughts about their functions, their mechanisms, and the causes and cures of their problems.

WHAT IS A CITY?

Like many words, "city" is used in several distinct but related senses. Legally, a city is a political subdivision, usually created by a state, provincial, or national government. It can be distinguished from other subdivisions, such as counties, boroughs, towns, and villages. But the practice in designating cities varies widely from country to country and from state to state in the United States. What is designated a city in one state may be designated a town in another state. More important, the part of an urban area included in a city varies from place to place and from time to time. The city of Boston contains 23 percent of the people in the Boston metropolitan area, whereas the city of Des Moines contains 70 percent of the people in its metropolitan area.

To the political scientist studying local government, the legal definition of the city is of primary importance. But to the urban economist, it is secondary. For the most part, we can assume that the boundaries of the legal city were chosen for historical and political reasons, and are exogenous to the urban economic system. They are of interest mainly because their locations may cause problems in the provision of local public services. These problems are discussed in Chapter 12. (City boundaries are sometimes moved on the basis of the provision of public services. In some arid parts of western United States, provision of municipal water to new developments has been made conditional on their agreeing to annexation by the city.)

Much more fundamental for the urban economist than legal designations is the variability in the density of population and employment from one place to another. At any point in time, a country contains a number of people and a number of square miles of land. The ratio of the two is the country's average population density. In the United States in 1970, the average population density was about sixty per square mile. It is conceivable that every square mile in the country might have about the same number of people. The beginning of urban economics is the observation that population density varies enormously from place to place.

There are about 230 places in the United States where population density reaches extremely high levels relative to the average, and relative to the level a few miles away. In New York City, for example, the 1960 population density was about 24,700 per square mile. Fifty miles away in Sussex County, New Jersey, it was 93. A less dramatic, but instructive, example is Wichita, Kansas. In 1960, its population density was 4900 people per square mile, whereas twenty miles away in Butler County, Kansas, the density was 27. Such places are clearly urban areas. They contain more than half the residents of the nation, and they constitute the popular image of a metropolitan area. But they do not exhaust the list of urban areas. Outside of these 200 or so areas, there are hundreds of small cities and towns, many of which have population densities that exceed those in the surrounding area by a factor of 100 or 200. They are also urban areas.

Thus, an urban area is fundamentally a place with a much higher population density than elsewhere. At least a few such places have existed since the beginning of recorded history, and they are now found in every country in the world. For many purposes, this crude definition is perfectly adequate. But for purposes of data collection and analysis, ambiguities arise, and some warnings are in order.

First, an urban area is a relative concept. A place with a population density of 2000 per square mile might be thought of as an urban area in a country in which the average density is 50, but not in a country in which the average density is 500. In fact, this is rarely a problem because variations in density within countries are large relative to variations in average densities between countries.

Second, although in most cases the data make it clear whether or not a place is an urban area, it is not certain that the same theoretical analysis will apply to all urban areas. Miami, Florida, Washington, D.C., and Flint, Michigan, are all large urban areas, but quite different theories may be required to explain their existence, functions, and structure.

Third, urban areas come in a continuum of sizes, and there is inevitable ambiguity in the designation of small areas. The problem exists, regardless of the definition used. Official statistics necessarily employ an arbitrary population cutoff, of, say, 2500 to 50,000 in presenting data on urban areas.

Fourth, what happens when two formerly separate urban areas grow together? Suppose there are two places, separated by thirty or forty miles, where population densities are much higher than in the surrounding areas. Draw a straight line through the two places, compute population density along the line at two points in time, and suppose the results to be as shown in Figure 1-1. Earlier, they were clearly two separate urban areas. But what about later? Should they be called one or two? The answer is that we cannot decide without additional criteria.

Possible criteria might involve the amount of movement of people and freight between the two centers. For many purposes, it does not matter much whether the two places are designated as one or two urban areas. For almost all purposes, the kinds of relationships that exist between the places are much more important than the numbers game of counting urban areas. Several formerly separate urban areas have in fact grown together in the United States. The New York/northeastern New Jersey and Chicago/Gary areas are the most prominent examples. In such cases, the U.S. Census Bureau wisely presents separate data so that users can put them together as they please.

Figure 1-1

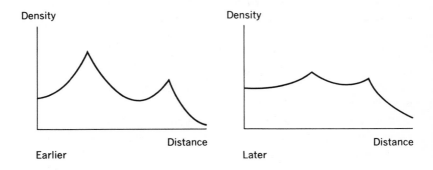

A NOTE ON STATISTICAL DATA

Much of the U.S. data available to the urban economist, and most of that which is comparable among urban areas on a nationwide basis, comes from the U.S. censuses of population and housing, manufactures, and business and government. Every student of urban economics should get to know these data sources. Despite many inadequacies, there are none better in the world.

Most U.S. federal government data pertaining to urban areas are now based on the same set of definitions regarding the area covered. But the federal government distinguishes among several urban concepts, depending on the way data became available and the purposes for which measures are intended.

An *urban place* is any concentration, usually in an incorporated town, borough, or city, of at least 2500 people. But since an urban place is usually defined by political boundaries, it does not correspond to the economist's notion of an urban area. Data pertaining to urban places are therefore of relatively little value to the urban economist. In fact, an urban area usually contains many urban places. In the 1960 U.S. census of population, there were 5445 urban places containing 125 million people, about 70 percent of the country's population of 179 million at that time.

The concept that corresponds to the economist's notion of an urban area is called an *urbanized area* by the federal government. An urbanized area consists of one central city (or sometimes two) of at least 50,000 residents, and the surrounding closely settled area. The urbanized area is thus the physical city, defined without regard for political boundaries. In 1960, the U.S. census identified 213 urbanized areas in the United States. They contained 95 million people, or 53 percent of the country's population.

A geographically more inclusive concept is the *standard metropolitan statistical area*, or SMSA. An SMSA includes one central city (or possibly two) of at least 50,000 residents, and one or more contiguous counties that are metropolitan in character, as determined by the percentage of the labor force that is nonagricultural and by the amount of commuting between the county and the city. Thus SMSAs do not include parts of counties. Although the list of SMSAs is virtually the same as the list of urbanized areas, the SMSAs include nonurbanized parts of contiguous metropolitan counties. Not surprisingly, SMSAs have somewhat greater populations than urbanized areas and much more land. In 1960, 113 million people, 63 percent of the country's population, lived in 212 SMSAs—19 percent more people than in the urbanized areas. But the SMSAs contained 12 times as much land. Some SMSA counties, particularly in the west, are geographically very large, although their nonurbanized parts contain few people. To take the most dramatic example, the San Bernardino SMSA in California extends through the desert to the eastern boundary of the state.

The urbanized area corresponds much more closely to the economist's notion of an urban area than does the SMSA. Why then should an economist be interested in SMSA data? The answer is easy: more data are available for SMSAs than for urbanized areas because some data become available by county and can therefore be put together for SMSAs, but not for urbanized areas.

The largest urban concept recognized by the federal government is the *standard consolidated area*, which consists of several contiguous SMSAs. In 1960, the U.S. census recognized only two standard consolidated areas, New York/northeastern New Jersey and Chicago/northwestern Indiana. The former had a population of 15 million in 1960, and the latter 7 million.

(The term *megalopolis*, sometimes applied to part of the eastern seaboard from Boston to Richmond or from New York to Washington, is unofficial and somewhat unreal. An interesting series of high-altitude aerial photographs of New York/Washington megalopolis was published in *Scientific American* in September 1965. Anyone who doubts that the term is unreal should look at the photographs. With only some exaggeration, it can be said that they give the impression that it is mostly farmland.)

That the urbanized area is a significant urban concept is revealed by overall density data. In 1960, population density for the United States was 51 people per square mile. In urbanized areas it was 3752. By contrast, for SMSAs it was 364.

In this book, the term *urban area* refers generically to places of high population density. The term *city* refers to the legal city. The terms *urban place*, *urbanized area*, and *SMSA* refer to U.S. census concepts.

WHY URBAN AREAS?

If the urban area is to be defined by dramatically high population densities relative to those found elsewhere, the next question is, "Why do we have urban areas?" In fact, there is no single answer. Historians, geographers, sociologists, political scientists, and economists tend to emphasize somewhat different sets of factors in explaining the existence of urban areas. But we can begin with the proposition that urban areas exist because people have found it advantageous to carry on various activities in a spatially concentrated fashion.

Most of the differences of opinion about the reasons for urban areas result from the fact that these activities may be of very different kinds: military activities, religious practice or religion administration, government, and production and distribution of goods and services. At various times in history, many urban areas had defense as their major function. It was simply more economical and effective to defend a large group of people if they were spatially concentrated. The word "was" is used intentionally, because weapons technology in the nuclear age may make it easier to defend a dispersed than a concentrated population. In such urban areas, people commuted out of the city to carry on the predominant economic activity, farming. Some urban areas began as cathedral towns or centers for religion administration. Finally, some cities grew because they were seats of civil government. Washington, D.C., is the most obvious U.S. example.

However, most urban areas do not owe their existence or size to military, religious, or governmental activities. In countries where economic decisions are mainly privately made, the sizes of most urban areas are mainly determined by market forces. Households have found that income and employment opportunities, and prices and availability of consumer goods, are more favorable in urban than in other areas. And business firms have found that returns are higher on investments made in urban than in rural areas.

In the United States, seats of government are almost the only substantial exceptions to the determination of urban sizes by market forces. Washington, D.C., is a clear exception. So, to some extent, are most state capitals. But most state capitals were intentionally located in small towns away from major centers, and many have remained small towns. European national capitals, such as London, Paris, and Rome, are harder to classify. They certainly owe part of their size to their being seats of government. But the opposite is also true. They were made seats of government partly because they were major cities.

People unsympathetic to economic location theory sometimes claim that historical, rather than economic, forces have determined the locations of major urban areas. They claim, for example, that a certain urban area is where it is because some settlers happened to land there first. But this idea assumes that settlers, or other founders, were unresponsive to the advantages and disadvantages of alternative locations. Much more important, the map is dotted with places where settlers happened to settle. Some became major urban centers, but most remained just dots on the map, despite elaborate local plans and efforts to make them metropolitan centers. Those that developed into major centers did so because their economic potential induced thousands of people and institutions to decide to work, live, and produce there. The best assumption is that economic factors affect location decisions to about the same extent that they affect other types of decisions, such as pricing by firms, and demand for goods and services by consumers.

Scale Economies

How do market forces produce urban areas? We have said that most urban areas arise mainly because of the economic advantages of large-scale activities. The economist's term for this phenomenon is "indivisibilities" or, more generally, *scale economies*. General price theory says that a firm's production function displays scale economies if a proportionate change in all inputs leads to a greater proportionate change in output. In this book we say that scale economies exist at any level of output at which, with all input prices constant, long-run average total cost is falling. Thus, diseconomies of scale exist if long-run average cost is rising.

What is the relationship between scale economies and spatial concentration? Economists usually assume that most scale economies are realized within a plant, which is usually a contiguous set of production facilities. But even if they are contiguous, they may be more or less concentrated; that is, the ratios of capital or other inputs to land may be high or low. Which ratio entails lower costs?

In some cases, the mechanism by which proximity provides scale economies is clear. When a raw material is subject to several processing stages, greater spatial separation of the stages entails more movement of the material. This is particularly significant for cases where material must be at extreme temperatures during processing: to move molten steel over substantial distances would be highly impractical. But contiguity does not always seem to be a requirement for scale economies. It is easy to imagine that a firm with two plants might find it economical to provide a service facility, such as maintenance, for its plants and that it might therefore have lower average costs than a firm with one plant that either bought maintenance services from another firm or produced them itself. Although examples are easy to come by, economists have paid to date relatively little attention to the spatial aspects of scale economies.

Scale economies are important for the existence of urban areas. Consider a simple model of a country in which there are no scale economies.

In the economy, a finite, but possibly large, number of different goods is produced. Inputs in each industry are: the outputs of other industries; a single kind of labor, which is mobile; and a single nonproduced natural resource, which is distributed uniformly over the total land area. Suppose that all input and output markets are competitive, and that there are neither economies nor diseconomies of scale at any output in any industry. Thus production can take place on however small a scale is necessary to meet local demands. There is no loss of efficiency, so no need for transportation from one area to another. Each small area would contain the same mix of production and mix of people with different tastes. Markets would be in equilibrium because population and employment densities were uniform, with all demands satisfied by local production.

The density of population or employment in any one area could not be greater than elsewhere: competition for land in a high-density area would drive its land values above the land values in areas of lower density, so households and businesses in the high-density area would move to an area of lower density with lower land costs. They would not be held back by lower production costs or lower prices of consumer goods and services resulting from economies of scale in the high-density area.

The crux of the argument here is that, if there are no scale economies, production can take place on a very small scale near each consuming location, and population and production density—and land values—will thus be uniform.

Now change the model by supposing that one industry (S) does have scale economies, at least at small outputs. Now it pays to concentrate spatially the production of industry S in order to obtain a lower average cost. The amount produced in one place depends on the extent of the scale economies, on the nature of demand, and on transportation cost. In addition, workers in industry S live near their place of work to avoid commuting costs. Moreover, it is advantageous to other industries, without scale economies, to locate nearby if they sell their products to industry S or to its employees. It is also advantageous to their employees to live nearby. Again, the same advantages apply to industries selling to these industries and their employees; and so on.

The process produces a spatial concentration of economic activity that legitimately can be called an urban area. Although the process makes it appear that everything might end up in one urban area, at some size the advantages of proximity are balanced by high transportation and land costs, and the urban area's growth ceases. Thus there will be several urban areas, each of which has one firm of industry S. In addition, the urban areas do not trade with each other, although industry S may export its output to the surrounding countryside. Each urban area satisfies its own demands for the product of industry S and for the products of all industries without scale economies. So there is as yet no specialization among urban areas.

The foregoing description is perhaps the simplest model of urban areas. Such models, based on scale economies, are referred to as *central place theory*, which has had a long and distinguished history. (One of the curiosities of that history is that, until after World War II, most contributions were made by German-speaking writers, and central place theory was practically unknown to English-speaking economists. August Lösch, the father of modern location theory, was the most important contributor. The English translation of his *The Economics of Location*, published in 1954, did a great deal to familiarize English-speaking economists with central place theory.)

Specialization of a kind results from the next step toward reality in our model. Economists tend to think of scale economies mainly in manufacturing. In terms of absolute scale, that may be appropriate. In a manufacturing plant, scale economies may not be exhausted until employment numbers in the hundreds. But scale economies are pervasive in all industries, at least at low levels of output. In retailing, wholesaling, and services, scale economies also exist, but may be exhausted when employment reaches only a dozen or a few dozen. It is not the absolute scale at which economies are exhausted, but rather *the scale relative to market demand* which determines whether there can be one, two, or a hundred firms in an industry. Many service industries, for example, are highly specialized and have extremely low per capita demands. Scale economies may preclude such industries from locating in towns and small cities, or may permit so few firms that they have substantial monopoly power. Thus, large urban areas provide specialized cultural, legal, medical, financial, and other services that are not available in small urban areas.

The fact that scale economies exist in all industries rather than in just one, and that scale economies may be exhausted at different levels of output or employment in different industries, greatly enriches our hypothetical landscape. All industries tend to concentrate spatially to some extent, and transportation costs can be kept low if they concentrate near each other. Thus, it is now possible to account for variety among urban-area sizes, and for a certain kind of trade between large and small urban areas. The small urban areas would contain only those industries whose scale economies were exhausted by the demands of small populations. The larger urban areas would contain, in addition to small-scale industries, industries whose scale economies were exhausted only by the demands of a larger population. The larger urban areas would supply such products not only to their own residents but also to residents of small urban areas. The largest urban areas would contain all types of industries, and would be the only urban areas to contain those industries whose scale economies required the demands of the largest population to exhaust them.

Thus, urban areas of a given size would export to urban areas of smaller sizes, but there would be no other kind of trade between urban areas. In particular, it is not yet possible to account for mutual trade, in which one urban area both exports to and imports from another.

Lösch used a model of the foregoing kind to explain not only a hierarchy of urban area sizes, but also their spatial distribution. (His model is discussed further in Chapter 7.) But his results are based on an assumption that, for our purposes here, is unduly restrictive. He assumed each industry's average cost curve to be L-shaped, which means that no output can be produced below a certain level at any cost and that there are no scale economies at outputs above that level. Such a model cannot accommodate the fact that some goods and services are produced in both large and small urban areas, but are produced on a larger scale or in more competitive industries in large urban areas than they are in small urban areas.

Agglomeration Economies

So far, the existence of urban areas has been explained entirely in terms of scale economies in production, a concept that economists understand relatively well. Urban economists also often refer to the *agglomeration economies* of urban areas. In part they mean by the term the advantages of spatial concentration resulting from scale economies. Of course, it must be remembered that scale economies exist not only in the private sector, but also in mixed public/private or regulated sectors, such as transportation, communication, and public utilities. Also, scale economies may exist in such public-sector activities as education, police protection, water supply, and waste disposal.

Urban economists also use the term "agglomeration economies" to refer to the advantages of spatial concentration that result from the scale of an entire urban area but not from the scale of a particular firm. The most important of such agglomeration economies is statistical in nature, and is an application of the law of large numbers. Sales of outputs and purchases of inputs fluctuate in many firms and industries for random, seasonal, cyclical, and secular reasons. To the extent that fluctuations are imperfectly correlated among employers, an urban area with many employers can provide more nearly full employment of its labor force than can an urban area with few employers. Likewise, a firm with many buyers whose demand fluctuations are uncorrelated will have proportionately less variability in its sales than a firm with few buyers. It can therefore hold smaller inventories and employ smoother production scheduling.

A second agglomeration economy is complementarity in labor supply and in production. Different kinds of labor are to some extent supplied in fixed proportions. Industries with large demands for female workers are attracted to areas where women live because of their husbands' workplaces. Complementarity in production works the same way. If two commodities can be produced more cheaply together than separately, then users of both commodities will be attracted to areas where they are produced.

A third agglomeration economy has been emphasized by Jane Jacobs. Although her argument is complex, it is based on the contention that spatial concentration of large groups of people permits a great deal of personal interaction, which in turn generates new ideas, products, and processes. She views urban areas generally as the progressive and innovative sector of society. Hers is a fascinating theory, which ties in with economists' interest in sources of technical progress, and deserves careful attention.

Other types of agglomeration economies have been claimed, but on analysis they usually turn out to be special cases of the mechanisms just described.

Comparative Advantage

The foregoing analysis has assumed a single, uniformly distributed natural resource. It accounts for large and small urban areas, but for trade between urban areas of only a very special kind. Thus the last step in our argument is to recognize that regions have comparative advantage for certain products because of the variability of available natural resources. Land is a natural resource used in all economic activity, but its qualities vary from place to place. Although fertility is not important for most urban activities, other qualities are, such as drainage, grade, and the nature of subsoil formations.

In addition, most manufacturing and to some extent other industries directly or indirectly process mineral or other natural resources. The uneven occurrence of such resources produces regional comparative advantage for particular products. A characteristic of much technical progress is the increase in the number of processing stages to which natural resources are subjected. Presumably, proximity to the natural resource thereby becomes gradually less important relative to the other locational factors already discussed. At the same time, increases in population and per capita income make greater demands on certain replenishable natural resources, especially air and water. The availability of pure air and water becomes increasingly important as a determinant of comparative advantage.

A final factor in comparative advantage is climate. Temperature and humidity affect heating, air conditioning, and construction costs. Rainfall affects drainage and water supply in complex ways, but is otherwise unimportant. Snowfall makes most kinds of transportation expensive, slow, and dangerous.

There is an obvious similarity between the factors that determine comparative advantages among urban areas and those that determine comparative advantages among countries. International trade specialists usually list differences in technology, costs and skills of labor, and costs and availability of capital, in addition to natural resources, as determinants of international comparative advantage. The state of technology obviously varies much less within than between countries, but recent studies of production functions have shed little light on regional differences in technology within the United States. Labor is obviously much more mobile within than between countries. Within the United States, regional differences in wage rates and education of the labor force have become smaller over time. But they are not negligible, and they have persisted for long periods. Much existing physical capital is nearly immobile—although there are notable exceptions, such as airplanes and trucks. Investment of new capital, however, responds quickly to regional differences in rates of return, and such differences are therefore small in a growing economy. Thus, differences in natural resources are much more important, relative to other factors, in determining the comparative advantage of regions within a country than between countries.

Another factor that determines urban size and location is proximity to economical interurban transportation. The transportation way may be man-made—a road, railroad, or airport, for example—or it may be of natural origin—a navigable river or an ocean port. The argument is that, other things being equal, goods for interurban shipment are produced near interurban transportation terminals to avoid extra unloading and reloading of goods. This argument must be used with care, however. Transportation access is a determinant of urban area size and location if there is some reason for interurban trade, but it is not itself a reason for interurban trade. In the absence of regional comparative advantage or other reasons for such trade, proximity to interurban transportation would be irrelevant. In fact, almost all large U.S. urban areas are located on navigable bodies of water, which is evidence not only that navigable waterways permit profitable interurban trade, but also that regional differences in comparative advantage are strong. Furthermore, if there are international differences in comparative advantage, there will be international trade, providing a reason for urban areas at major ports of entry and exit. Most large urban areas on the eastern seaboard of the United States owe their prominence to international differences in comparative advantage.

Up to this point, the discussion of natural resources has been concerned entirely with their direct effects on comparative advantage in production. But natural resources may also have direct effects on people's welfare, and hence indirect effects on production costs. Suppose that climate, topography, and other natural conditions cause workers and their families to prefer to live in some areas rather than others. Labor costs would be lower in the more desirable areas and production would concentrate there. It has been claimed by Perloff that these "amenity resources" have become increasingly important in recent decades, as industry has become less tied to location near natural resources and therefore more "footloose." Those parts of the country claimed to have the most amenity resources are Florida and the southwest, and these have indeed been among the most rapidly growing parts of the country since World War II. (Amenity resources can also be used to account, in part, for the decentralized structure of the Los Angeles area. The amenity resources there are presumably climate, topography, and proximity to ocean beaches, which more or less pervade the basin and generate no need for an urban area with a high central density. Unfortunately, man-made disamenities, such as smog, also pervade the Los Angeles basin.)

To what extent do regional comparative advantages pertain directly to production, and to what extent indirectly by their effects on people's welfare? The question is answerable but unanswered. It is necessary to know to what extent firms in, for example, the southwest have lower costs than they would have elsewhere because of lower labor costs and to what extent because of lower nonlabor costs. It does not answer the question to point out that the southwest is a high-wage area. Many of the industries that have been attracted there demand highly skilled labor. One of the reasons firms have located there so rapidly is that highly skilled workers are more mobile than others.

In summary, regional comparative advantages occur for a variety of reasons, mostly related to natural resources. Regional comparative advantage accounts for mutual interurban trade, and for the tendency of major urban areas to be located near economical interurban transportation.

LIMITS TO URBAN SIZE

So far the discussion has been entirely in terms of the reasons for the existence of urban areas. Only incidentally have the limits to the size of large urban areas been mentioned. One limit to urban area size is the demand for the products in which it specializes. In other words, an urban area's size may be limited by the demand for its exports. Another limit is the natural resources which provide its comparative advantage; if they run out, the comparative advantage disappears. Even if they are not depleted, their rate of extraction may be subject to diminishing returns. Alternatively, if natural resources are not extracted, they may be subject to congestion. Only so many ships can be handled economically by a port, and only so many people can live comfortably in the Los Angeles basin. Even replenishable resources, such as clean air and water, are limited in supply— as we are now becoming painfully aware—and if they are overused, they deteriorate.

Some writers have speculated that there is also an intrinsic limit to urban size in the sense that the entire urban area is subject to diminishing returns, at least beyond some point. Suppose that an entire urban area is in equilibrium. No change in the location or level of any activity can increase either consumer welfare or producer profits. Suppose that all industries, including local transportation, have constant returns to scale at outputs greater than those that exist. Suppose the output of each industry in the urban area is to be doubled. Can that be done by doubling the urban area's population, and the labor and other inputs in each industry? To double inputs in all industries efficiently requires that floors be added to some buildings and that others be demolished to make way for increased transportation.

Doubling inputs in the transportation system will produce twice as many passenger miles and ton-miles of transportation services. However, transportation per person and per ton of output will be unchanged, since population and output have also doubled. Is this enough transportation for the larger urban area? The land area has doubled, so it seems reasonable to assume that trip lengths must increase. If so, transportation must grow faster than the urban area's population, and real income and output per capita must fall. Whether trip lengths increase, and diminishing returns therefore occur, depends on precisely how spatial arrangements change as urban areas grow. At present, too little is known to decide whether or not increased trip lengths are a significant cause of diminishing returns to urban size. But the theoretical case seems persuasive.

Even if this analysis is correct, it does not imply that traffic congestion is inevitably worse in large than in small urban areas. Some congestion is desirable in large urban areas, as is explained in Chapter 11. In addition, some congestion occurs in large urban areas because, as traffic increases, not enough land is taken from buildings and other uses to handle the increased transportation without increased congestion. But failure to tear down buildings for more transportation is not perfidy on the part of public officials. It results from the fact that, once buildings have been put in place, it is often prohibitively expensive to tear them down. Thus, one reason for downtown congestion is the historical fact that the land-use decisions for structures and transportation were made in an earlier era when transportation needs were slight.

This fact illustrates a common characteristic of urban problems. Important aspects of many problems can be understood by long-run equilibrium analysis. But many are made more serious and complex by the fact that structures have long lives, and thus urban spatial relationships are strongly influenced by decisions made long ago.

SUMMARY

The subject matter of urban economics is the generic city or urban area, not the legal central city. The basic characteristics of urban areas are high population densities, high ratios of other inputs to land, and high land values.

Urban areas exist because of the advantages of scale and proximity in the production and exchange of goods and services. Economies of scale in manufacturing and in other productive activities are the most important reasons for urban areas. Other agglomeration economies result from statistical averaging of fluctuations, from complementarity in labor supply and production, and from the rapid generation and spread of new ideas that can occur in large urban concentrations. The sizes and locations of urban areas are also affected by regional comparative advantage resulting from uneven distribution of natural resources and by the locations of economical interregional transportation networks.

Theoretical analysis suggests that limits to the sizes of urban areas may come from limits on the demands for products produced in an urban area or from decreasing returns to production and transportation activities in an urban area.

DISCUSSION QUESTIONS

1. Suppose there were economies of large-scale production so that larger urban areas exported to smaller urban areas, but not vice versa. How would smaller urban areas pay for their imports? (Hint: use the analogy with triangular exchange in international trade.)
2. Most U.S. population growth since World War II has taken place in urban areas on the edges of the country, which have easy access to ocean shipment. (This includes the ports on the Great Lakes.) How do you explain this?
3. Commuting times and distances are greater in large than in small urban areas. Is this fact evidence of diminishing returns in large urban areas?

REFERENCES AND FURTHER READING

Martin Beckmann, *Location Theory*, 1968, Chapter 5.

Kingsley Davis, "The Urbanization of Human Populations." *Scientific American*, Vol. 213, No. 3 (September 1965), 41–53.

Edgar Hoover, *The Location of Economic Activity*, 1948.

Jane Jacobs, *The Economy of Cities*, 1969.

August Lösch, *The Economics of Location*, 1954.

Paul Meadows and Ephraim Mizouchi (editors), *Urbanism, Urbanization and Change: Comparative Perspectives*, 1969.

Harvey Perloff and others, *Regions, Resources and Economic Growth*, 1960.

Chapter 2

Urbanization and the Growth of Urban Areas in the United States

During a period of less than two hundred years, the United States has been transformed from a predominantly rural and agricultural society into a predominantly urban and industrial society. Next to industrialization, urbanization is perhaps the most prominent and widely discussed trend in U.S. economic history. Many of the nation's dreams and accomplishments, as well as its conflicts and frustrations, must be defined in relation to urbanization. In this chapter, the major components of U.S. urbanization are presented and analyzed. Although causes of major trends are identified along the way, the major goal is to present a historical context for the more analytical chapters that follow.

LONG-TERM TRENDS

The simplest statistical picture of U.S. growth and urbanization is as presented in Table 2-1, which shows the urban and rural population from 1790, the time of the first U.S. census, to 1970. The urban population consists of people living in urban places. In Chapter 1 the urban place is identified as the least useful of all the urban concepts employed by the Census Bureau, but it is the only measure available for the entire period of U.S. history. Its main defect is that it usually constitutes only part of an urban area, and therefore there are many more urban places than urban areas. But the total number of people living in urban places is about the same as the total number of people living in urban areas. The total population of urban places is therefore representative of the total urban population, but not of the population of particular urban areas. It should be remembered that an urban place can contain as few as 2500 people, and urban places therefore include many villages and small towns.

Table 2-1   Urban and Rural Population of the Coterminous United States, 1790–1970 (population figures in millions)

Year	Total Population	Urban Population		Rural Population	
1790	3.9	0.2	5.1%	3.7	94.9%
1800	5.3	0.3	6.1	5.0	93.9
1810	7.2	0.5	7.3	6.7	92.7
1820	9.6	0.7	7.2	8.9	92.8
1830	12.9	1.1	8.8	11.7	91.2
1840	17.1	1.8	10.8	15.2	89.2
1850	23.2	3.5	15.3	19.6	84.7
1860	31.4	6.2	19.8	25.2	80.2
1870	38.6	9.9	25.7	28.7	74.3
1880	50.2	14.1	28.2	36.0	71.8
1890	62.9	22.1	35.1	40.8	64.9
1900	76.0	30.2	39.7	45.8	60.3
1910	92.0	42.0	45.7	50.0	54.3
1920	105.7	54.2	51.2	51.6	48.8
1930	122.8	69.0	56.2	53.8	43.5
1940	131.7	74.4	56.5	57.2	43.5
1950	150.7	89.7	59.6	60.9	40.4
1960	178.5	112.5	63.1	65.9	36.9
1970ᵃ	203.2	149.3	73.5	53.9	26.5

a) Based on new urban place definition; not comparable with earlier data.
Source: United States censuses of population, 1960 and 1970.

Total U.S. population grew from 3.9 million in 1790 to more than 200 million in 1970. In 1790, only 5 percent of the country was urban, even under the inclusive measure represented in Table 2-1. In 1960, 63 percent was urban. Since 1950, the Census Bureau has used a new and somewhat broader definition of urban places, which increases the urban percentages for 1950 and 1960 in Table 2-1 by about 7 percent. Only data based on the new definition are available in the 1970 U.S. census.

The percentage of the U.S. population that is urban has grown steadily from 1790 to 1970, with the exception of an insignificant drop between 1810 and 1820. But the country's total population has grown fast enough that the number of people in rural areas has also grown each decade, even though its percentage of the total population has declined. Indeed, the number of rural residents in 1960 exceeded the country's entire population of each decade up to 1890.

Table 2-1 also suggests the close historical relationship that has existed between urbanization and industrialization. Historians place the beginning of rapid U.S. industrialization at about 1840. Table 2-1 shows that, between 1790 and 1940, the urban percentage of the population increased by about 1.1 percent per decade. Between 1840 and 1930, the increase averaged about 5 percent per decade. Urbanization thus proceeded very rapidly during the second half of the nineteenth century and the early part of the twentieth century, when industrial employment and output were also increasing rapidly.

It is not widely appreciated that urbanization has decelerated since about 1930. Between 1930 and 1960 the percentage of the population that was urban increased by an average of only 1.7 percent per decade. Industrialization has become more widespread, and the growth rate of employment in manufacturing has slackened relative to that in other sectors. Also, despite the massive urbanization of society, rural areas are by no means drained of people. Even under the new urban place definition, more than 50 million people still live in rural areas. Another popular misconception is that most rural people live on farms. In 1960, the United States farm population was only 15 million.

In the early years of U.S. history, the cities and towns in which the urban population lived were very small indeed. In 1790, only 62,000 people lived in the only two cities (New York and Philadelphia) whose populations exceeded 25,000. By 1840, three cities (New York, Baltimore, and New Orleans) had populations in excess of 100,000 but the three cities together contained little more than half a million people. In 1840, Chicago had fewer than 5000 people. During the last half of the nineteenth century, statistics on the growth of cities become difficult to interpret because of the common tendency to annex suburban areas to the central city. For example, between 1890 and 1900, New York City's population increased from 1.5 million to 3.4 million, mostly as a result of the consolidation of the five boroughs that now constitute the city. But by 1900, six cities (New York, Chicago, Philadelphia, Baltimore, St. Louis, and Boston) had at least half a million people each. Los Angeles, now the nation's second largest metropolitan area, had little more than 100,000 people.[1]

Employment data are fragmentary for the early years of the nation's history, but they make it possible to trace the rough outlines of the industrialization process. Table 2-2 shows the number of gainful workers in the total labor force and in agriculture and manufacturing at 20-year intervals from 1820 to 1960, and for 1969.

Table 2-2 shows vividly the transformation of the U.S. economy. Farm workers fell from 71.9 percent of all workers in 1820 to a mere 4.6 percent in 1969. Manufacturing workers increased from 12.2 percent to 25.9 percent during that period. It can be seen that, even in 1820, many

---

1. All statistics are from the U.S. census of population, 1960.

Table 2-2   Industrial   Distribution   of   Gainful   Workers,   1820–1969
(employment figures in thousands)

Year	Total	Agriculture		Manufacturing		Other and Not Allocated	
1820	2,880	2,070	71.9%	350ᵃ	12.2%	460	16.0%
1840	5,420	3,720	68.6	790ᵃ	14.6	910	16.8
1860	10,530	6,210	59.0	1,930ᵃ	18.3	2,390	22.7
1880	17,390	8,610	49.5	3,170	18.2	5,610	32.3
1900	29,070	10,710	36.8	6,340	21.8	12,020	41.3
1920	41,610	11,120	26.7	10,880	26.1	19,610	47.1
1940	45,070	8,449	18.7	10,650	23.7	25,951	57.6
1960	64,639	4,257	6.6	17,513	27.1	42,869	66.3
1969	77,902	3,606	4.6	20,169	25.9	54,127	69.5

a) Includes construction.

Sources: 1820–1920: Historical Statistics of the United States. 1940 and 1960: United States census of population, 1960. 1969: Survey of Current Business, 1970.

rural people were nonfarm. In that year, as seen in Table 2-1, 92.8 percent of the population was rural, but only 71.9 percent of the workers were on farms. Table 2-2 also shows that the period of rapid industrialization was between about 1840 and 1920. During that period, the percentage of all workers employed in manufacturing increased by an average of 1.4 percent per decade. But between 1920 and 1960, the percentage of all workers in manufacturing hardly changed. By 1969, it had fallen below its 1920 value. (The 1940 figure is strongly influenced by the large amount of unemployment that still existed that year. The figures in Table 2-2 are workers, not labor force, and employment fell much more in manufacturing than in agriculture during the depression. Therefore, the 23.7 percent of the workers in manufacturing would be closer to the 1920 and 1969 percentages had there been full employment in 1940.)

Table 2-2 shows the magnitude of the agricultural revolution that has been in progress for fifty years. As a result of mechanization and other changes, productivity per farm worker has risen at an unprecedented rate. Despite the fact that food consumption has increased substantially, agricultural workers have decreased, not only as a percentage of all workers, but also in numbers. Between 1940 and 1969, more than half the jobs in agriculture disappeared. Since the rural population grew, or under the new definition, remained about constant during the period, nonfarm people have become an increasingly large percentage of the rural population.

Food is one of the prime requirements for life, and its provision has the highest priority in every society. A poor society must devote most of its labor force to the production of food, or of exports to get the foreign exchange needed to import food. But in wealthy societies, high productivity in agriculture and low income elasticities of demand for food free much of the labor force to produce other goods and services. In such societies, increases in agricultural productivity come from technical progress both in agriculture and in industry. In the United States, large increases in agricultural productivity have resulted from technical progress in the design and production of farm machinery, which is part of the manufacturing sector. The process of freeing workers from food production has gone much further in the United States than in other countries that produce enough food to nourish their population.

But nonagricultural workers can, and often do, find rural employment in manufacturing and other sectors. Rapid urbanization has occurred because manufacturing and other employers found it increasingly advantageous to locate in large population centers. Since about 1920, there has been a deceleration of growth in manufacturing employment. One consequence has been deceleration in the growth of urban areas. Another consequence has been that urban employment has grown more rapidly in other sectors.

RECENT TRENDS

SMSA Population

Much more accurate and comprehensive data regarding urbanization are available for the period since 1940. Most important has been publication by the Census Bureau of comprehensive demographic and economic data for SMSAs (see Table 2-3). These data confirm the observation that the populations of urban places and SMSAs are of similar magnitude. Some

Table 2-3   Population of United States and SMSAs, 1940–1970 (population figures in millions)

Year	U.S. Population	SMSA Population	SMSA Population as a Percentage of U.S. Population
1940	131.7	72.8	55.3%
1950	150.7	89.3	59.3
1960	178.5	112.9	63.2
1970	203.2	136.3	67.1

Source: U.S. censuses of population, 1960 and 1970.

urban places are outside SMSAs, and some parts of each SMSA are rural. But there is a large overlap between SMSA and urban place populations, and the two nonoverlapping groups approximately cancel out.

The SMSA data provide the best picture of the metropolitan character of the U.S. population. Table 2-3 shows that in 1970 more than two thirds of the U.S. population lived in metropolitan areas. The table also confirms the deceleration in the growth of urban areas shown in Table 2-1. Between 1940 and 1960, the percentage of the population living in SMSAs grew an average of 0.4 percent per year. Between 1960 and 1970, it grew an average of less than 0.3 percent per year. But some of the rapid growth of SMSAs after World War II was undoubtedly the result of postponed growth because of the depression and the war. The deceleration may reflect no more than the end of that process.

SMSA Employment

By and large, SMSAs are labor-market areas. Most people who work in an SMSA also live there, and vice versa. In fact, there is some commuting between SMSAs. Some people live in Gary and work in Chicago, and some people live in Newark and work in New York. It is for this reason that the Census Bureau has defined the two standard consolidated areas. But there is relatively little commuting between SMSAs and nonSMSA areas. The number of workers employed in SMSAs is therefore about the same as the number of workers living in SMSAs. Another way to say this is to say that it is not necessary to distinguish workers by place of employment from workers by place of residence, although the distinction is crucial in discussing data on suburbanization (Chapter 6).

Table 2-4 shows U.S. and SMSA employment in 1950 and 1960 for 12 major industry groups. Aside from those who did not report the industry in which they were employed, the groups are exhaustive; that is, they include all workers. The names of the groups are self-explanatory. Not all SMSAs are included in Table 2-4, unlike Table 2-3. Table 2-4 includes only those SMSAs with at least 250,000 population. They should be called medium and large SMSAs, but for brevity they can be referred to as large SMSAs. In 1960, 100 of the 212 SMSAs were in this category. In 1950, just over one half of all workers lived in large SMSAs; in 1960, it was 56.5 percent. For each year, Table 2-4 shows the percentage distribution of total U.S. and large-SMSA employment by industry; it also shows the percentage of all workers found in large SMSAs in each industry.

Table 2-4   Industry Groups of Employed Persons: United States and SMSAs with at Least 250,000 Population, 1950 and 1960 (employment figures in thousands)

Industry	1950 U.S.		1950 SMSA		1950 Percentage in SMSAs	1960 U.S.		1960 SMSA		1960 Percentage in SMSAs
Agriculture, forestry, fisheries	7,034	12.5%	564	2.0%	8.0%	4,350	6.7%	559	1.5%	12.9%
Mining	931	1.6	216	0.8	23.2	654	1.0	157	0.4	24.0
Construction	3,458	6.1	1,709	6.0	49.4	3,816	5.9	2,028	5.6	53.1
Manufacturing	14,685	26.0	8,676	30.6	59.1	17,513	27.1	10,643	29.1	60.8
Transportation, communication, utilities	4,450	7.9	2,551	9.0	57.3	4,458	6.9	2,764	7.6	62.0
Wholesaling, retailing	10,507	18.6	5,936	20.9	56.5	11,793	18.2	6,862	18.8	58.2
Finance, insurance, real estate	1,920	3.4	1,358	4.8	70.7	2,695	4.2	1,930	5.3	71.6
Business and repair services	1,308	2.3	784	2.8	59.9	1,610	2.5	1,057	2.9	65.7
Personal services	3,465	6.1	1,811	6.4	52.4	3,859	6.0	2,032	5.6	52.7
Entertainment, recreation	493	0.9	355	1.3	72.0	503	0.8	330	0.9	65.6
Professional services	4,826	8.6	2,489	8.8	51.6	7,578	11.7	4,345	11.9	57.3
Public administration	2,514	4.5	1,523	5.4	60.6	3,203	5.0	2,024	5.5	63.2
Not reported	843	1.5	371	1.3	44.0	2,608	4.0	1,788	4.9	68.6
Totals	56,435	100.0	28,351	100.0	50.2	64,639	100.0	36,520	100.0	56.5

Source: United States censuses of population, 1950 and 1960.

It should be possible to prove that, for any industry and either year, the percentage figure in the last column of Table 2-4 will exceed the national total at the bottom of the table if, and only if, the percentage figure in the SMSA column exceeds the percentage figure in the U.S. column. In other words, if the percentage of the workers in a certain industry who are in large SMSAs exceeds that for all workers, then that industry's workers must constitute a larger percent of SMSA than of U.S. workers. For example, in 1950, 59.1 percent of manufacturing workers were in large SMSAs, which exceeds the 50.2 percent of all workers who were in large SMSAs. Therefore, manufacturing workers constitute a larger percentage of large SMSA workers, 30.6 percent, than of U.S. workers, 26.0 percent.

It should be expected that some industries are predominantly located in SMSAs, whereas others are predominantly outside SMSAs. In 1960, the percentage of workers living in large SMSAs ranged from less than 13 percent in agriculture, forestry, and fisheries to more than 71 percent in finance, insurance, and real estate. Although manufacturing is the largest employer in both the United States and in large SMSAs, it is not, contrary to popular belief, among the most highly urbanized industries by the measure in Table 2-4. In 1960, five industries had larger percentages of their employment in large SMSAs than did manufacturing. Manufacturing was only slightly more urbanized than total employment. Not surprisingly, agriculture, forestry, fisheries, and mining are the least urbanized industries, whereas the service industries are most urbanized.

If 1950 is compared with 1960, the percentage of total employment that was in large SMSAs rose from 50.2 to 56.5. Manufacturing employment fell slightly from 30.6 percent of large SMSA employment in 1950 to 29.1 percent in 1960. But the percentage of manufacturing employees who were in SMSAs rose slightly from 59.1 to 60.8. In percentage terms, the largest growth in both United States and large SMSA employment was in service industries: finance, insurance, and real estate; business and repair services; professional services; and public administration. Not only did these industries grow rapidly; they also became increasingly urbanized. We now see clearly what is suggested by the data presented in the foregoing section on "Long-Term Trends": recent growth in SMSA employment has taken place to a considerable extent outside manufacturing.

The major lesson of Table 2-4 is that manufacturing and other industrial jobs (construction, transportation, communications, and utilities) are no longer the major sources of SMSA employment growth. A secondary lesson is that highly urbanized service industries are not only major sources of increased SMSA employment; they are also becoming more urbanized.

The shift of employment toward services parallels the national trend, and results mainly from high-income elasticities of demand and the slow growth of productivity in service industries. One reason for the increased urbanization of service industries is that they find it increasingly advantageous to locate near hospitals, medical laboratories, law courts, financial markets, and other institutions found mainly in large population centers. Another reason is that improved transportation and communication have increased the ability of service industries to provide services to customers whose residences are farther away.

An anomaly in Table 2-4 is that the percentage of agricultural, forestry, and fishery employment in large SMSAs rose from 8.0 percent in 1950 to 12.9 percent in 1960. There was a smaller drop in large-SMSA than in U.S. employment in this sector, probably caused by two factors. First, land prices in the rural parts of SMSAs have probably risen relative to prices of other factors of production in agriculture, so SMSA agriculture became increasingly labor-intensive. Second, there was probably a tendency near population centers to substitute production of labor-intensive agricultural products.

SMSA Manufacturing Employment

Most U.S. federal government industrial statistics are now based on a consistent industrial classification scheme. The data in Table 2-4 are based on what is called the one-digit standard industrial classification (SIC) code. The next level of detail is the two-digit level. For example, all manufacturing industries are in one-digit groups two and three. Two-digit numbers are numbers from 20 to 39 that represent twenty more-detailed manufacturing industries.[2] These two-digit groups are successively divided into three, four, five, and seven-digit groups. For example, food processing is the two-digit manufacturing industry bearing the SIC code 20. Within the food-processing category, there are several three-digit industries, one of which is meat products, given the three-digit code 201. Within the three-digit meat products category, there are several four-digit industries, one of which is slaughterhouses, given the four-digit code 2011. Altogether there are 149 three-digit industries and 427 four-digit industries. There are also five and seven-digit codes. Disclosure rules limit the detail that govern-

---

2. In 1963, a new two-digit industry (ordnance, with SIC code 19) was added, but is not included in data discussed in this section.

ment agencies can publish. In addition, most five and seven-digit data are too detailed for economists' purposes. Only at the two-digit level are comprehensive data available for large SMSAs.

Table 2-5 provides complete two-digit data for the largest industry, manufacturing. The table shows U.S. and large-SMSA employment data for all two-digit manufacturing industries for 1947 and 1963. The set of SMSAs included consists of those with at least 40,000 manufacturing employees. This is roughly, but not quite, the group of SMSAs included in Table 2-4.

It should not be surprising to find that some two-digit manufacturing industries are much more urbanized than others. In 1963, large-SMSA employment ranged from a low of 17.4 percent of total employment in lumber products to a high of 73.8 percent in scientific and technical instru-

Table 2-5 Manufacturing Employment in United States and in Large SMSAs by SIC Industry Groups, 1947 and 1963 (employment data in thousands)

SIC Code	Industry	1947 Employment			1963 Employment		
		U.S.	SMSA	Percentage in SMSAs	U.S.	SMSA	Percentage in SMSAs
20	Food	1442	717	49.7%	1643	858	52.2%
21	Tobacco	112	33	29.5	77	25	32.5
22	Textiles	1233	384	31.1	863	233	27.0
23	Apparel	1082	759	70.1	1280	745	58.2
24	Lumber products	636	87	13.7	563	98	17.4
25	Furniture	322	158	49.1	377	181	48.0
26	Paper	450	207	46.0	588	286	48.6
27	Printing	715	511	71.5	913	658	72.1
28	Chemicals	632	370	58.5	737	411	55.8
29	Petroleum refining	212	133	62.7	153	75	49.0
30	Rubber products	259	176	68.0	415	260	62.7
31	Leather	383	159	41.5	327	143	43.7
32	Stone, clay, glass products	462	203	43.9	574	258	44.9
33	Primary metals	1157	839	72.5	1127	687	61.0
34	Fabricated metals	971	698	71.9	1082	751	69.4
35	Nonelectrical machinery	1545	1018	65.9	1459	958	65.7
36	Electrical machinery	801	614	76.7	1512	1029	68.1
37	Transportation equipment	1182	901	76.2	1601	1170	73.1
38	Instruments	232	184	79.3	305	225	73.8
39	Miscellaneous	464	339	73.1	391	278	71.1
	Totals	14,294	8490	59.4	15,987	9329	58.4

Source: Compiled from data in the U.S. censuses of manufactures, 1947 and 1963.

ments. Generally, the least urbanized industries are those whose major material inputs originate in rural areas. Food processing, tobacco products, textiles, lumber products, furniture, paper, chemicals, petroleum refining, and leather, stone, clay, and glass products fall in this category. The most urbanized industries tend to be those in which material inputs have already gone through several processing stages. For example, the transportation equipment industry buys metal products from the fabricated metals industry. But these metal products have already been processed by another industry, primary metals. Other industries in this category are printing, machinery, and instruments.

It is not surprising that industries which process materials grown in or extracted from the ground tend to locate near the predominantly rural sources of such materials. Industries that mainly process the products of other industries tend to locate near centers of population where they find their customers and their labor force.

Table 2-5 shows a drop of 1 point in the percentage of manufacturing employment in large SMSAs. This finding is in slight contrast with Table 2-4, which shows a slight increase in the percentage of manufacturing employment in large SMSAs. But neither the years nor the SMSAs are exactly the same in the two tables. In any case, the discrepancy is small, and the major point of both tables is that the percentage of manufacturing employment in large urban areas has remained stagnant, while the percentage of population in these areas has grown.

If changes in urbanization among particular two-digit industries are considered, an interesting pattern emerges. The percentage of employment that was in large SMSAs fell in most two-digit industries and in those employing most manufacturing workers. The percentage fell in 13 of the 20 two-digit industries. In 1947, the 13 industries employed 69.5 percent of manufacturing workers in large SMSAs and 70.6 percent of manufacturing workers in the country. Furthermore, the percentage decreases are much larger in the industries that became less urbanized than the percentage increases in industries that became more urbanized.

How can it happen that most manufacturing industries became substantially less urbanized at a time when the total hardly changed? This apparent paradox occurs frequently in economic statistics, and it is worthwhile to explore it. Although it did not happen, it is logically possible for urbanization to decrease in every manufacturing industry at a time when urbanization increases in total manufacturing employment. An example will make the phenomenon transparent. Suppose a country has two industries, A and B, and that SMSA and total employment data for years one and two are as shown in Table 2-6. Between years one and two, urbanization decreased from 80 percent to 71 percent in industry *A* and from 20 percent to 7 percent in industry *B*. Yet urbanization of total employment increased from 50 percent to 52 percent. This peculiar pattern is made possible by a shift in employment in the direction of the more highly urbanized industry. Thus, even though a smaller percentage of workers is in SMSAs in year two than in year one in each industry, the percentage of all workers in SMSAs has increased because the more urbanized industry employs a larger percentage of all workers in year two than in year one.

A less extreme form of the phenomenon is illustrated in Table 2-5. In 1947, 39.7 percent of manufacturing employees were in two-digit industries whose urbanization was below the national average of 59.4 percent. By 1963, these industries employed only 36.0 percent of manufacturing employees. Thus, as in the example of Table 2-6, manufacturing employment has shifted in the direction of relatively urbanized two-digit industries.

So much for the apparent statistical paradox. Why did employment shift toward the more highly urbanized industries? The answer involves a certain amount of guessing, but appears to be as follows: Technical change is pervasive and rapid in manufacturing. An inevitable characteristic of technical progress is an increase in the number of processing stages through which raw materials go before they reach the final consumer. Indeed, the Industrial Revolution itself imposed the factory between the farmer as producer and the farmer as consumer. And current technical change continues to create further stages of raw-material processing. The greater is the number of processing stages, the greater is the number of workers who will be found in those two-digit industries representing later processing stages. But, as has been seen, industries engaged in later stages of processing are precisely those that are not tied to location near predominantly rural sources of raw materials.

Table 2-6   Increasing/Decreasing Urbanization

Industry	Year One			Year Two		
	National Employment	SMSA Employment	Percentage in SMSA	National Employment	SMSA Employment	Percentage in SMSA
A	25	20	80%	35	25	71%
B	25	5	20	15	1	7
Totals	50	25	50	50	26	52

Increased fabrication of raw materials explains the shift of employment toward urbanized two-digit industries, but it does not explain the decreased urbanization of these industries. All two-digit industries have substantial employment outside urban areas. There is no reason to expect that the percentage of employment in large SMSAs will remain constant in any industry. But the particular pattern of decreased urbanization of the most highly urbanized industries calls for study and explanation.

There are of course special explanations for the changes in particular industries. The decreased urbanization of the textile industry is part of the migration of that industry from New England to predominantly rural parts of the south. The movement has been extensively studied. Decreased urbanization in the apparel industry is partly explained by the movement of that industry out of New York City. There are undoubtedly reasons that are peculiar to other industries. But it would be interesting to know the importance of factors that are common to most industries.

The pattern observed in this section is rather slight increases since World War II in the percentages of population, total employment, and manufacturing employment found in large SMSAs. But there is evidence of slowing down in urbanization in all three categories. Nobody knows what future censuses will show, and it is dangerous to project trends based on only two or three decades of evidence.

SUMMARY

In less than two hundred years, the United States has been transformed from a country in which 95 percent of the population was rural to one in which three fourths is urban. In broad outlines, the transformation has been associated with dramatic decreases in agricultural employment and with industrialization of the economy. Since about 1920, urbanization has proceeded steadily, despite constancy in the percentage of the labor force in manufacturing.

There is great variation in the extent of urbanization among industries. Manufacturing is more urbanized than most industries, but less urbanized than many industries in the service sector. Within manufacturing, industries that process raw materials are least urbanized, whereas those that process materials previously processed are more urbanized. Since World War II there has been a shift in manufacturing employment toward more highly urbanized industries, but a decrease in urban location in most manufacturing industries.

DISCUSSION QUESTIONS

1. Do you think that manufacturing industry will be less urbanized by the year 2000 than it is now?
2. What part of the population do you think will live in SMSAs in the year 2000?
3. Do you expect service sectors to urbanize more rapidly than population during the remainder of the century?

REFERENCES AND FURTHER READING

Oscar Handlin and John Burchard (editors), *The Historian and the City*, 1963.

Eric Lampard, "The Evolving System of Cities in the United States: Urbanization and Economic Development," in *Issues in Urban Economics* (1968), edited by Harvey Perloff and Lowdon Wingo.

Harvey Perloff and others, *Regions, Resources and Economic Growth*, 1960.

Chapter 3

Theory of Land Rent and Land Use

It was shown in Chapter 1 that urban areas are places where market activity results in much more intensive use of land than elsewhere. Tall, closely spaced buildings and high population densities are visible representations of high ratios of capital and labor to land in the urban production of goods and services. Thus, most important to the urban economist is a theory of the way markets allocate urban land among alternative uses—although the theory of land rent and allocation does not by itself constitute a theory of urban structure. If it did, David Ricardo, the father of modern rent theory, would have been the world's first urban economist. Rather, the theory of land rent and allocation can be used to analyze land use in any context, urban or rural. To provide insight into urban phenomena, however, the theory must be placed in a specifically urban context. That is the task of Chapters 4 and 5. This chapter concentrates on an understanding of the basic theory.

The theory of market allocation of land is a part of microeconomic theory concerned with the allocation and pricing of factors of production.[1] However, modern price theory textbooks hardly mention land rent, except in an agricultural context. This chapter therefore concentrates on the way land fits into the general framework of production theory, and on some special characteristics which distinguish land from other factors of production, and which make rent theory so intriguing.

Just as the wage rate is the price of labor services, so land rent is the price of land services. And just as a large part of labor-market theory is concerned with wage-rate determination, so much of land-market theory is concerned with land-rent determination. Prices are, of course, the mechanism by which uses of inputs and outputs are rationed in a market economy. It is no less true of land than of any other commodity or service. But

---

1. For review, Stigler offers a good discussion of production theory.

the special character of land rent as the price of a nonproduced factor of production has stimulated some of the most interesting scientific and political controversy in history. (Some comments on this controversy are made later in this chapter.)

SOME TERMS

It is necessary here to define carefully several closely related terms. *Land value* and *land rent* are related in the way that the price of any asset is related to the price of the service that it yields. Stocks of physical assets are valuable because they yield flows of services during considerable periods of time. Land rent is the price of the services yielded by land during a specific time period, such as a year. Land rent therefore has the dimension of the time period as well as of the unit in which land is measured. For example, land rent might be quoted as dollars per acre per year. The price of an asset is the present value, or capitalized value, of the rent the asset will yield during its useful life. For example, if a tract of land will yield a rent of R dollars per year forever, and if the appropriate interest rate to use in discounting is $100i$ percent per year, the price (P) of the land is

$$P = R/i \qquad (3\text{-}1)$$

An asset price has the dimension only of the unit in which the asset is measured (e.g., dollars per acre).

Man-made assets, such as buildings and machinery, inevitably deteriorate with time and use, and eventually cease to be valuable. Land used —or rather abused—in agriculture may also deteriorate. But most urban uses of land do not cause physical deterioration, and the land therefore yields a perpetual stream of services, as assumed in Equation 3-1.

The second set of terms to define are *unimproved* and *improved land values*. Most urban uses of land require that structures be built on the land. In other words, the urban production of goods and services normally requires both land and capital, among other factors of production. Unimproved land value means the price of the land with no structure on it, whereas improved land value means the price of the land and the structure on it. Since structures are usually expensive to move or demolish, it is often difficult to estimate the unimproved value of land that has a structure on it. Furthermore, in many urban areas very little unimproved land appears on the market, especially near city centers. There are therefore few transactions from which to estimate unimproved land values, which are among the scarcest and poorest of the data needed by urban economists.

There are also many ways of improving land in addition to building on it, if the term "improving" is taken literally. It can be drained and graded, provided with pipes for water supply and waste disposal, and planted with or cleared of trees. These are simply different kinds of capital investment in land, and like buildings, they can affect its market value. Some of the ambiguity of unimproved-land-value data results from the fact that various amounts of nonbuilding capital may have been invested in it.

Although nonstructural land improvements present real problems in applied research, as well as in real-estate tax assessment, they are not important in this book. The terms *land value* and *land rent* refer here to the prices and rents of unimproved land, that is, before any capital has been invested in it. *Improved land values* include the value of buildings and other capital invested in the land. Much of the analysis here is concerned with equilibrium situations in which land values and land rents are proportionate to each other, as in Equation 3-1.

THEORY OF LAND RENT AND LAND USE

In this section and throughout much of the book it is assumed that factor and product markets are perfectly competitive, that is, that each market participant can buy and sell unlimited quantities without affecting the price set by the market. There are two compelling reasons for this assumption. First, most urban phenomena and problems can be best understood and analyzed within the competitive framework. Although monopoly and oligopoly may worsen some urban problems, they are not important explanations of most urban phenomena. Racial discrimination, poverty, poor housing, congestion, and pollution would hardly be less serious problems in competitive than in noncompetitive markets. (The analysis to support this claim is presented in Part II.) Second, spatial models, such as those used to analyze urban markets, are usually much simpler to formulate and analyze if perfect competition is assumed than if other market structures are considered. There are basic difficulties (discussed later on) which economists have not yet solved in formulating spatial relationships in noncompetitive markets.

It is also assumed, as it is in other branches of economic theory, that people own productive land and capital assets because of the return they yield. Owners will therefore seek the use of the asset that yields the greatest return available.

These are powerful assumptions and they yield many insights. Among them is the statement that, in equilibrium, all equally productive units of land will command the same price—which does not imply that all urban land will have the same price or rent. Productivity may vary greatly from one unit of land to another within an urban area.

The theory of land rent was one of the most hotly debated topics in economics during the nineteenth century. Fuel for the fires of debate was provided by the fact that economic theory was closely related to urgent social issues regarding the distribution of wealth and income. In one view of the nature of land rent, held by Henry George and others, all the fruits of economic progress would go to landlords who produced nothing, whereas workers would be able to earn no more than a subsistence wage. But although social relevance caused the rhetorical fires to burn brightly, they were kept alight by difficult theoretical problems, which required many decades to resolve.

Two ideas dominated the nineteenth century debate over land rents. The first, which was first stated clearly by Ricardo in 1817, is that land rent is a residual, equal to the excess of revenues from the sale of goods produced on the land over remunerations to nonland factors used in production. The second, which was formulated by Wicksteed and other marginal-productivity theorists writing late in the century, is that land rent, like the remuneration for any other factor of production, is determined by the value of its marginal product.

Ricardo's Theory

Ricardo's theory can be formulated as follows: Suppose that lands of varying fertility are available to produce the food needed by a country's population. For simplicity, suppose that all land can be placed in one of several fertility classes, 1, 2, . . . m, so that all land in a given class has the same fertility, and classes with lower numbers designate more fertile land. Suppose also that a certain amount of labor, and perhaps other nonland inputs, is required per acre of land regardless of its fertility. Finally, suppose that land available for agriculture has no other use.

If all the food needed can be produced on land in fertility class 1, then no other land will be used, since that land requires the least land and nonland input relative to output. If more land is needed, that in fertility class 2 will be brought into production, and so on. Suppose that at some stage, food production requires all the land in the first four fertility classes and some of that in the fifth. Then the price of food will just cover nonland production costs on class 5 land, leaving a rent of zero for class 5 land. If any owner of class 5 land charged a positive rent, the farmer could rent unused class 5 land at a lower rent. Furthermore, the rent of class 4 land will equal the price of food times the excess productivity of class 4 over class 5 land. At any lower rent, farmers would make higher incomes on class 4 than on class 5 land. Farmers on class 5 land would therefore offer owners of class 4 land a higher rent. Following the argument, land rent in any fertility class will be proportionate to the excess of the productivity of land in the class over that of the least productive land in use.

Now suppose there is an increase in the demand for food caused by population growth, and that land in fertility class 6 is brought into production. Suppose also, as Ricardo did, that the increased population provides a proportionate increase in the supply of farmers. Then the rent of land in classes 1 to 5 will rise, and farmers will be no better off. Indeed, Ricardo believed (following Malthus) that population would grow until such infertile land was needed in production that no more people could be supported at a subsistence income. (This is why economics was termed the "dismal science.") For the purpose of this book, Ricardo's dubious iron law of subsistence wages is not needed, but only the notion that wages and other nonland factor prices are set in competitive markets. In this case, Ricardo's theory is that land rent will equal the residual revenue after remunerating competitively priced nonland factors, and will be proportionate to the excess of fertility over that of the least fertile land in use.

However, whatever causes high land values in large urban areas, it is clearly not fertility. We can make Ricardo's theory much more relevant to urban economics if we substitute distance for fertility. Suppose, to take the specific assumptions made by von Thünen, a contemporary of Ricardo's, that a city is surrounded in all directions by a plain of uniform fertility, and that the city's food is grown on the plain. Parts of the plain not used for the city's food production have no other use. Retain Ricardo's assumption of constant amounts of nonland inputs per acre, and the assumption of competitive determination of nonland factor prices. Suppose food can be shipped straight to the city from any point on the plain, and that transportation cost per ton-mile is a constant. Then the furthest land from the city brought into production commands a rent of zero, and land rent increases linearly toward the city. The slope of the linear relation is proportionate to the ton-mile transportation cost. All the land a given distance from the city commands the same rent.

The land rent function is shown in Figure 3-1. In the figure, u is distance from the city, and $R(u)$ is the land rent per acre u miles from the city.

Figure 3-1

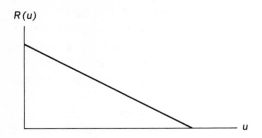

It is worthwhile to show this algebraically. Suppose that p is the price per ton of food in the city, A is the tons of food produced per acre per year, w is the cost of nonland inputs required per acre per year, and t is the ton-mile cost of food shipment. Then land rent per acre at a distance of u miles from the city is the value $R(u)$ that absorbs the excess of revenue over nonland costs. Define the farmer's profit per acre, $\pi(u)$, as the revenue left over from the sale of the acre's output after paying land and nonland production costs and the cost of transporting the output to the city. Then $R(u)$ is the value that makes $\pi(u)$ zero at each u, that is,

$$\pi(u) = pA - w - R(u) - tAu = 0$$

or

$$R(u) = (pA - w) - tAu \qquad (3\text{-}2)$$

Equation 3-2 is the equation of the straight line shown in Figure 3-1.

If land rent at any distance u were different from that indicated by Equation 3-2, some farmers would have reason to move. If at some u, land rent were less than indicated by Equation 3-2, farmers elsewhere would try to move there to obtain positive profits, and would thus bid up land rent there. If land rent were more than $R(u)$, farmers would move away or go out of business to avoid losses, and land rent would fall. It makes no difference to the analysis whether the land is owned by the farmer or by an absentee landlord, provided that (as has been assumed) the owner tries to find the use of his asset that yields the highest return. It makes a great deal of difference to the farmer's welfare whether or not he owns the land he farms, but not to the rent paid or imputed to the landowner.

The Ricardo/von Thünen model can be given a distinctly urban flavor which will yield insight into urban land-rent determination, if the interpretation is changed again. Suppose a harbor, railhead, or expressway interchange, to which locally produced goods must be shipped to be exported outside the urban area. Surrounding land is used to produce goods for export. The term p becomes the price of the export good at the point of export, w is nonland production costs per acre per year, A is output per acre, and t is the ton-mile cost of shipping the commodity to the point of export. Then Equation 3-2 shows how urban land rent will vary with distance from the city center.

The above is not intended to be a realistic model of urban land rent and land use; more realistic models are presented in Chapters 4 and 5. It is, however, intended to show how reinterpretation of the 150-year-old Ricardo/von Thünen model can help in understanding an important reason for high city-center land values. In this model, proximity to the city center permits producers to economize on transportation costs, which makes centrally located land more valuable than distant land.

Neoclassical Theory

During the latter part of the nineteenth century and the early part of the twentieth century, economists gradually acquired sharper and more sophisticated tools of microeconomic analysis. Foremost among these tools was marginal productivity theory, which forms the basis of the modern theory of factor price determination.

Suppose a commodity is produced with the aid of several inputs, say land, labor, and capital. Output and inputs are continuously variable. The production function shows how much output can be produced with various combinations of inputs. It indicates that more or less substitution is possible among the inputs, unlike the fixed-proportions technology of the Ricardo/von Thünen model. Input and output markets are assumed to be competitive. A profit-maximizing firm employs the amount of each input that equates the value of the marginal product (VMP) of that input to its price, or in the case of an asset, to its rental rate. This important result is proved in most intermediate price theory textbooks, and can be established as follows:

The marginal product (MP) of a factor of production is the change in production that results from a small change in the amount of the input employed. The VMP is the output price multiplied by the MP of the input. It shows the change in the firm's revenue resulting from a small change in the employment of an input, holding constant the amounts of other inputs. The factor price shows the change in cost resulting from a one-unit change in the employment of the input. If the *VMP* exceeds the factor price, it means that employment of additional units of the input would add more to revenue than to cost. Profit would therefore increase. If the *VMP* is less than factor price, a decrease in the employment of the factor would reduce cost by more than revenue. Profit would therefore increase. It follows that profit is largest when an amount of the input is used that equates the *VMP* and the input price.

The result is illustrated in Figure 3-2. The term n stands for the amount of the input, say labor, employed. S_n is the perfectly elastic supply curve of labor, and w is the competitive wage rate. The VMP_n decreases with n because the labor *MP* falls as more labor is employed with fixed amounts of other inputs. The term $\bar{n}$ shows the profit-maximizing employment of labor for the firm, in that it equates VMP_n to w.

Since profit maximization requires equality between *VMP* and price for each factor of production, a diagram like Figure 3-2 holds for each input, land and capital as well as labor. Generally, the *MP* of one factor depends not only on the employment of that factor but also on the employment of other factors. Normally, the *MP* of each factor falls with the employment of that factor and rises with the employment of other factors. Therefore, the equations between the *VMP* and price of each factor are simultaneous and must be solved together. In the three-input example, simultaneous solution of the three equations for land, labor, and capital tells the firm the amounts to employ of all three inputs. A fourth equation, the production function, indicates the firm's output.

Until now, the discussion has been entirely concerned with the firm. In a competitive factor market, factor price is fixed to the firm and is deter-

Figure 3-2

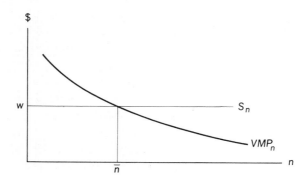

mined by industry supply and demand. To understand land-rent determination, we must therefore pass on to a discussion of the industry as a whole. In a competitive factor market, each firm faces the same fixed factor price. Industry demand is computed by adding the demands of all firms for the factor at the fixed factor price. The industry factor-demand schedule is obtained by repeating the procedure at each factor price. Like the firm's VMP curve, it is downward-sloping. Although the factor supply curve is horizontal for the firm, it is normally upward-sloping for the industry. The factor price is determined by the equality of demand and supply for the factor in the industry as a whole.

Factor price determination is illustrated in Figure 3-3. N refers to labor employment in the entire industry. S_N and D_N are the labor supply and demand curves for the entire industry, w is the equilibrium wage rate, and $\bar{N}$ is total employment of labor in the industry. The term w equals the common value of VMP_n in all the firms in the industry.

To the marginal-productivity theorists, the only peculiarity of land is that, being a nonproduced input, its total supply is fixed. Therefore its supply curve to the industry is vertical or perfectly inelastic. But the competitive supply to the individual firm is nevertheless horizontal or perfectly elastic. Thus, the foregoing analysis applies in full, and the appropriate diagram is Figure 3-4. L is land used by the entire industry, D_L is industry demand for land, and S_L is the vertical industry supply curve. R and $\bar{L}$ are the equilibrium land rent and land employed in the industry. As with labor or any other input, land rent equals the common value of its VMP in all land-using firms.

Figure 3-3

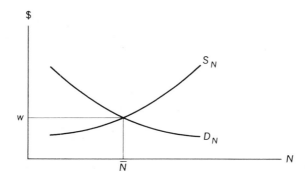

Figure 3-4

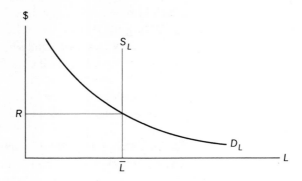

Synthesis

This completes our outline of Ricardian and marginal-productivity, or classical and neoclassical, theories of land rent. To what extent are they really different? Although Ricardo lacked a clear notion of marginal productivity, the idea is implicit in his writing, and the term "productivity" was used several times in the foregoing exposition. After all, if the residual revenue after competitive compensation of other factors is greater on one tract of land than on others, it seems reasonable to suppose that its *VMP* must be greater, either because of greater fertility or because of more favorable location. This suggests that the residual and marginal-productivity theories may come to about the same thing. But Wicksteed was the first economist to see clearly the precise circumstances in which the two theories are equivalent, and Wicksell provided a rigorous proof and generalization of Wicksteed's result.

Wicksteed's theorem is that, if the production function has constant returns to scale and if input and output markets are competitive, land rents can both exhaust residual revenues and satisfy the productivity criterion. The result is an easy consequence of Euler's theorem,[2] which says that if the production function has constant returns to scale at all input and output combinations (is homogeneous of degree 1), every combination of inputs and outputs satisfies the following identity:

$$x \equiv MP_l \cdot l + MP_k \cdot k + MP_n \cdot n \tag{3-3}$$

---

2. Proved in many calculus and mathematical economics textbooks.

Here x is output; l, k, and n are inputs of land, capital, and labor; and MP is the marginal product of each of the three inputs. If input and output markets are competitive, then each input's VMP equals its price or rental rate. These equations can be written as

$$p \cdot MP_l = R \qquad p \cdot MP_k = r \qquad p \cdot MP_n = w$$

or

$$MP_l = R/p \qquad MP_k = r/p \qquad MP_n = w/p \qquad (3\text{-}4)$$

where p is the product price, R and r are the rental rates on land and capital, and w is the wage rate. If the expressions in Equation 3-4 are substituted for the three MP expressions in Equation 3-3, and both sides are multiplied by p, the result is

$$px = R \cdot l + k \cdot r + w \cdot n \qquad (3\text{-}5)$$

Equation 3-5 says that the sum of competitive payments to the three factors of production is exactly equal to total receipts from the sale of the product on a competitive market. This remarkable result is a basic reconciliation of the classical and neoclassical theories of land rent. Furthermore, the result does not depend on the number of factors of production.

Wicksell's generalization showed that Wicksteed's theorem may hold even if the production function does not have constant returns to scale. Suppose that input and output markets are competitive, and that the production function and the fixed competitive factor prices yield a conventional U-shaped long-run average cost curve (LAC), as shown in Figure 3-5. LMC is the firm's long-run marginal cost curve. The term p is the industry's long-run equilibrium price, and $\bar{x}$ is the firm's long-run equilibrium output.

Figure 3-5

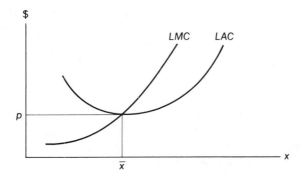

Then, as the diagram illustrates and as Wicksell proved, price equals average cost, and factor payments therefore just exhaust revenues.

The foregoing statement indicates the equivalence of the classical and neoclassical rent theories, but only in situations that permit input and output markets to be perfectly competitive. They are extremely important results, and economists took about a century to establish them clearly and carefully. They form the theoretical foundation of much of the analysis in the chapters to follow.

But constant returns to scale and U-shaped cost curves do not exhaust the situations in which economists want to understand land rent. Unfortunately, we do not know whether there can be equivalence of the classical and neoclassical theories with other kinds of production functions, such as those with increasing returns to scale. And if there is no equivalence, what is the correct theory? Economists, having solved some of the basic problems, lost interest in land rent in the twentieth century. Perhaps the recent surge of interest in urban economics will stimulate a revival of interest in rent theory.

WELFARE AND ETHICAL ASPECTS OF LAND RENT

Two things account for the passionate feelings of nineteenth century economists toward land rent. First was the theory held by Ricardo, Henry George, and others, that land rents would absorb all the fruits of economic progress, with wages continuing at a subsistence level. Second was the view that land, not having been produced by man's efforts, should yield no return to its owners.

It is fortunate that the Ricardo/George theory turned out to be wrong. Ricardo's view rested on Malthus's population theory and on an underestimate of the speed of technical change. However important Malthusian theory may be for other parts of the world, it does not appear to pose a threat for the foreseeable future in Western Europe and North America. Henry George's laboratory was the open spaces of nineteenth century United States, and he rejected Malthus's population theory. But, writing before the important contributions of the marginal-productivity theorists, he had only a confused theory of wage determination.

Even if Ricardo's and George's theories were sound, facts speak louder than theories. And the facts are clear. During most of U.S. history, real wages in the United States have risen rapidly and fairly steadily. The share of wages in national income has changed little if at all. The facts speak less clearly about long-term trends in land rents. But the best study on the subject (Keiper) concludes that land rent may have been 7.7 percent of U.S. national income in 1850, and may have fallen to about 6.4 percent by 1956. The obvious explanation of a fall in the national income share of land rent is the massive shift (discussed in Chapter 2) of economic activity from agriculture, where the share of land is high, to urban production, where it is low.

Thus the first of the nineteenth century concerns over land rent seems unimportant in the United States in the 1970s. But what about the second? Henry George proposed a "single tax" on land. Since the supply of land is perfectly inelastic, he argued correctly that a tax equal to its entire rent would have no effect on its supply or use. He called it a "single" tax because he thought its yield would be sufficient to finance all government activity, making other taxes unnecessary. He was probably right at the time he wrote, but government now spends and taxes a much larger part of national income than the 6.4 percent that goes to land rent. Nevertheless, many economists believe that a 100 percent tax on land rent would be a good idea, and that it should replace other taxes to the extent that its yield would permit.

An analogy between land rent and wages may help to clarify some of the issues. Labor, like land, is a nonproduced factor of production, in the sense that procreation is not undertaken mainly for the monetary return its issue provides to those who make the decision, the parents. Should income from land be taxed rather than that from labor? Not necessarily. First, ownership of land, and other assets, is much less equally distributed than ownership of labor. Therefore an 8.5 percent tax on wages, which might have about the same yield as a 100 percent tax on land rent, would be a much less progressive tax. This argument is perfectly correct, but land redistribution is a considerably less drastic change in public policy than a 100 percent tax on land rent. Therefore, if inequality of land ownership is the problem, land redistribution would seem preferable to a single tax.

Second, a large part of what we call "wage income" is really a return on investment in human capital, such as education and training. A tax on wages would reduce the return on investment in human capital and hence discourage it. But it is also difficult to separate the return of land from the return of capital investment, or improvements, on it. Thus, in principle, land and labor are similar. Both are typically "improved" by investments which should not be discouraged. Practically, it is much easier to separate the return on improved and unimproved land than the return on improved and unimproved labor. But the same kinds of problems are present in both cases.

Third, a major justification for competitive pricing of any factor of production is to provide its owner with an incentive to use it efficiently. A central result of modern welfare economics (demonstrated in Chapter 8) is that if all factors of production are priced competitively, and if their owners use them where the return is greatest, goods and services will be produced efficiently. Thus, if wages are taxed heavily, owners of labor (i.e., workers) will lack incentive to find the occupation with the highest return.

Again the situation is nearly symmetrical with respect to land and labor. If central planners knew the best use for each plot of land and each unit of labor, they could allocate both without the help of market transactions. But central planners do not know the best use of each unit of each input. We therefore use market prices as rewards to encourage input owners to find their best uses. An important difference between land and labor is that people are rightly much more bothered by bureaucratic controls over the use of labor than over the use of land. The former violates a human right, whereas the latter violates a property right. But the problem with the single tax remains.

To levy the right tax, the assessor must know the best use and the resulting rent for each plot of land. If he levies an excessively high tax, resource misallocation will result. Thus, the single tax would assign to the tax assessor the task now assigned to real estate markets. This is a serious matter, because urban land is a valuable resource and it is important that it be used efficiently. Whatever the deficiencies in the ways competitive markets allocate land (discussed in Chapter 10), it is clear that the job should not be given to the tax assessor. Tax assessors are skilled at tax assessment, not at urban land allocation.

A final point is that a 100 percent tax on land rent is, economically speaking, the same as land confiscation. It is not desirable public policy in the United States to institute such a tax without compensation of land owners at fair market values. But if government and land owners hold the same expectations of future land rents, compensation will equal capitalized future land rents, and the government will be in no better financial position with the single tax than without it.[3]

The theoretical merits of the single tax seem slight. Most concern with land rents is probably based on concern with the distribution of asset or wealth ownership. If that is the case, asset redistribution is the appropriate reform, and one less drastic than adoption of the single tax.

---

3. This statement assumes that the government's discount rate equals the land owners' discount rate less the marginal income tax rate. It may not be quite true, because public and private risk premiums may differ.

Although the single tax may not be desirable, higher tax rates on land than on improvements may be justifiable. In the United States, real estate taxation is almost the exclusive preserve of local governments. They now tax both land and improvements at high rates, especially in urban areas. It can be argued that less distortion of resource allocation would result if land were taxed at higher rates and improvements at lower rates than they are at present. This practical policy issue is discussed in Chapter 12.

CONCLUSION AND SUMMARY

In Chapters 4 and 5, the basic theory of land rent and land allocation is used to develop the theory of urban structure. It is worth emphasizing here that land rent and allocation theory are tools to help us understand other urban phenomena, and are not themselves of primary concern. Reasons for direct concern with land rents are those discussed above. Otherwise, land is merely one of several inputs used in urban production, and its remuneration certainly accounts for less than 10 percent of total incomes.

The theory and social implications of land rent were among the most hotly debated subjects in economics during the nineteenth century. David Ricardo, the father of land-rent theory, believed that land rent equals residual revenues remaining after other inputs are compensated at competitive prices. Neoclassical writers believed that land rents were set, like other factor prices, by marginal productivity. Wicksteed and Wicksell proved that the two theories are equivalent if there are constant returns and competitive input and output markets.

Nineteenth century writers were agitated about land rents because land is a nonproduced input and because they feared that land rents would absorb the fruits of technical progress, leaving wages at the subsistence level. Historical evidence shows that the second concern was misplaced, but the first is still a subject of controversy.

DISCUSSION QUESTIONS

1. Would you expect land rents to be a larger share of national income in the United States or in Great Britain?
2. Would you expect land rents to be a larger share of value added in New Jersey, the most densely populated state, or in predominantly rural Iowa?

3. What would be the effect of a single tax in Iowa on Iowa land values and corn prices?
4. Property income is more unequally distributed than earned income. Do you think land ownership is more unequally distributed than ownership of other property?

REFERENCES AND FURTHER READING

Henry George, *Progress and Poverty*, 1879.
Joseph Keiper and others, *Theory and Measurement of Rent*, 1961.
David Ricardo, *Principles of Political Economy and Taxation*, 1951.
George Stigler, *Theory of Price*, 1966.
Johann von Thünen, *Isolated State*, 1966.
Knut Wicksell, *Lectures on Political Economy*, 1934–1935.
Philip Wicksteed, *Alphabet of Economic Science*, 1955.

Chapter 4
Theoretical Analysis of Urban Structure

The goal in theorizing about urban structure is to understand how the urban economy "ticks." Why are certain goods and services produced in urban areas? Why are some produced downtown and some in the suburbs? Why do suburbs grow more rapidly than central cities? Why are certain areas so much more intensively developed than others? Most important, what are the causes and cures of the problems that afflict urban areas?

As is shown in Chapter 1, urban areas are places where large amounts of labor and capital are combined with small amounts of land in producing goods and services. Intensive development of central cities is another way of saying that the ratio of nonland to land inputs is greater there than in the suburbs. A major determinant of location of production within an urban area is the extent to which large amounts of capital and labor can be combined economically with small amounts of land. Other things being equal, goods and services are produced downtown if their production functions permit substitution of capital and labor for land. If not, they are produced in the suburbs, or as in the case of agriculture, outside urban areas altogether. Furthermore, goods and services produced both downtown and in the suburbs are produced with much higher ratios of nonland-to-land inputs downtown than in the suburbs. Therefore, understanding how the urban economy ticks is mainly a matter of understanding how markets combine land with other inputs in varying proportions at different places to produce goods and services.

This chapter presents the basic ingredients of models of urban structure, and puts them together in models of increasing complexity and realism.

AN URBAN AREA WITH A SINGLE INDUSTRY

Suppose a region with a comparative advantage in production of a certain commodity. The commodity is exported from the region at a certain point, which may be a port or a railhead. Wherever the commodity is produced in the region, it must be shipped to the point of export. It is therefore an advantage to produce it as close to the point of export as possible.

A circle of radius u has a circumference of $2\pi u$ and an area of πu^2. Therefore, within u miles of the point of export, there are πu^2 square miles of space. Some of the space may be covered by water, or have other topographical features which make it unusable for production. And some space may be needed for intra or interurban-area transportation. But obviously the greater the distance from the point of export, the more space is available for production. Quite generally, the supply of such space can be represented by a function of the square miles of land within u miles of the point of export. For simplicity, suppose that ϕ radians of the circle are available for production at every distance from the point of export. Then the supply of land for production within u miles of the point of export is $(\phi/2)u^2$ square miles. Of course, ϕ cannot exceed 2π.

Production Conditions

Labor inputs and the production of housing services play no role in this model. They are introduced in the next section. Here it is assumed that only one commodity is produced in the urban area. Equivalently, it can be assumed that all commodities have the same production functions. The commodity can be sold locally as well as exported, but all units of the commodity are assumed to be shipped to the point of export for distribution in all cases. The demand for the commodity is a function of price at the point of export.

The commodity is produced with land and capital. The production function has constant returns to scale, and permits substitution between capital and land. Suppose a building with a certain number of floors and a certain number of rooms. Then the inputs and the output of usable floor space can be doubled by constructing an identical building adjacent to it.[1] This is the meaning of constant returns to scale. Now suppose the building

---

1. This is not quite true. Some economy is made possible by sharing common walls. But this economy becomes unimportant in a building with a modest number of rooms.

is extended up rather than out to economize on land. Suppose, for example, that an identical second floor is added to a one-story building. The land input is unchanged, but the amount of capital has more than doubled; although the second story requires the same amount of materials as the one-story building, the walls of the first story and the foundation must be strengthened to hold the second story, as well as the first. In addition, the output of usable floor space is less than double because part of the first story must be used for stairs to provide vertical transportation to the second story. Similar considerations apply to additional floors on the building. Thus, capital can be substituted for land, but with diminishing returns to the use of additional capital with a fixed amount of land.

It is assumed that input and output markets are perfectly competitive. A competitive output market means that all units of the commodity must be sold at the same price at the point of export, wherever they are produced. Competitive input markets mean that producers take rental rates on land and capital as given at each location. It is assumed that the supply of capital is perfectly elastic to the urban area as a whole, and that the rental rate on capital is the same throughout the urban area. Land rent, on the other hand, is determined by the model, and depends on distance from the point of export.

Finally, it is assumed that shipment costs of the commodity to the point of export depend only on the straight-line distance between the location of production and the point of export. This is an approximation, since shipments must follow the road network. But studies have shown that actual transportation time and distance are very strongly correlated with straight-line distance in urban areas. Thus transportation cost per commodity unit per mile is assumed to be constant, independent of the distance shipped and of the point of origin.

The dependent variables in the model are the amounts of capital employed on different plots of land, the rental rates on the various plots, and the total output and price of the commodity. Since transportation cost to the point of export depends only on distance and not on direction, it follows that all the land available around a circle of radius u centered on the point of export has the same rent; that is, land rent also depends only on distance and not on direction.

As shown in Chapter 3, in any place that production of the commodity occurs, producers use amounts of the capital and land inputs that equate the VMPs of the inputs to their rental rates. We can write these equations as

$$MP_{K(u)}(p - tu) = r \qquad (4\text{-}1)$$

$$MP_{L(u)}(p - tu) = R(u) \qquad (4\text{-}2)$$

$MP_{K(u)}$ and $MP_{L(u)}$ are the marginal products of the amounts of capital and land used at a distance u miles from the point of export. Each MP depends on the amounts of both factors used. The term p is the price of the commodity at the point of export, and t is the unit-mile shipment cost to the point of export. The term $p - tu$ is therefore the price at the point of production for units of the commodity produced u miles from the point of export, that is, the price net of shipment cost to the point of export. The terms r and $R(u)$ are the rental rates per unit of capital and land.

We know from the Wicksteed-Wicksell theorem discussed in Chapter 3 that a rent function $R(u)$ that satisfies Equations 4-1 and 4-2 will also make profit exactly zero at each u. It is worthwhile to investigate carefully the shape of the rent function. If no input substitution were possible, then $MP_{L(u)}$ would be a constant, and Equation 4-1 and 4-2 would not have to be solved simultaneously. The rent that equated profit to zero at each u would decrease linearly as u increased.

This is the special case that was shown in Figure 3-1 (Chapter 3). In that special case, the only saving from locating production close to the point of export is lower transportation cost. Therefore, to make profit just zero at each u, land rent increases just enough to offset the reduced transportation cost as u decreases. But in the model here, some factor substitution is possible. Then it is easy to show that $R(u)$ must rise faster than linearly as u decreases; that is, $R(u)$ must have the general shape shown in Figure 4-1.

To establish the result, suppose the contrary. Specifically, suppose $R(u)$ at a level that makes profit just zero at some large value of u, and that $R(u)$ increases linearly as u decreases. Then profit would be just zero at small values of u, if the same factor proportions were used there as at large

Figure 4-1

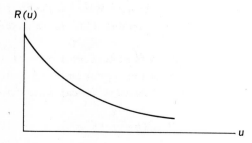

values of u. But they would not be the same. At small values of u, land is more expensive relative to capital than at large values of u. This means that at small values of u, production cost is lower if a larger capital/land ratio is used than the ratio appropriate at a large u. Therefore, if $R(u)$ increases linearly as u decreases, profit will be positive at small values of u. Thus, $R(u)$ must increase faster than linearly as u becomes small if profit is to be just zero at each u. Of course, the more rapidly $R(u)$ rises at small u, the more capital is substituted for land. The urban area is in equilibrium when the capital/land ratio at each u is appropriate for $R(u)$, and $R(u)$ makes profit just zero at each u. $R(u)$ must satisfy both properties to be a solution of Equations 4-1 and 4-2.

Thus, $R(u)$ must increase faster than linearly as u becomes small. Of course, the ratio of capital to land inputs is an increasing function of the ratio of land rent to capital rent. Therefore, as land rent rises rapidly and u decreases close to the city center, the capital/land ratio also rises rapidly. The expression "rising capital/land ratio" is a graphic one, since it is precisely measured by the rising height of buildings.

The result is important. If it were not possible to substitute capital for land, urban rent functions would be linear, and land used for each purpose would be used with the same intensity in all parts of the urban area. But land rent, population density, and capital/land ratios fall very rapidly with distance close to city centers and flatten out in the suburbs. The pattern is a consequence of factor substitution, and the precise form of the rent function depends on the ease with which capital can be substituted for land. Nonlinear rent functions sometimes appear to be mysterious in models with linear transportation costs. Why should land rent increase more with a move from three to two miles toward the city center than with a move from nine to eight miles? After all, the saving in transportation cost is the same in the two moves. The answer, as we now see, is factor substitution.

Market Equilibrium Conditions

So far, only the marginal productivity conditions of Equations 4-1 and 4-2 have been discussed. The model is completed by several additional equations. First, all the land available within the urban area must be used to produce the commodity. It would never pay to use land at a certain distance from the point of export if closer land were unused. Thus, for each u within the urban area, we must have $L(u) = \phi u$.

Second, the production function tells us how much of the commodity is produced by the land and capital employed at each u.

Third, overall demand and supply for the commodity must be equal for the urban area as a whole. Overall supply is the sum, or integral, of the amounts produced at each u within the urban area. The overall demand equation shows the amount that can be sold, both locally and for export, at each p. Although each competitive producer in the urban area takes p as given, p depends on the total amount produced by the entire area. A decrease in p increases exports in two ways. The commodity is then cheaper in the area in which it was previously exported, and customers there buy more. In addition, a decrease in p increases the area in which the urban area's exports are competitive.

Finally, urban areas compete for land with nonurban users, such as agriculture. Suppose, for simplicity, the nonurban land surrounding the urban area commands a rent of $\bar{R}$. Then the urban area includes only the land that can be bid away from nonurban users. The edge of the urban area occurs at a distance $\bar{u}$ miles from the point of export where urban land rent falls to the level $\bar{R}$. The urban area has a radius of $\bar{u}$ miles where $R(\bar{u}) = \bar{R}$.

This completes the model. The two marginal productivity conditions, the equation relating land use to land available and the production function, give us four equations to determine land and capital inputs, output, and land rent at each u in the urban area. Then the equation of overall demand and supply and $R(\bar{u}) = \bar{R}$ determine the price of the commodity at the point of export and the radius of the urban area.[2]

The model here cannot in any sense be thought of as a realistic model of urban structure. Its purpose is to introduce the use of land rent and allocation theory in models of urban structure. It is, however, possible to deduce from the model the single most pervasive characteristic of urban structure, namely, high land rents and intensive land use near the city center, both falling rapidly near the center and much less rapidly in the more distant suburbs. Although there are many unrealistic simplifications in the model, the most significant is that the urban area here has no people in it. Labor does not appear as a factor of production, and households do not appear as consumers of housing and other goods and services.

---

2. Despite its drastic simplifying assumptions, computations with the model discussed here can be rather cumbersome. Nevertheless, a clearer understanding of it can be developed by working through the calculations of the more complex model in Chapter 5; then returning to this model and the other models in this chapter and working out some examples, using production and demand functions of your own invention or that you have studied in other courses.

HOUSEHOLDS IN A SPATIAL CONTEXT

There are important similarities between the foregoing model of industrial location and the theory of household location. Firms are assumed to maximize profits by choosing a location for production, and shipping the commodity they produce to the city center. Households are assumed to maximize their utility or satisfaction in choosing a residential location (among other goods and services). It is the worker himself who gets shipped, or rather commutes, to the city center. Thus, production of housing services is analogous to industrial production, and commuting is analogous to the shipment of commodities. (Of course, not all workers actually work in the city center, any more than all goods are really shipped to the city center. More realistic assumptions along this line are introduced later. Here it is assumed that all commuting is to the city center in order to maintain the parallelism of the model with the model of industrial location.)

Housing services, like other goods and services, are produced with land, labor, and capital inputs. The provision of housing services bears the same relationship to the housing construction industry that the downtown provision of legal services bears to the office construction industry. In both cases, the construction industry produces a capital good which is used as an input in the production of a service to consumers. The cost of housing services includes labor cost, for maintenance and repairs, plus the rent on the land and capital used. Provided that competitive markets supply the inputs to everyone on the same terms, the cost of a given amount of housing services at a given location is the same to all, and the distinction between ownership and rental of housing is immaterial. Real-estate mortgage markets are highly competitive, and mortgages are highly secure loans in that land and houses are durable, easily insured, and unlike cars virtually impossible to steal (in a physical sense).

In the United States, there are only two important reasons for the cost of a particular house in a particular location to vary from person to person. First, and most important, is racial discrimination. In many parts of most urban areas, whites sell or rent real estate to blacks only at premium prices, if at all. Second, mortgage interest payments and real-estate taxes are deductible for federal income tax purposes, whereas rent payments for housing are not. Thus, housing services are provided on more favorable terms to owners than to renters. (This is important only to those people in a high marginal income-tax bracket.) More is said about racial discrimination and tax considerations in housing markets in Chapter 10. Here it is assumed that the cost of housing services is independent of ownership.

Capital and land can be, and are, substituted for each other in the production of housing services in the same way as for commodity production. A downtown high-rise apartment has a high capital/land ratio. There is, however, an additional consideration, more important in the production of housing services than it is in commodity production. The value of housing services is affected by the amount of uncovered land surrounding the house. Presumably householders are as well off with a big house surrounded by a small amount of uncovered land as with a somewhat smaller house surrounded by a larger amount of uncovered land. Although suburban industrial buildings sometimes have considerable amounts of uncovered land around them, it is usually held for parking, future expansion, or speculation.

Assumptions of the Model

We can formulate a theory of household location choice as an extension of consumer behavior theory. Suppose that the household has a utility function or set of indifference curves for its tastes or preferences for housing services and for nonhousing goods and services. As is true of nonspatial consumer behavior theory, the theory presented here depends in only minor ways on the number of goods and services available. But to facilitate diagrammatic exposition, it is assumed that only one nonhousing commodity, called "goods" for short, is available.

The most general way to introduce location choice into the model would be to include u in the utility function. It could then represent all the subjective costs of commuting, such as time forgone from other activities, fatigue, strain, and boredom. Although little is known about some of these factors, it is reasonable to assume that the marginal disutility of additional time spent in commuting increases with the time spent commuting, at least beyond some number of minutes. (Some interesting research has been done on commuters' valuation of travel time; it is discussed in Chapter 11.) Practically no results can be demonstrated unless restrictions are placed on the way commuting affects utility. In this section, a very special assumption is used, the commuting costs enter linearly in the budget constraint but do not otherwise affect utility. The important restriction implied by this assumption is that the marginal disutility of additional time spent commuting is a constant. In Chapter 5, it is shown that the disutility of a given amount of commuting may nevertheless increase with income.

Households maximize their satisfaction with respect to the consumption of housing, goods, and commuting, subject to a budget constraint. The budget constraint says that expenditures on housing, goods, and commuting must not exceed income. Using the assumption that the disutility of travel appears in the budget constraint, income must be interpreted as money income plus income foregone as a result of commuting. Part of this potential income is "spent" on commuting. It is assumed that the household can buy as much of goods and housing services as it wants without affecting their prices. The price of goods is assumed not to vary with residential location, but the price of housing services depends on u, since the price depends on land rents, which in turn vary with u. In addition to subjective costs, commuting entails monetary costs in the form of fares or vehicle operating costs. The money cost per mile of commuting is assumed to be a constant, and commuting cost, like the cost of commodity shipment, is assumed to depend on the straight-line distance from the residence to the city center. The coefficient of distance in the budget equation (t in Equation 4-4 below) includes both money and the subjective or time costs of commuting.

Wherever the household decides to live, it consumes the amount of housing services and goods that yields the greatest satisfaction at that location. Figure 4-2 illustrates the equilibrium choice for a household located u miles from the center. The term $x_1(u)$ is the consumption of goods, and $x_2(u)$ is the consumption of housing services. The straight line is the budget line for a household living u miles from the center. The term I is the highest indifference curve that can be reached, attained by consuming $\bar{x}_1(u)$ units of goods and $\bar{x}_2(u)$ units of housing services. The equilibrium condition is the familiar equation between the marginal rate of substitution, or the slope of the indifference curve, and the ratio of the prices of the two consumer goods.

Figure 4-2

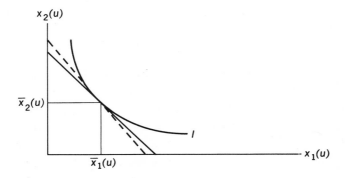

If we write Δx_1 and Δx_2 for small changes in the consumption of x_1 and x_2 that keep the household on the indifference curve, the slope of the indifference curve is $\Delta x_2/\Delta x_1$; and equilibrium requires the consumption of amounts of x_1 and x_2 such that

$$\frac{\Delta x_2}{\Delta x_1} = -\frac{p_1}{p_2} \tag{4-3}$$

The household must also decide how far from the city center to live. If its residence is close to the center, housing services are expensive, but commuting is cheap. If its residence is far from the city center, housing services are cheap, but commuting is expensive.

Now suppose that the workplaces in the city center occupy a space small compared with the rest of the urban area, which is occupied by residences. Approximate the area occupied by workplaces with a point at the city center. Suppose also that $(\phi/2)u^2$ square miles of land are available for housing within u miles of the city center. Finally, suppose that all households have the same tastes or indifference curves and the same money income. Then an equilibrium location pattern requires that households achieve the same satisfaction level wherever they live. If they did not, some households would move.

Suppose, for example, that households living five miles from the city center could achieve a higher indifference level than those living ten miles from the center. By moving closer in those living ten miles away could achieve the same satisfaction as those five miles away, since they have the same tastes and income and face the same market prices. Thus, some households at the more distant location would move in. This would increase land and housing prices at the closer location, and reduce them at the more distant location. Thus, satisfaction levels would fall at the closer location and rise at the more distant location. Movement ceases only when equal satisfaction levels are achieved at all distances from the center.

Implications of the Model

What land-rent function shape is implied by this model? It is an interesting and important fact that the model has a land-rent function steeper close to the city center than in the suburbs, as did the model in the previous section. This can be seen as follows: the household budget constraint can be written

$$p_1x_1(u) + p_2(u)x_2(u) + tu = w \tag{4-4}$$

Here p_1 is the price of goods, which does not depend on u, and $p_2(u)$ is the price of housing services, which does depend on u. The term t is the cost per two miles of commuting. A worker who lives u miles from his work must commute $2u$ miles per day. The term w is income. Now consider the effect on p_2, x_1, and x_2 of a small change Δu in u. Since the budget constraint must be satisfied at both values, Equation 4-4 implies that

$$p_1\Delta x_1(u) + \Delta p_2(u)x_2(u) + p_2(u)\Delta x_2(u) + t\Delta u = 0 \qquad (4\text{-}5)$$

Here Δx_1, Δx_2, and Δp_2 are the resulting small changes in x_1, x_2, and p_2. If the Δ terms are sufficiently small, the cross-product $\Delta p_2\Delta x_2$ is nearly zero, and has been ignored in Equation 4-5.

Now Equation 4-3 can be written

$$p_1\Delta x_1(u) + p_2(u)\Delta x_2(u) = 0$$

Subtracting it from both sides of Equation 4-5 yields

$$\Delta p_2(u)x_2(u) + t\Delta u = 0$$

Rearranging terms, this equation can be written as

$$\frac{\Delta p_2(u)}{\Delta u} = -\frac{t}{x_2(u)} \qquad (4\text{-}6)$$

The left-hand side of Equation 4-6 is the slope of the housing price function. The minus on the right-hand side shows that the slope is negative; that is, housing is more expensive close to the city center than in the suburbs.

Equation 4-6 also implies that the housing price function is steep wherever x_2 is small. Therefore the housing price function is steeper close to the city center than in the suburbs if suburban residents consume more housing than those living closer in. But suburban residents must consume more housing or they could not achieve the same utility level as those living closer in. Therefore, the budget line of a suburban resident must be steeper than that of a close-in resident in Figure 4-2, since the housing price is lower for the surburban resident. But the surburban resident also spends more on commuting. Since equilibrium requires that the suburban and close-in residents achieve the same indifference curve, the combined effect of increased commuting cost and lower housing prices must make the suburban resident's budget line tangent to the same indifference curve as is that of the close-in resident. Thus, the broken line in Figure 4-2 is the budget line of a suburban resident, and the solid line is that of a close-in resident. It is clear from Figure 4-2 that the suburban resident consumes more housing than the close-in resident.

The foregoing result can be stated in terms of income and substitution effects. As one moves further from the city center, the price of housing falls. But the increased commuting cost exactly offsets the income effect of the decline in housing price. Thus, the new budget line is tangent to the indifference curve achieved before the move. It follows that the only effect of the move on housing consumption is the substitution effect of the decrease in housing price. It is a basic theorem of consumer behavior analysis that the substitution effect on the consumption of a product whose price falls is to increase the consumption of the product.

It is easy to see that the assumption that u does not appear directly in the utility function is crucial in the foregoing demonstration. If u did appear in the utility function, a move away from the city center would shift the indifference curve in Figure 4-2, and it would not be possible to predict the effect on housing demand.

It has now been shown that suburbanites consume more housing than close-in residents in equilibrium. It follows from Equation 4-6 that the housing price function must be steeper close to the city center than in the suburbs. If nonland factor prices do not vary with distance, housing price can be steep only where the land-rent function is steep. Thus, the land-rent function becomes steep close to the city center in the consumer model, just as in the producer model.

The consumer model has two very realistic implications. First, suburbanites consume more housing than residents close to the city center. Second, since land is cheaper relative to other housing inputs in the suburbs than it is close to the city center, suburban housing will use lower capital/land ratios than downtown housing. These two implications entail lower suburban population densities than those near the city center. (None of the above implies that suburbanites are better off than those living close to the city center. In this model, all households have the same income and all achieve the same satisfaction level. This assumption is dropped in the next section.)

The consumer model here can also provide insight into the process of suburbanization. Suppose that all incomes rise in the urban area. There is considerable evidence that housing demand rises rapidly with income, that is, that the income elasticity of demand for housing is greater than 1.0. Therefore we should expect housing demand to rise considerably. The increase in housing demand may cause the price of housing to rise, but it cannot rise enough to offset completely the effect of the increase in income on housing demand. Even if p_2 rises, Equation 4-6 shows that the housing price function becomes less steep as x_2 increases. Therefore, as income rises, housing prices vary less between downtown and suburb, as do the demand for housing and the land intensity of housing. Thus, population density varies less with u as incomes and the resulting housing demand rise. As can be seen from Equation 4-6, the effect also results from a decrease in t, which represents the cost of commuting. A reduction in t not only has a direct effect on flattening the housing price function, it also may increase the demand for housing, since more income is left after paying commuting costs. This, of course, further flattens the housing price function.

Reductions in the variability of population density with distance from the city center have been observed in U.S. and other urban areas for many decades. (Some of this evidence is reported in Chapter 6.) Consumer behavior theory provides an explanation of the observed trend. Real incomes have risen rapidly. In addition, although this is less well documented, it is likely that the money cost per mile of commuting has fallen relative to other prices. This is the probable result of a succession of urban transportation innovations, such as the mass production of automobiles and improved urban roads.

SEVERAL URBAN SECTORS

We have now considered two one-sector models in which the urban area contains only producers or only households, thus developing the basic location theory of firms and households. In this section, the theory is extended to explain the location pattern of several sectors in one urban area. A sector is defined as a set of institutions that have the same rent functions. Firms' rent functions are affected by their production functions, prices of nonland factors of production, and product demand functions. Households' rent functions are affected by their incomes, their tastes for housing, commuting, and other goods and services, and by the prices of consumer goods other than housing. Thus, there are many distinguishable sectors in even a fairly small urban area. For theoretical purposes, the number of sectors makes little difference, but for applied research and for ease of exposition, it is important to keep sectors to a manageable number. This necessitates the grouping of similar, but not identical, institutions as an approximation of a sector. In applied research, the way data are collected and published usually dictates the definition of sectors.

The key to understanding the location pattern of several sectors in an urban area is the notion, introduced in Chapter 3, that land owners want the largest return possible from their asset and hence allocate their land to the institution that offers the highest rent.

Two Industries

Suppose that two industries bid for land in an urban area. The rent that firms in each industry can offer for land at each distance from the center is found in the way discussed at the beginning of the chapter. From here on, the rent that each industry can pay at each u will be referred to as the industry's *rent-offer function*. Designate the industries as 1 and 2, and suppose that their rent-offer functions are as shown in Figure 4-3. At values of u less than u_o, industry 1 can offer higher rent than industry 2, and at values of u greater than u_o, the opposite is true. Land close to the city center is used by industry 1, and land beyond u_o is used by industry 2. At each u, the rent actually paid is the higher of the two rent-offer functions. That is, the rent function is the *envelope* of the rent-offer functions.

Why should firms in industry 1 pay much more for land than $R_2(u)$ at small values of u? After all, industry 1 firms can rent the land if they offer just a little more than industry 2 firms. The answer is that industry 1 firms are competing not only with industry 2 firms but also with each other. Remember that the entire analysis here rests on the assumption that firms enter each industry until profit is just zero. Thus, the complete set of equilibrium conditions for our two-industry urban area is as follows:

1. Wherever firms in each industry locate, they must make zero profit.
2. Each plot of land goes to the highest bidder.
3. Supply and demand for land must be equal.
4. Supply and demand for the product of each industry must be equal.

Figure 4-3

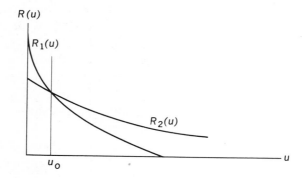

There is a very simple rule for the urban location pattern of industries with linear rent-offer functions. Suppose an arbitrarily large set of industries, each of which is able to bid successfully for land somewhere in the urban area, and each of which has a linear rent-offer function. The industries are ranked by distance from the city center in the order in which they are ranked by the steepness of their rent-offer functions. The industry with the steepest rent-offer function is closest to the city center, followed by the industry with the next steepest function, and so on. This is illustrated in Figure 4-4. The heavy line is the rent function, constructed as the envelope of the industries' rent-offer functions. It is easy to see that in an urban area with a large number of sectors, the rent function would be nearly smooth, and would become flatter the greater distance from the center, even if each industry had a linear rent-offer function.

Although Figure 4-4 shows the shape of the rent function, it does not indicate which industries will locate in the urban area. It is not necessarily true that industry 1 will locate in the urban area at all. This possibility is illustrated in Figure 4-5. Here, $R_1(u)$ is steeper than $R_2(u)$, but $R_1(u)$ is nowhere above R_2u, so industry 1 therefore does not locate in the urban area.

As we have seen, factor and product substitution mean that industry and household rent-offer functions are typically not straight lines. In that case, no simple rule indicates the locational pattern to be expected in the urban area. But the locational pattern must satisfy the four equilibrium conditions listed above.

Figure 4-6 illustrates a realistic possibility. Here, the industry 1 rent-offer function is steep at the beginning and flattens as it moves out, whereas the industry 2 function is more nearly linear. The result is that industry 1 lo-

Figure 4-4

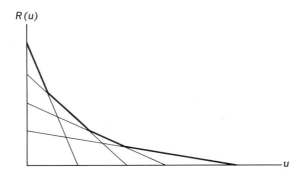

R (u)

u

Figure 4-5

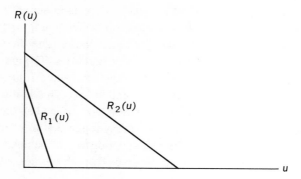

cates at values of u less than u_o and at values of u greater than u_1, whereas industry 2 locates at distances between u_o and u_1. There are, however, some reasonable sets of assumptions that preclude multiple intersections. Suppose that each industry has a Cobb-Douglas production function (discussed in detail in Chapter 5). Suppose further that the two industries differ only in that their production functions have different land intensities. Then their rent-offer functions cannot intersect twice. Alternatively, if the industries differ only in elasticity of demand for their products, their rent-offer functions cannot intersect twice. But there are some realistic situations discussed in the next section in which multiple intersections should be expected.

Figure 4-6

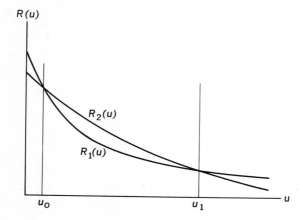

Households and Industries

An industry's rent-offer function is unique because zero profit is a well-defined notion. But in considering the rent-offer functions of households, zero *utility* is not a sensible notion. In fact, in modern ordinal utility theory, any "bundle" of goods and services whatever can be assigned zero utility. All that matters is whether one bundle yields more or less utility than another. For a sector of households with given tastes, income, and prices for nonhousing goods and services, a rent-offer function exists for each utility level. The lower the rent-offer function, the higher is the utility level, since paying less land rent leaves more money to spend on housing and other goods and services. This is illustrated in Figure 4-7, where $R_1(u)$ is the rent-offer function corresponding to a low utility level for the set of households, and $R_2(u)$ corresponds to a high utility level.

Which rent-offer function is relevant? The lowest one is, that is, the one representing the highest utility that equates supply and demand for labor provided by these households. Figure 4-8 illustrates this notion. Here $R_1(u)$ is the rent-offer function of an industry that employs labor. $R_2(u)$ is a rent-offer function for the households that supply labor to the industry; it represents a high utility level and a small supply of labor. $R_3(u)$ is another household rent-offer function representing a low utility level and a large supply of labor. If labor demand and supply are equal when the household rent-offer function is $R_2(u)$, it is relevant. But if labor demand exceeds supply, and if the wage rate is high enough to attract more workers to the urban area, the household rent-offer function rises to one like $R_3(u)$, the labor supply ex-

Figure 4-7

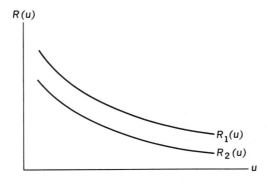

Figure 4-8

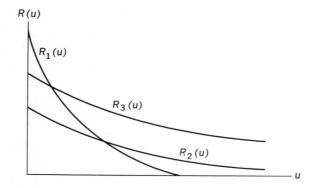

pands, and utility falls. Thus, the equilibrium conditions for households location are similar to those for industrial location:

1. Wherever households with given tastes and income reside, they must achieve the same utility levels.
2. Each plot of land goes to the highest bidder.
3. Supply and demand for land must be equal.
4. Supply and demand for labor provided by the households must be equal.

In addition, household utility levels in this urban area must be at least as high as can be achieved elsewhere. For some kinds of labor, the lowest rent-offer function that commands land anywhere in the urban area may be so high that the households to which the labor belongs achieve lower utility levels than those that can be achieved elsewhere. Households of this type simply do not locate in this urban area. Farmers rarely reside in large urban areas, and highly specialized labor, such as an eye surgeon, is rarely found in small towns.

As was shown in Figure 4-6, not all the firms in an industry necessarily locate in a contiguous area. The same is true of households. In Figure 4-6, $R_2(u)$ might be the rent-offer function of an industry employing labor, and $R_1(u)$ might be the household rent-offer function that produces equilibrium in the urban area's labor market. Then, some households would live downtown and some in distant suburbs. The two residential areas would be separated by an industrial area. The two groups of households would, however, be equally well off, and neither would benefit from a move.

We can now use the analysis to understand one of the most interesting of urban phenomena, namely the location effects of differences among households. Some differences are easy to dispose of. Households with unusually strong preferences for housing tend to live far out because housing is relatively cheap there. Likewise, workers who attach relatively little disutility to commuting, perhaps because it enables them to escape noisy telephones at the office and noisy children at home, also live in distant suburbs.

The most interesting issue has to do with the effects of income differences on location. Suppose there are two household sectors with identical tastes but with different incomes. Does the high or low-income group live closer in? Other things being equal, the high-income group will demand more housing than the low-income group, which encourages the high-income group to move out where housing is cheap. But the marginal disutility of commuting also depends on income, and it may (theoretically) rise so fast with income that the high-income group will stay put and spend its money on other things. A remarkably simple and realistic result (proved in Chapter 5) can be stated:[3] Suppose that the disutility of a mile of commuting is proportionate to the wage rate, and that the factor of proportionality is no greater for high than for low-income workers. Then, if the income elasticity of demand for housing exceeds 1, high-income workers live further from the city center than do low-income workers. If the income elasticity is less than 1, high-income workers nevertheless live farther out, provided the demand for housing is not too inelastic with respect to its own price.

The result does not, of course, depend on the existence of only two income groups. Even if there is an arbitrarily large number of income groups, if all satisfy the conditions of the theorem, their residences will be ranked by distance from the city center inversely to their rank by income; that is, the lowest income group will be closest in, the next lowest will be next closest, and so on. This is a remarkably realistic result, and it mirrors closely the predominant pattern in U.S. urban areas.

The result does not rest on coercion. In the model, the poor live close to the city center because it is the best place for them to live. But in no sense is it a justification for coercion. First, it is not best for all low-income people to live near city centers. As has been indicated, not everyone has the same tastes for housing, commuting, and other things. Realistically, at least some low-income people want to live in the suburbs and commute long distances,

---

3. This result had been seen intuitively, but the first satisfactory proof was by Muth, pp. 29 et seq.

and at least some high-income people want to live close in and commute short distances, as a matter of taste.

Much more important, not everyone actually works in the city center. As is discussed in the next section and in Chapter 6, an increasingly large amount of urban employment is located in the suburbs. In the absence of discriminatory treatment, some low-income people would qualify for suburban jobs and would want to live in the suburbs. But, as has been pointed out, low-income, and especially black, people are discriminated against in suburban housing markets. Whites often refuse to rent or sell to blacks and make them unwelcome if they succeed in finding suburban housing. Most insidiously, suburban zoning rules require that all housing be on large lots that represent optimum land input for high-income suburban housing, but which make suburban housing prohibitively expensive for low-income groups. The advantage of suburban employment for whites is that they can use low-cost suburban land for housing and still avoid long work trips. But if blacks want to work in the suburbs, they must nevertheless live on high-priced center-city land and commute long distances.

Finally, if the poor were better off in inner cities, enforced segregation would not be needed to keep them there. Only if at least some are better off in the suburbs is coercion necessary to keep them in the inner city.

Until now, no explicit mention has been made of the fact that the land rent a sector can offer at a particular place depends on where other sectors are located. Most important, the land rent or housing price that a household can pay, and nevertheless achieve a given utility level, depends on the locations of its members' workplaces. A household can make a higher rent offer for suburban land if its labor-force participants work in the suburbs than it can make if they work in the city center. Similarly, the land rent a retailer can offer depends on how many households and other retailers are located nearby. Theoretically, the implication of interdependency is merely that the equilibrium conditions for the various sectors must be solved simultaneously. Practically, it vastly complicates the solution of realistic models. In addition, interdependencies of rent-offer functions are difficult to represent and analyze diagrammatically.

REALISTIC URBAN LOCATION PATTERNS

Ideally, this section should review several empirical studies of urban rent-offer functions for a variety of sectors. Unfortunately, few such studies exist. Housing is the only sector that has been studied carefully. Although housing is the most important urban sector, studies are also needed for the employment sectors. To understand the location patterns of employment sectors, it is necessary to know more about their production functions, and about the relative advantages to each of central and suburban location. It is particularly unfortunate that, despite the outpouring of industrial production-function studies in recent years, practically none, except in the housing and agricultural sectors, has included land among the inputs. It is therefore difficult to know to what extent industrial suburbanization has resulted from shifts in production functions and to what extent from other changes, such as in transportation costs. Nevertheless, a good deal is known about where in urban areas various kinds of activities tend to locate, and somewhat informal research has shed light on some of the reasons for the observed patterns.

There seem to be two important reasons for the central location of production in urban areas. First, some manufacturing industries produce goods that are exported from the urban area, and possibly from the country, at centrally located port or rail facilities. Similarly, some manufacturing industries use inputs imported into the urban area through these facilities. Firms in such industries find it advantageous to locate near the terminal facility. Usually, the bulkiness of the inputs and outputs justifies rail and water shipment, and it also necessitates the manufacturer's locating near the terminal facility. Examples are petroleum refining, shipbuilding, and some chemical and primary metal manufactures. Although location near terminal facilities is still important in some industries, it is of decreasing importance as road transportation becomes more important.

Second, firms in many specialized service industries require the demand of the entire urban area to exhaust their scale economies. For such firms, central location is valuable. Examples are specialized legal, financial, retailing, and medical services, and cultural and governmental activities.

Most of the above are office activities, and there is another important reason for their central location that has not been emphasized in the literature. Office activities entail much less rapidly diminishing returns with increases in the capital/land ratio than do most kinds of manufacturing. In office activities, labor is almost the only important input other than land and the capital structure, whereas manufacturing requires large amounts of raw and processed materials. In relationship to value, workers are much less expensive to transport vertically than are materials. VMP per pound of office labor transported is much greater than VMP per pound of manufacturing materials transported. Thus, although it pays to transport executives to the top of a tall office building, it does not pay to transport steel that far up to make cars.

Thus inability to produce economically with a high capital/land ratio is a deterrent to central location for most manufacturing industries. Much more important is the fact that, increasingly in recent decades, manufacturing inputs and outputs have been shipped by road. If a firm's inputs come from, and its outputs go to, places outside the urban area, and if they are shipped by road, suburban location provides the "best of both worlds." High central-city land values are avoided and so are congested downtown streets. Much has been written about the increasing use of road transportation as a cause of increasing suburban location of manufacturing. There seems to be little doubt that it has had a major effect. Indeed, Table 2-5 (Chapter 2) shows that the percentage of manufacturing employment in large SMSAs has fallen since World War II. Road transportation may have decreased the attractiveness of large urban areas to manufacturing firms. It has certainly permitted them to locate on the peripheries of urban areas in large numbers.

A large class of urban service industries requires the demand of a substantial part, but not all, of an urban area to exhaust its scale economies. Such industries tend to locate in subcenters away from the main center of the urban area. The suburban shopping center is the most prominent example. In addition, suburban centers providing a variety of office activities have sprung up in recent years. The larger the urban area and the more affluent its citizens, the more subcenters there are. The higher the residents' incomes, the fewer people are needed to generate the demand that will support a given activity, unless it produces an inferior good. Thus, urban subcenters have become more important since World War II, both because the population of urban areas has grown and because of rising real incomes.

Housing is of course the most suburban of urban industries. As was shown in the previous section, high incomes induce households to choose suburban locations because low land values permit low-cost and low-density housing. In addition, suburban manufacturing and other employment enables households to live further out without increased commuting.

The industries described above do not fit easily into a small number of sectors. Many industries ship some inputs and outputs by rail and some by road. Most industries engage in both materials handling and office activities. Household incomes and tastes are continuously variable. Nevertheless, many of the salient characteristics of urban structure can be represented schematically, as in Figure 4-9. Urban activities are classified into four sectors, and the rent offer of each is portrayed. Section A is nearest the city center, representing centrally located manufacturing and office activities. Sector B is the next nearest the center, representing low-income housing.

Figure 4-9

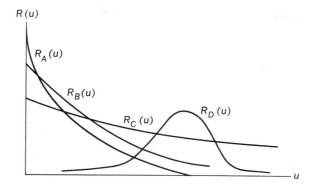

Sector *C* represents suburban high-income housing. Sector *D* represents suburban manufacturing and office activities. In Figure 4-9 it is assumed that sector *D* can pay more rent for suburban than for central-city land since intercity road shipments of freight are cheaper from suburban than from central-city locations.

Figure 4-9 is intended to represent dominant activities in various parts of urban areas. It is no more than an illustration of a typical way that the ingredients are put together to make an urban area. There is, of course, no guarantee that all urban areas have the same location pattern. Moreover, in most urban areas at least some of several activities are found at most distances from the city center. For example, in suburbs dominated by housing, at least some retailing is found. Graphically, this means simply that the rent offers of two or more activities are the same at some values of *u*. To make them the same, the activities may need to be present in certain proportions. If there is too much retailing relative to the number of households at some values of *u*, the retailers' rent-offer function will fall below that of the housing sector. Only when the two are present in equilibrium proportions do their rent offers coincide.

SOME QUALIFICATIONS

The theoretical analysis in this chapter and in Chapter 3 has employed long-run competitive equilibrium as its tool. Many people resist any application of equilibrium analysis to urban phenomena because they believe the durability of structures prevents equilibrium from being achieved. The view here is that one should expect neither too much nor too little from equilibrium analysis.

There can be no doubt that adjustments from one equilibrium to another take a long time when the construction and demolition of buildings are required. The result is that many detailed urban phenomena can only be understood within the historical context of the particular urban area in question. For example, the fact that the very worst housing in many urban areas is adjacent to the central business district undoubtedly results in part from the fact that the area's oldest housing is there.

Whether or not equilibrium analysis is appropriate depends on the specific question one wants to answer. Suppose, for example, that one wants to study the massive decentralization of urban areas that has been observed in the United States and in other countries during the last century or so. Such decentralization has been in response to basic and pervasive determinants of long-run equilibrium; thus, equilibrium analysis is the only way to identify and analyze such shifts carefully. For such analysis to be instructive, it is not necessary that the urban area be continuously in equilibrium.

The underlying contention in Part II is that practically all the important and pervasive urban problems are characteristics of equilibrium and can best be analyzed in equilibrium models. Poverty, poor housing, racial discrimination, pollution, and congestion are all, unfortunately, properties of urban equilibrium. Nevertheless, their detailed effects may depend on disequilibrium considerations and on historical and other characteristics that are peculiar to each urban area. The question to keep in mind in reading Part II is: to what extent would the analysis be more enlightening if disequilibrium were introduced?

SUMMARY

Microeconomic theory of producer and consumer behavior can be extended to an urban spatial context. Assuming that a commodity is to be produced and exported from the urban area at a predetermined point, and assuming the conditions of the Wicksteed-Wicksell theorem, a spatial allocation of inputs and outputs and a land-rent function can be derived. Factor substitution insures that the rent-distance function will be flatter at greater distances from the center.

If workers commute between their homes and workplaces located at the city center, the theory of consumer behavior implies a spatial distribution of housing and a rent-distance function in residential areas. The rent-distance function will be steeper closer to the city center.

If there are several sectors in the urban area, their locations must be determined simultaneously. An important theorem shows that households with higher incomes are likely to locate at greater distances from city centers than households with lower incomes. Although realistic urban location patterns are complex, the model can be used to understand certain important characteristics of urban areas.

DISCUSSION QUESTIONS

1. How would you introduce real estate taxes into an urban location model?
2. How would an urban area's household location pattern be affected if congestion made commuting more expensive near the center than elsewhere?
3. Is it possible in equilibrium that land rent might increase with distance from the center of the urban area?
4. Evaluate the economic logic of the argument that employment has moved to suburbs because central business district land values have gone so high that employers can no longer afford to locate there.

REFERENCES AND FURTHER READING

William Alonso, *Location and Land Use*, 1964.
Benjamin C. Chinitz (editor), *City and Suburb*, 1964.
Edgar Hoover, "The Evolving Form and Organization of the Metropolis," in *Issues in Urban Economics* (1968), edited by Harvey Perloff and Lowdon Wingo.
Edwin S. Mills, *Studies in the Structure of the Urban Economy*, 1972.
Richard Muth, *Cities and Housing*, 1969.

Chapter 5
A Simplified Mathematical Model of Urban Structure

In this chapter are introduced some of the mathematical techniques that have proven useful to urban economists as well as to researchers in other specialties. One purpose of the chapter is to prove some of the statements made in Chapter 4. A much more important purpose is to show that mathematics is a useful tool in understanding urban processes and problems. The fundamental characteristic of an urban area is that many forces interact to determine land rents, land uses, and other interesting urban characteristics. In other words, an urban area is a system with a large amount of simultaneity. Mathematics is indispensable in analyzing such systems.

It is not necessary to be a professional mathematician to be an urban economist. In any specialty in economics, it is desirable to have a mixture of scholars with different levels of mathematical interest and background. But a specialist in any branch of economics ought to be able to follow the relevant literature. For that purpose the minimum requirement is a knowledge of elementary calculus. That background is sufficient to follow this chapter and, indeed, practically all the important work in urban economics. Anyone lacking that background should try to understand the assumptions and conclusions in this chapter, but should not concern himself with the derivations.

A MODEL OF URBAN STRUCTURE

The model analyzed here[1] is mainly concerned with the urban area residential sector. It is the most important urban sector and the one that has been studied most carefully. Most models that include more than one sector are too large to present here and require the help of a computer to solve.

---

1. The model is a simplified version of those analyzed by Mills and Muth.

Assume that the urban area has a predetermined center, perhaps at a port or railhead. At each distance from the center, ϕ radians of a circle are available for urban uses. Since a circle has 2π radians, ϕ must not exceed 2π. The rest of the land, $2\pi - \phi$ radians, is either unavailable for urban use, perhaps because of topographical characteristics, or is used for transportation, parks, and other public purposes.

Assume that all the urban area's employment is located in a semicircular central business district (CBD) with a radius of $\underline{u}$ miles. Thus, the CBD has an area of $(\phi/2)\underline{u}^2$ square miles, and it is assumed that N people work there. The terms ϕ, $\underline{u}$, and N are given from outside the model.

The available land outside the CBD is used for housing as far away from the center as is necessary to house the N workers employed in the CBD. The total amount of land available for housing within u miles of the city center is $(\phi/2)u^2 - (\phi/2)\underline{u}^2$.

Housing Supply and Demand

Equations can now be introduced that express the conditions for location equilibrium in the residential sector. It is assumed that commuting cost depends only on the straight-line distance between place of residence and the city center. It follows that land rent and the intensity of land use also depend on straight-line distance, so that all the land u miles from the center commands the same rent and is used with the same capital/land ratio. This is an important simplification in urban models, since it implies that activities can be located with only one variable, distance from the center, rather than two, distance and direction. The value of each variable at a distance u miles from the center is designated with a u in parentheses following the variable. For example, $K(u)$ and $L(u)$ represent inputs of capital and land in the production of housing services u miles from the center. This notation shows that the variables are functions of u, and solving the model consists in deducing from the equations in the model the functional relationship between the variables and u.

It is also assumed that housing services are produced with land and capital inputs. The production function is assumed to be the Cobb-Douglas one, which economists have used to study many production activities. Using this function, the output of housing services at u, $X_s(u)$, depends on the inputs of land and capital employed at u in the following way:

$$X_s(u) = AL(u)^\alpha K(u)^{1-\alpha} \tag{5-1}$$

where A and α are constants. A is a scale parameter and depends on the units in which inputs and output are measured. The term α is called the distribution parameter, and must lie in the interval $0 < \alpha < 1$. (It is discussed later.) It can be verified that Equation 5-1 has constant returns to scale, so the Wicksteed-Wicksell theorem applies.

It is assumed that input and output markets are perfectly competitive, so that firms will use amounts of inputs equating VMP to input rental rates at each u. It is assumed that the market for housing capital is national, so that its rental rate r is independent of both u and the amount used in the entire urban area. Land rent $R(u)$ and the rental rate for housing services $p(u)$ are determined by the model, and of course depend on u.

If Equation 5-1 is differentiated, it is seen that the MPs of land and capital are

$$MP_{L(u)} = \alpha AL(u)^{\alpha-1}K(u)^{1-\alpha} = \alpha X_s(u)/L(u)$$

and

$$MP_{K(u)} = (1 - \alpha)AL(u)^{\alpha}K(u)^{-\alpha} = (1 - \alpha)X_s(u)/K(u)$$

Therefore the equations relating factor VMPs to their rental rates are

$$\frac{\alpha p(u)X_s(u)}{L(u)} = R(u) \tag{5-2}$$

and

$$\frac{(1 - \alpha)p(u)X_s(u)}{K(u)} = r \tag{5-3}$$

If Equations 5-2 and 5-3 are multiplied by their respective input amounts and divided by $p(u)X_s(u)$, they show that the ratio of each input's remuneration to total revenue equals the input's exponent in Equation 5-1. These ratios are the shares of the factors in housing rental revenues; thus, it can be seen why α is called the distribution parameter. The value of α determines the distribution of housing rental revenues between the two inputs. Since the exponents in Equation 5-1 add to 1, competitive remuneration of land and capital exhausts total revenue, thus verifying the Wicksteed-Wicksell theorem. A typical house may be worth four times the land it occupies, which suggests that α might be about 0.2.

It is assumed that all workers receive the same income w, determined outside the model, and that all have the same tastes. The demand function for housing services per worker living at u, $x_D(u)$, is assumed to be

$$x_D(u) = Bw^{\theta_1}p(u)^{\theta_2} \tag{5-4}$$

where B is a scale parameter, and depends on the units in which housing services are measured. The terms θ_1 and θ_2 are the income and price elasticities of demand for housing, as can be verified by computing the elasticities from Equation 5-4. Unlike other demand functions, Equation 5-4 assumes the elasticities to be constant, and has been used in many applied studies of demand theory. Housing per worker depends on u, as Equation 5-4 indicates. Housing is not an inferior good; hence, $\theta_1 > 0$. The housing demand function slopes downward; hence, $\theta_2 < 0$. Recent studies of housing demand suggest that θ_1 may be about 1.5 and θ_2 about -1.0. $X_D(u)$, total housing demand at u, is housing demand per worker multiplied by $N(u)$, the number of workers living at u:

$$X_D(u) = x_D(u)N(u) \qquad (5\text{-}5)$$

In equilibrium, housing demand and supply must be equal at each u:

$$X_D(u) = X_s(u) \qquad (5\text{-}6)$$

In addition, it was shown in Chapter 4 that locational equilibrium in housing requires that Equation 4-6 be satisfied. That equation can be written

$$p'(u)x_D(u) + t = 0 \qquad (5\text{-}7)$$

Here $p'(u)$ is the slope of $p(u)$, and t is the cost per two miles of commuting. Equation 5-7 says that families are unable to increase utility by moving their households if the change in the cost of housing from a move is just offset by the change in commuting cost.

Other Equilibrium Conditions

It has already been assumed that ϕ radians of land are available for housing at each u, so that ϕu is the length of the semicircle available for housing u miles from the city center. Land used for housing cannot exceed what is available, and no available land can be left unused out to the edge of the urban area. Thus

$$L(u) = \phi u \qquad (5\text{-}8)$$

It is assumed that nonurban uses of land command a rent $\bar{R}$. Therefore, the urban area can extend only as far as households can bid land away from nonurban uses. Thus, the distance from the center to the edge of the urban area is $\bar{u}$ miles, where

$$R(\bar{u}) = \bar{R} \qquad (5\text{-}9)$$

Finally, the land available for housing must house all N workers in the urban area. If $N(u)$ workers live u miles from the center, the total number of workers in the urban area is the sum or integral of $N(u)$ for values of u from u to $\bar{u}$, that is

$$\int_{\underline{u}}^{\bar{u}} N(u)du = N \qquad (5\text{-}10)$$

The model is now complete. The first eight equations relate the eight variables $X_s(u)$, $L(u)$, $K(u)$, $p(u)$, $R(u)$, $x_D(u)$, $X_D(u)$, and $N(u)$ at each value of u. Their solution provides the value of each variable at each u between $\underline{u}$ and $\bar{u}$. Equation 5-7 contains a derivative of $p(u)$ with respect to u. A differential equation, its solution requires a predetermined value of the variable at some u. It is shown below how Equation 5-7 can be expressed as a differential equation in $R(u)$. Equation 5-9 then provides the required value of $R(u)$ at $\bar{u}$, known as an initial condition for the differential equation. Finally, Equation 5-10 can be solved for the variable $\bar{u}$.

Once the model is solved, it shows a complete picture of the housing sector of the urban area. For each value of u, it shows land rent and the rental rate of housing services. From the solution for $K(u)$ and $L(u)$, it is easy to compute the capital/land ratio at each u. From the solution of $N(u)$, population density can be computed at each u.

SOLUTION OF THE MODEL

The land-rent function is the key to the foregoing model. Once it has been found, all the other variables can be calculated easily. The first step in solving $R(u)$ is to derive a well-known relationship between input and output prices for the Cobb-Douglas production function. Solving Equation 5-2 and 5-3 for $L(u)$ and $K(u)$ gives

$$L(u) = \frac{\alpha p(u)X_s(u)}{R(u)} \qquad K(u) = \frac{(1-\alpha)p(u)X_s(u)}{r}$$

Substituting these expressions for $L(u)$ and $K(u)$ in Equation 5-1 and rearranging terms gives

$$p(u) = [A\alpha^{\alpha}(1-\alpha)^{1-\alpha}]^{-1}r^{1-\alpha}R(u)^{\alpha} \qquad (5\text{-}11)$$

which shows that $p(u)$ is proportionate to $R(u)$ raised to a power between zero and 1. Thus, housing prices are high wherever land rents are high, but housing prices rise less than proportionately with land rents because of factor substitution. If α is 0.2, than a 10 percent rise in land rent will lead to a 2 percent rise in housing prices.

The derivative of Equation 5-11 with respect to u is

$$p'(u) = A^{-1} \left(\frac{\alpha r}{1 - \alpha} \right)^{1-\alpha} R(u)^{-(1-\alpha)} R'(u) \qquad (5\text{-}12)$$

where $R'(u)$ is the slope of $R(u)$. Now substitute Equation 5-4 for $x_D(u)$ in Equation 5-7, substitute Equation 5-11 for $p(u)$ and Equation 5-12 for $p'(u)$ and collect terms. The result is

$$E^{-1}R(u)^{\beta-1}R'(u) + t = 0 \qquad (5\text{-}13)$$

where E and β stand for collections of constants,

$$E^{-1} = \alpha B w^{\theta_1}[A\alpha^{\alpha}(1 - \alpha)^{1-\alpha}]^{-(1+\theta_2)} r^{(1-\alpha)(1+\theta_2)}$$

and

$$\beta = \alpha(1 + \theta_2)$$

Equation 5-13 expresses the differential equation 5-7 in terms of $R(u)$. Using the initial condition of Equation 5-9, the solution is

$$R(u) = [\bar{R}^{\beta} + \beta t E(\bar{u} - u)]^{1/\beta} \qquad \text{if } \beta \neq 0 \qquad (5\text{-}14a)$$

and

$$R(u) = \bar{R}e^{tE(\bar{u}-u)} \qquad \text{if } \beta = 0 \qquad (5\text{-}14b)$$

In Equation 5-14b, the term e is the base of the natural logarithm. This equation therefore indicates that, when β is zero, land rent decreases exponentially as u increases. Both equations indicate that $R(u)$ equals $\bar{R}$ when u equals $\bar{u}$. Both have the characteristic shape established in Chapter 4 and illustrated in Figure 4-1. It can be seen from the definition of β that $\beta =$ zero, and Equation 5-14b thus applies, when $\theta_2 = -1$. But it was indicated above that θ_2, the price elasticity of demand for housing, is probably about -1, and the exponential function of Equation 5-14b should therefore be a good approximation of urban land-rent functions. The term β is positive if $\theta_2 > -1$, that is, if housing demand is price-inelastic. Regardless of the sign of β, $R(u)$ is steep at small values of u and flat at large values of u.

Equations 5-14a and 5-14b contain the variable $\bar{u}$, representing the radius of the urban area. So far, Equation 5-10 has not been used and $\bar{u}$ has not been computed. Using the equilibrium condition of Equation 5-6, Equation 5-5 can be written:

$$N(u) = \frac{X_s(u)}{x_D(u)} \qquad (5\text{-}15)$$

Taking the ratio of Equation 5-2 to Equation 5-3, $K(u)$ can be expressed in terms of $L(u)$:

$$K(u) = \frac{1-\alpha}{\alpha r} R(u)L(u)$$

Now substitute this expression for $K(u)$ in Equation 5-1. The result is

$$X_s(u) = A\left(\frac{1-\alpha}{\alpha r}\right)^{1-\alpha} R(u)^{1-\alpha}L(u) \qquad (5\text{-}16)$$

Substitute Equation 5-11 for $p(u)$ in Equation 5-4. Then, in Equation 5-15, substitute Equation 5-4 for $x_D(u)$ and Equation 5-16 for $X_s(u)$. Rearranging terms gives

$$\frac{N(u)}{L(u)} = ER(u)^{1-\beta} \qquad (5\text{-}17)$$

If both sides of this equation are multiplied by $L(u)$, Equation 5-8 is substituted for $L(u)$, and the result is integrated from $\underline{u}$ to u, an expression for the left-hand side of Equation 5-10 results. Equating it to N provides the equation from which $\bar{u}$ can be calculated. The result, however, is cumbersome and so is not presented here.

Equation 5-17 shows how the number of resident workers per square mile varies with u. Except for a multiplicative factor equal to the reciprocal of the labor force participation rate, it is the same as population density, and so will be referred to as "population density" from here on. Equation 5-17 expresses a remarkable result: population density is proportionate to land rent raised to the power $1 - \beta$. The term $1 - \beta$ must be positive, since θ_2 is negative. Thus, as would be expected, population density is high wherever land rent is high. More important, if $\beta = 0$, so that Equation 5-14b applies, population density is proportionate to land rent, and therefore declines exponentially with u just as land rent does. Exponential functions have been used in many applied studies of urban population density (some of which are reported in Chapter 6) and have been found to fit the data very well. Thus, Equation 5-17 provides a link between theory and observation.

A universal conclusion of urban population-density studies is that density functions become flatter through time. Many writers have guessed that increasing incomes and falling commuting costs have caused the density functions to flatten. The mathematical model here shows that the guess is correct. The population density function of Equation 5-17 will be flatter, the larger is the coefficient of u in Equation 5-14a or 5-14b; that is, the closer is the coefficient to zero. Both increases in w and decreases in t

flatten the density function by increasing the coefficients of u in Equations 5-14a and 5-14b.

It is easy to see that finding $R(u)$ is the key to solving the mathematical model. Many of the other variables have already been expressed as functions of $R(u)$; the term $p(u)$ can be calculated from Equation 5-11; the term $L(u)$ is given by Equation 5-8; the term $X_s(u)$ can be calculated from Equation 5-16; and the term $N(u)$ can be calculated from Equation 5-17. As an exercise, calculate $x_D(u)$, which shows how housing demand per worker varies with u, and prove that it is exponential if $R(u)$ is exponential.

TWO HOUSEHOLD SECTORS

In this section, the mathematical model is generalized to study the effects of income differences on the household location pattern. In particular, a proof is provided for the statement in Chapter 4 that, under realistic conditions, high-income households live farther from the city center than do low-income households.

Until now, the time cost of travel has simply been included in t. In this section, it is assumed that commuters value travel time proportionately to the wage rate w. Thus, t is written

$$t = t_o + t_w w \qquad (5\text{-}18)$$

where t_o represents operating cost per two miles of travel, about 20–25 cents if travel is by automobile; t_w represents the time cost or disutility of two miles of travel per dollar of income; and t_w is inversely proportional to travel speed. For example, suppose commuting speed is 25 miles per hour. Then two miles of travel require $2(1/25) = 0.08$ hours (4.8 minutes). If travel time is valued at the wage rate, $t_w = 0.08$. If the wage rate is $5 per hour, the time cost of two miles of commuting is 40 cents. If t_o is 25 cents, two miles of commuting have a total cost of 65 cents. In this example, location equilibrium requires that the worker's housing expense must fall by 65 cents per day, or about $14 per month (assuming a 22-day working month), if he moves one mile further from the city center.

If travel time is valued at less than the wage rate, t_w is less than in the example. If commuting speed is faster than 25 miles per hour, t_w is also less than in the example. As was indicated in Chapter 4, the assumption that the marginal disutility of commuting is independent of commuting distance is a special case. It is shown below that the assumption is crucial to the results obtained here.

Suppose two household sectors, distinguished only by income. Household sector 1 has income w_1, and household sector 2 has income w_2. All households have the same tastes and therefore the same housing demand function, but the amount of housing demanded differs from one sector to another.

For convenience, the household sector closer to the city center is designated number 1, and its rent-offer function as $R_1(u)$. The sector farther from the center is number 2, and its rent offer $R_2(u)$. Then the two rent-offer functions must be as shown in Figure 5-1. If sector 1 is to be close to the center, its rent-offer function must be above that of sector 2 for small values of u. Household sector 1 occupies the available land at values of u between $\underline{u}$ and u_o, and sector 2 occupies the land between u_o and $\bar{u}$. Suppose u_o and $\bar{u}$ satisfy all the equilibrium conditions.

$R_2(u)$ has the initial condition $R_2(\bar{u}) = \bar{R}$, and its solution is Equation 5-14a if $\beta \neq 0$; that is,

$$R_2(u) = [\bar{R}^\beta + \beta t_2 E_2(\bar{u} - u)]^{1/\beta} \tag{5-19a}$$

where w affects E and t, but not β. Therefore, E_2 and t_2 designate the values of E and t when the wage rate is w_2.

$R_1(u)$ has the initial condition $R_1(u_o) = R_2(u_o)$, and its solution is

$$R_1(u) = [\bar{R}^\beta + \beta t_2 E_2(\bar{u} - u_o) + \beta t_1 E_1(u_o - u)]^{1/\beta} \tag{5-19b}$$

It can be verified that Equation 5-19b satisfies its initial condition, and that $R_1(u)$ and $R_2(u)$ can have only one intersection.

Is sector 1, close to the center, the high-income or the low-income sec-

Figure 5-1

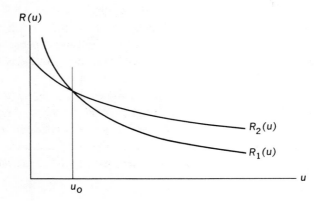

tor? The condition that $R_1(u)$ be greater than $R_2(u)$ at values of u less than u_o is

$$[\bar{R}^\beta + \beta t_2 E_2(\bar{u} - u_o) + \beta t_1 E_1(u_o - u)]^{1/\beta} > [\bar{R}^\beta + \beta t_2 E_2(\bar{u} - u)]^{1/\beta} \qquad (5\text{-}20)$$

for $u < u_o$. If β is positive, Inequal. 5-20 reduces to the condition that the term in square brackets on the left-hand side exceed the term in square brackets on the right-hand side; that is,

$$\bar{R}^\beta + \beta t_2 E_2(\bar{u} - u_o) + \beta t_1 E_1(u_o - u) > \bar{R}^\beta + \beta t_2 E_2(\bar{u} - u)$$

for $u < u_o$, or

$$t_1 E_1 > t_2 E_2 \qquad (5\text{-}21)$$

If β is negative, Inequal. 5-20 reduces to the condition that the term in square brackets on the left-hand side be less than the term in square brackets on the right-hand side; that is,

$$\bar{R}^\beta + \beta t_2 E_2(\bar{u} - u_o) + \beta t_1 E_1(u_o - u) < \bar{R}^\beta + \beta t_2 E_2(\bar{u} - u)$$

Canceling terms and remembering that $\beta < 0$, this inequality also reduces to Inequal. 5-21.

Thus, it is only necessary to establish the relationship between w_1 and w_2 that is equivalent to Inequal. 5-21. The following theorem provides the key relationship: If $\theta_1 \geq 1$, then Inequal. 5-21 holds if and only if $w_2 > w_1$. To prove the theorem, first note that E is w^{θ_1} multiplied by terms that cancel on both sides of Inequal. 5-21, which therefore can be written

$$\frac{t_o + t_w w_1}{t_o + t_w w_2} > \left(\frac{w_1}{w_2}\right)^{\theta_1} \qquad (5\text{-}22)$$

by substituting Equation 5-18 for t.

1. Suppose $w_2 > w_1$. Then Equation 5-22 holds for $\theta_1 = 1$, since

$$\frac{t_o + t_w w_1}{w_1} = \frac{t_o}{w_1} + t_w > \frac{t_o + t_w w_2}{w_2} = \frac{t_o}{w_2} + t_w$$

reduces to $w_2 > w_1$. But the right-hand side of Inequal. 5-22 becomes smaller as θ_1 becomes larger than 1. Therefore, $w_2 > w_1$ implies Inequal. 5-22.

2. Suppose $w_2 < w_1$. The left-hand side of Inequal. 5-22 has a maximum value of w_1/w_2 when $t_o = 0$, and decreases asymptotically to 1 as t_o becomes large. But the right-hand side of Inequal. 5-22 exceeds w_1/w_2 if $\theta_1 > 1$. Therefore, Inequal. 5-22 cannot hold.

This proves the theorem. Using Equation 5-14b, the theorem can be verified if $\beta = 0$. Thus, in this model, an income elasticity of demand for housing of at least 1 implies that low-income workers live closer to the city center than high-income workers. Generally, any number of household sectors, differentiated only by income, will be ranked by distance from the city center inversely to their rank by income.

The theorem only proves that low-income groups live close to the city center if $\theta_1 \geq 1$. It does not prove that they will live elsewhere if $\theta_1 < 1$. Inequal. 5-22 may still hold for $w_2 > w_1$ even if $\theta_1 < 1$. For example, suppose that t_o and t_w have the values 0.25 and 0.08 used in the foregoing example. Suppose further that $w_1 = \$2$ and $w_2 = \$4$. Then Inequal. 5-22 holds if $\theta_1 \geq 0.48$.

It is easy to see that the theorem may not hold if high-income workers value travel time higher in relationship to the wage rate than do low-income workers, or if the marginal disutility of commuting increases with the amount of commuting. In the former case, t_w is larger for the high-income group than for the low-income group. In the latter case, t_w is larger for the sector residing farther from the city center. It can be easily verified that the theorem does not hold if either change is made in the model. But it is still true that a sufficiently large income elasticity of housing demand will result in the location pattern implied by the model.

SUMMARY

This chapter has shown how mathematical models can be used to explain important characteristics of urban areas. First, land values are extremely high near the centers of large urban areas. Near the center they fall rapidly with distance; in the suburbs they flatten. Downtown land values may be 100 or 200 times as high as those ten or twenty miles away in the suburbs. The model shows how transportation costs and the substitution of land and other inputs cause the pattern.

Second, urban population densities have been widely observed to decline exponentially with distance from city centers. The model shows that the exponential density pattern results from empirically verified parameter values in production and demand functions.

Third, it has been observed that population density functions flatten through time, and that high-income families typically live farther from city centers than do low-income families. The model explains that these are closely related phenomena resulting from the effects of income on housing demand.

These are dramatic results from a simple model. Somewhat more so-phisticated urban models are presented in the references at the end of the chapter. But urban model building is in its infancy. Hardly any models con-tain realistic transportation systems, so that the effects of the transportation system on urban structure can be studied. And hardly any of the models provide insight into the determinants of employment location, so that the interaction between housing and employment location and the causes of employment suburbanization can be studied. Important scientific questions and urgent social issues hinge on the outcome of such studies.

DISCUSSION QUESTIONS

1. What are the relative merits of a discrete model like Lowry's and a con-tinuous model like that presented in this chapter?
2. Alter the model in this chapter by using the CES production function in-stead of the Cobb-Douglas in Equation 5-1. How would the pattern of residential land use and land rent be affected, depending on whether the elasticity of substitution were large or small?
3. What does your economic intuition tell you should happen to $\bar{u}$, the radius of the city, if t falls, in the model with one household sector? Can you check your intuition mathematically?

REFERENCES AND FURTHER READING

Ira Lowry, *A Model of Metropolis*, Rand Corporation, RM-4035/RC, August 1964.
Edwin S. Mills, *Studies in the Structure of the Urban Economy*, 1972.
Richard Muth, *Cities and Housing*, 1969.
Lowdon Wingo, *Transportation and Urban Land*, 1964.

Chapter 6

Trends in Suburbanization of Urban Areas in the United States

The theoretical analysis of Chapters 3–5 suggests that urban population and employment are likely to become less centrally located as time passes. Population decentralization is likely as the population of the urban area grows, as real incomes rise, and as commuting becomes cheaper and faster. Employment decentralization is likely as the population of the urban area grows and spreads out, and as road transportation replaces rail and water transportation in intercity freight movement.

Americans are strongly aware that suburbanization has proceeded rapidly since World War II. For reasons probably more comprehensible to the social psychologist than to the economist, the subject arouses strong emotion on all sides. The rapid growth of suburban populations reveals clearly that large numbers of people prefer suburbs to the available alternatives. But professionals concerned with urban affairs, such as city planners, sociologists, and economists, tend to be critical of the architecture, the life styles, the racial and ethnic groupings, and other aspects of suburbia. The terms "slurb" and "suburban sprawl" were invented to express the predominant attitude of disdain. Many criticisms are based on the strong personal likes and dislikes of the writers and have little to do with professional expertise. Of course, urban professionals are free to have personal opinions, but suburbanization seems to generate emotions out of proportion to the amount of serious study that has been devoted to the subject.

For a social scientist interested in evaluation of the suburbanization process, the obvious first question is whether there are reasons to believe that suburban land markets are inefficient in allocating resources to satisfy people's needs and tastes. No one has yet posed the question carefully enough to permit an answer, let alone presented persuasive reasons for inefficiency. Most critics content themselves with the claim that suburban housing is unplanned and therefore chaotic. But the issue is not planning versus chaos. Rather, it is whether competitive markets allocate resources efficiently. It is instructive that the only careful analysis of inefficiency in urban housing markets has been applied to inner-city slums. Eevn those who believe that inner-city housing markets operate inefficiently have been unwilling to draw the same conclusions regarding suburban markets. (This issue is discussed in Chapter 10.)

An example will indicate the kind of poorly reasoned criticism that is common. Writers often complain that low suburban population densities devour large amounts of land needed for agriculture and other purposes. In the first place, suburbanization results in large part from the growth of metropolitan areas as described in Chapter 2. But residential land per household is much less in metropolitan areas than in the small towns and rural areas from which migrants come. Therefore, urbanization and the resulting suburbanization decrease, rather than increase, the land required for residential purposes. In the second place, to the extent that suburban population densities are artificially low, it is because of artificially low density zoning, discussed in Chapter 10. But this is a failure of public policy rather than of private markets, and the remedy is removal of defective zoning rules.

As is often true of highly emotional subjects, the facts of suburbanization are prosaic enough. Much of the available data regarding suburbanizations of U.S. urban areas is surveyed in this chapter. The first task is to establish precise measures of suburbanization. Then, the measures are used to quantify post-World War II suburbanization of population and employment in U.S. metropolitan areas. Finally, measures of prewar suburbanization are surveyed to ascertain the extent to which postwar suburbanization differs from earlier periods.

MEASURES OF SUBURBANIZATION

Despite its familiarity, the notion of suburbanization is not really a simple one. The most readily available measure of suburbanization, and the one almost always used in newspaper and magazine accounts, concerns the numbers of people living in central cities and in the surrounding suburban rings of metropolitan areas. By this measure, a metropolitan area would be said to have suburbanized between two points in time if a larger fraction of the metropolitan area's residents lived in the suburban ring at time 2 than at time 1. It is a valuable measure and much can be learned from it. But it relies on the location of the boundary of the legal city, and has the defects of data based on the legal city discussed in Chapter 1.

First, it does not permit cross-sectional comparisons of suburbanization. It is desirable to be able to tell whether one urban area is more suburbanized than another, but the amount and proportion of the land and population included in the central city vary enormously from one urban area to another. Therefore, central-city/suburban-ring data do not permit meaningful comparisons.

Second, even time-series comparisons must be made with care. Central-city boundaries are sometimes moved outward as urban areas grow, so that the central city continues to encompass a large part of the urban area. Some census data are presented for old as well as for new boundaries. When they are not, it is sometimes possible to estimate population and employment within old boundaries from data based on new boundaries, but the estimates are approximate at best.

Third, the central-city/suburban-ring dichotomy yields data aggregated across space. For some purposes, it would be desirable to measure changes in location patterns within central cities and within suburban rings.

Ideally, the urban economist would like to know the numbers of people living and working in various industries in each census tract. Each large city contains several dozen census tracts, and in the densest places a census tract is only a few city blocks. Such data would permit comparisons among a variety of measures of suburbanization. For recent censuses, population data are available by census tract, and interesting studies of population suburbanization have been undertaken using them. But government disclosure rules forbid the census bureau to publish data pertaining to fewer than four people or firms. Disclosure rules pose no problems for census-tract population data, since most census tracts contain several thousand residents. But a census tract may contain only one or a few firms in a particular industry, so the data cannot be published. With only a few exceptions, census data are available for employment in detailed industries for entire metropolitan areas, and for broad industry categories for central cities and suburban rings. In addition, many cities and states publish directories that may contain very detailed data. But little information is comparable among a large group of urban areas.

When dealing with census data, it is important to distinguish between employment by place of residence and employment by place of employment. Census-tract data give the industry of employment for working residents. In these data, workers are located in the tract in which they reside, and the data are referred to as employment data by place of residence. Employment data by place of employment identify workers by the places where they work. These are the data needed for measures of employment suburbanization, and whose availability is mainly limited to the central-city/suburban-ring dichotomy. Unless otherwise indicated, employment data here refer to employment by place of employment.

The foregoing can be summarized by the statement that urban employment data are mainly available for the central-city/suburban-ring dichotomy. The simplest processing of these data tells us a good deal about employment suburbanization. How much more can be learned from the data depends on what is already known or can be assumed about the location pattern.

POPULATION AND EMPLOYMENT SUBURBANIZATION SINCE WORLD WAR II

In this section, as much as possible of the postwar suburbanization story is told, using central-city/suburban-ring data. Since suburbanization is mainly a phenomenon of large metropolitan areas, we will begin with the list of 100 SMSAs that had populations of at least 250,000 in 1960. They are the SMSAs on which the 1960 data in Table 2–4 of Chapter 2 are based. We eliminate the six SMSAs that comprise the two standard consolidated areas (New York/northeastern New Jersey and Chicago/Gary) identified by the census in 1960. The reason for eliminating these SMSAs is that in standard consolidated areas, some central cities are to some extent suburbs of others. In such areas, the meaning of suburbanization is unclear, and considerable processing would be necessary to untangle the data. For the same reason, we eliminate the three contiguous SMSAs in the Los Angeles area. Finally, we eliminate the Washington, D.C., SMSA because its employment pattern is dominated by the federal government.

The result is a list of ninety SMSAs for which suburbanization can be measured with considerable precision. But keep in mind that the list excludes the three most populous areas in the country. As a reminder, the list will be referred to as medium-size SMSAs.

For the list of medium-size SMSAs, an approximate correction can be made to allow for boundary changes of central cities between 1950 and 1960. (The method of correction is given by Niedercorn and Kain.) All the data in Table 6–1 have been adjusted to approximate 1950 central-city

Table 6-1   Suburbanization of Population and Employment in 90 SMSAs,
1947–1963 (population and employment figures in thousands)

Sector	1947 or 1950				1960 or 1963			
	Central City		Suburban Ring		Central City		Suburban Ring	
Population	26,742	53.0%	23,506	47.0%	26,554	40.0%	39,487	60.0%
Employment								
Manufacturing	3,750	60.5	2,449	39.5	3,250	46.2	3,791	53.8
Retailing	2,032	71.5	811	28.5	1,667	48.7	1,756	51.3
Service	673	79.5	173	20.5	826	61.1	525	38.9
Wholesaling	980	85.2	171	14.8	943	65.2	503	34.8
Totals	7,435	67.3%	3,604	32.7%	6,686	50.4%	6,575	49.6%

Sources: United States censuses of population, 1950 and 1960; of business, 1948 and
1963; and of manufactures, 1948 and 1963.

boundaries. The table shows population and employment data for the central cities and suburban rings of the ninety SMSAs for two years since World War II. The years chosen are those in which relevant censuses were taken. Population data refer to 1950 and 1960. Employment data refer to 1947 and 1963. Employment data are for industries included in the censuses of manufacturers and business.

Only the service category of Table 6-1 is not self-explanatory. It includes finance, insurance, and real estate; business and repair services; personal services; and entertainment and recreational services. About two thirds of the SMSA employment is included in Table 6-1. The important excluded industries are construction; transportation, communication, and public utilities; professional services; and public administration.

Table 6-1 shows that population is more suburbanized than total employment and than any of the employment categories. In 1950, 47.0 percent of the residents of medium-size SMSAs lived in suburban rings, whereas in 1947 only 32.7 percent of the employees worked there. In 1960 and 1963, the figures were 60.0 percent and 49.6 percent. It should not be surprising that population is more suburbanized than employment, since it means merely that more people commute to work into than out of central cities. But it supports the suggestion made in Chapter 4 that, close to city centers, firms' rent-offer functions are generally steeper than those of households.

The ranking of employment sectors by degree of suburbanization remained unchanged during the period covered by Table 6-1. Manufacturing is the most suburbanized employment sector, followed by retailing, services, and wholesaling, in that order. These findings are also in keeping with the theoretical analysis of Chapter 4. There it was suggested that manufacturing should be highly decentralized because it is subject to rapidly decreasing returns on the ratios of other inputs to land, and because most of its output is exported outside the urban area and increasingly goes by road. Retailing is highly suburbanized because of the importance of locations near household customers. Services are centralized at least in part because the *VMPs* of other inputs fall slowly as their ratio to land is increased. Wholesaling is something of an enigma. One conjecture is that it is the most centralized employment category because firms in it need the demand of customers throughout the urban area to achieve a size that exhausts its scale economies.

Table 6-1 indicates that there has indeed been a great deal of suburbanization in medium-size SMSAs since World War II. Central-city populations fell from 53.0 percent of SMSA populations in 1950 to 40.0 percent in 1960. Central-city employment fell from 67.3 percent of SMSA employment in 1947 to 50.4 percent in 1963. Moreover, the total number of people living and working in central cities fell slightly during the period covered by the table. Almost beyond doubt, population suburbanization resulted mainly from rapidly rising real incomes, from growth in SMSA sizes, and from improved commuting conditions. Suburbanization of employment results from increasing SMSA size, from suburbanization of labor force and customers, and from the growing importance of trucks as the mode of intercity freight transport.

By one measure, population and manufacturing employment suburbanized least among the sectors included in Table 6-1. The percentage of the population living in the suburbs went from 47.0 to 60.0, an increase of 13 percentage points. For manufacturing, the increase was 14.3 points. But for the other employment categories, the figures are: retailing, 22.8; services, 18.3; wholesaling, 20.0. Some popular writing gives the impression that suburbanization has occurred mainly in residential and manufacturing location. The measure used here suggests the contrary—although it may be misleading. None of the percentages can go above 100, so there is less room for the large percentages to increase than for the small percentages to do so.

DENSITY FUNCTIONS

The defects listed above for central-city/suburban-ring data suggest the need for a measure of suburbanization alternative to that used in Table 6-1. It was shown in Chapter 5 that there are good theoretical reasons to expect population density to decline exponentially (approximately) with distance from the city center. Furthermore, several studies have shown that population densities do follow the exponential pattern closely. Most important, the exponential function has mathematical properties that make it useful as a measure of suburbanization. Changing the notation slightly from Equations 5-14b and 5-17 of Chapter 5, an exponential density function can be written as

$$D(u) = D_o e^{-\gamma u} \qquad (6\text{-}1)$$

where $D(u)$ is the density at a distance u miles from the center, e is the base of the natural logarithm, and D_o and γ are constants. Equation 6-1 has the general shape shown in Figure 6-1. Putting u equal to zero, it can be seen that D_o is the density at the city center, although it is a somewhat artificial notion for population, since very few people live extremely close to the centers of large metropolitan areas. The term γ is positive if density decreases with distance, and it is easy to see from Equation 6-1 that the density function is flatter the smaller is γ. In fact, it can be shown by differentiating Equation 6-1 with respect to u that γ is the percentage by which $D(u)$ falls as u increases. For example, if γ were 0.5, it would mean that population density would fall at a rate of 50 percent per mile at each value of u.

A final mathematical property shows the relationship between a measure of suburbanization derived from the exponential function and that presented in Table 6-1. If an urban area's population grows by increasing D_o, leaving γ unchanged, the percentage of the population living within any fixed distance from the center remains unchanged. In particular, the percentage of the urban area's population living within the central city remains unchanged if the urban area grows by increasing D_o, but with γ constant. It is therefore natural to say that, of two exponential density functions, the one with the smaller γ represents the more suburbanized urban area.

Figure 6-1

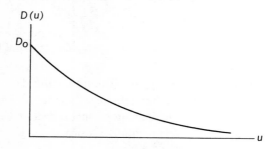

If changes in γ are precisely equivalent to change in the percentage of the urban area's population living in the central city, it might reasonably be asked: what is the advantage of the exponential function over the central-city/suburban-ring data as a measure of suburbanization? The answer is important. It is that the exponential function can be estimated with population and land-area data for any two dichotomous parts of the urban area.[1] In particular, estimates of exponential density functions from central-city/suburban-ring data are not affected by movements in the central city's boundaries if the central city's land area is known for each observation. This is extremely important because it eliminates the error in and work of adjusting for boundary changes, and far more important, because the adjustment cannot be made for pre-World War II data. The exponential function also permits cross-sectional comparisons. The term γ is a pure number, and if urban area A has a smaller γ than urban area B, it is safe to say that A is more suburbanized than B.

One warning is in order regarding exponential density functions. Although the evidence is strong that they provide a good approximation of urban population density patterns, there is almost no evidence as to their accuracy for employment density patterns. Thus, exponential density functions for employment should be viewed with much more suspicion than those for population.

Table 6-2 presents average values of γ estimated for a sample of eighteen of the ninety SMSAs represented in Table 6-1. Each entry in Table 6-2 is an unweighted average value of γ for the eighteen SMSAs, for the year and sector in question. In computing values of γ for population, the data were interpolated between census years to correspond to the years for which values of γ for employment were estimated.

Table 6-2 tells much the same story as Table 6-1. In all years, sectors are ranked in the same order by degree of suburbanization in the two tables. And both tables show that the SMSAs suburbanized greatly during the fifteen years covered. For example, Table 6-2 shows that population density fell at a rate of 58 percent per mile in 1948, but only 38 percent per mile in 1963.

Table 6-2 shows that, by one measure, suburbanization was more rapid during the early postwar years than in more recent years. Between 1948 and 1958, the average γ for population fell by 0.026 points per year, whereas between 1958 and 1963, it fell by 0.01 points per year. With the exception of

---

1. The estimation procedure is simple and is described by Mills. It relies on the fact that two observations permit an estimate of a two-parameter function. The density functions presented in the rest of this chapter are taken from the Mills study.

Table 6-2   Average Values of γ for 18 Metropolitan Areas

Sector	1948	1958	1963
Population	0.58	0.42	0.38
Manufacturing	0.68	0.48	0.42
Retailing	0.88	0.59	0.44
Services	0.97	0.66	0.53
Wholesaling	1.00	0.77	0.56

wholesaling, values of γ in the employment sector also decreased more rapidly during the early years covered by Table 6-2. In fact, it would be surprising if it were otherwise. The years between 1929 and 1945 contained a severe depression followed by an all-out war, both of which impede the normal process of suburbanization. Thus, a burst of suburbanization should be expected just after World War II, similar to the baby boom experienced at that time. Table 6-2 suggests that rapid suburbanization slackened in the late 1950s, at about the time the postwar baby boom ended.

Table 6-2 permits quantitative comparisons among sectors not possible with Table 6-1. For example, Table 6-2 permits us to say that population was almost twice as suburbanized as wholesaling employment was in 1948. This statement means that, with distance from the city center, the density of wholesaling employment fell almost twice as fast as that of population. (The value 1.00 for γ in the wholesaling sector in 1948 does not mean that wholesaling employment fell to zero at one mile from city centers. Rather, it means that, at each distance, wholesaling employment decreased at a rate of 100 percent per mile. It would only reach zero at one mile if the density function were linear, but of course the exponential function is not linear.)

An interesting conclusion from Table 6-2 is that the degree of suburbanization is becoming more nearly equal among the sectors represented. In 1948, wholesaling, the most centralized sector, was almost twice as centralized as population, the least centralized sector. In 1963 it was just less than one and a half times as centralized. If values of γ for population and employment were equal, it would be theoretically possible for no commuting to exist. The same percentage of employment as of population would be in any interval around the city center. For example, if the value of γ for both population and employment were 0.50, about 9 percent of both population and employment would be within one mile of the city center. Thus, it would be possible for each worker to work and live at the same distance from the center. Even if the value of γ for both was the same, there might be commuting. Equality of numbers of workers and jobs at each distance from the center does not necessarily mean that each worker is employed and lives the same distance from the city center. But there would be equal amounts of commuting in both directions at any distance from the center. If γ for population and employment continue to become more nearly equal, it should be expected that similar amounts of commuting into and out of central cities will be observed, and perhaps gradually decreasing amounts of commuting per worker.

PREWAR SUBURBANIZATION

Many people write as though suburbanization were a post-World War II invention. They do so because they tend to look at data on the numbers of people in central cities and suburban rings. As urban areas grow, more people inevitably live outside the central city, unless its boundaries are moved outward.

The methods discussed in the foregoing section make it possible to estimate employment, and especially, population density functions for periods considerably before World War II. But central-city/suburban-ring comparisons for prewar and postwar periods become meaningless because adjustments for boundary changes are almost impossible to make. And the amount of data available becomes much less the further back in history one goes, so the amount of processing the data require becomes much greater.

Table 6-3 shows average values of γ for population and available employment sectors, for selected years since 1920, for a sample of six of the eighteen metropolitan areas included in Table 6-2. The six metropolitan areas are Baltimore, Denver, Milwaukee, Philadelphia, Rochester, and Toledo. Although the number of large metropolitan areas was much smaller in the 1920s, six is nevertheless a small sample. Postwar values of γ for the six areas are included in Table 6-3 to facilitate comparison with the data in Table 6-2. Although the postwar values of γ for the six metropolitan areas are similar to those for the eighteen, they are by no means identical. Em-

Table 6-3   Average Values of γ for Six Metropolitan Areas

Sector	1920	1929	1939	1948	1958	1963
Population[a]	0.84	0.73	0.67	0.57	0.41	0.36
Manufacturing	0.95	0.82	0.77	0.76	0.60	0.48
Retailing	—	1.02	0.90	0.76	0.58	0.41
Services	—	—	1.12	0.88	0.70	0.55
Wholesaling	—	1.43	1.24	1.01	0.77	0.59

a) Population figures in columns headed 1929 and 1939 are for 1930 and 1940.

ployment density functions are impossible to estimate before the first years for which they are shown in Table 6-3 because the specialized industrial censuses were not collected before those years. Population density functions can be estimated for earlier years, and some are shown in Table 6-4. But they are presented separately because the sample is smaller yet, and because the data have been processed in somewhat subjective ways.

Table 6-3 shows that suburbanization did indeed occur before World War II. The population γ fell by an average of 0.011 points per year between 1920 and 1930, and the manufacturing employment γ fell by 0.013 points per year during the same period. As would be expected, there was much less suburbanization during the 1930s. But there was a surprising amount, especially in the population sector, between 1940 and 1948. Between 1958 and 1963, the population γ decreased by about the same number of points per year, 0.01, as between 1920 and 1930, which confirms the suggestion that the postwar burst of suburbanization had about exhausted itself by the late 1950s.

Table 6-3 also confirms the tendency toward convergence of values of γ observed in Table 6-2. In 1929, the largest γ was nearly twice as large as the smallest, whereas in 1963 it was less than two thirds larger than the smallest.

In summary, Table 6-3 shows about what we should expect. The 1920s were prosperous years in which automobile commuting became widespread and urban areas grew rapidly. Hence, suburbanization was rapid. The 1930s were depressed years, and suburbanization slowed almost to a standstill. After World War II, there was a burst of rapid suburbanization, caused by prosperity and rapid urbanization. By the late 1950s, there was evidence that the postwar burst of activity was over, but suburbanization was still rapid. Table 6-3 shows that employment sectors were still suburbanizing rapidly in the early 1960s, suggesting that they were still catching up to the rapid population suburbanization a few years earlier.

For population, it is possible to compute urban density functions back into the nineteenth century from census data. However, a great deal of hand processing of the data is necessary, placing a limit on the number of density functions that can be computed.[2] Average values of γ for a small sample of urban areas for selected years between 1890 and 1963 are shown in Table 6-4. It was not possible to compute density functions for years before 1900 for two of the six metropolitan areas included in Table 6-3. Hardly anybody lived outside the central city in the Toledo area, and Den-

---

2. The processing of the data and computation of the density functions are described by Mills.

Table 6-4   Average Values of γ of Population Density Functions for Four
Metropolitan Areas, 1890–1963

Year	Average γ	Year	Average γ
1880	1.22	1930	0.63
1890	1.06	1940	0.59
1900	0.96	1948	0.50
1910	0.80	1958	0.35
1920	0.69	1963	0.31

ver was too small to be included in the census. Therefore, the values of γ in Table 6-4 are averages for four metropolitan areas: Baltimore, Milwaukee, Philadelphia, and Rochester. Obviously, four metropolitan areas cannot be considered representative of even the small number of large metropolitan areas contained in the United States in 1880. Indeed, comparison between Tables 6-3 and 6-4 for overlapping years show that the four metropolitan areas are by no means entirely representative of even the six among which they are included.

For the four urban areas on which it is based, Table 6-4 presents a remarkable historical record of suburbanization. By 1963, the average value of γ of the four urban areas had fallen to one fourth of its 1880 value, representing a massive decentralization of the four urban areas during the 83-year period. The dramatic scale of the change can be put another way. Consider a metropolitan area whose γ equals the average for the four urban areas. In 1880, half the people in the representative metropolitan area lived within 1.3 miles of the city center. In 1963, half the people in the area lived within 5.5 miles of the center.

There is of course considerable variability from period to period in the rate at which the metropolitan areas suburbanized. Measured by the average decrease in γ per year, the fastest suburbanization occurred between 1880 and 1890 and between 1948 and 1954. But γ decreased almost as fast in the 1900–1930 and 1954–1958 periods. Generally, suburbanization proceeded most rapidly during prosperous periods, and slowed during depressions.

The findings presented in this chapter can be summarized by the statement that suburbanization has been a massive and pervasive characteristic of metropolitan areas in the United States as far back as the record has been examined. Population and employment density functions have flattened, especially during prosperous periods, throughout the twentieth century, and probably before. There is no reason to believe that the suburbanization process has been significantly different in the post-World War II period from that in other prosperous periods before the war.

SUMMARY

Census data show the percentages of people living and working in central cities and suburbs in metropolitan areas. These data must be used with care for several reasons, mainly resulting from the fact that central city boundaries are set for historical reasons and are changed from time to time. Census data show that population is more suburbanized than employment, and that manufacturing is the most suburbanized employment sector. Both population and employment have suburbanized rapidly since World War II.

An alternative to the use of raw census data as a measure of suburbanization is changes in exponential density functions. Density functions for U.S. metropolitan areas show that suburbanization has been rapid in prosperous periods as far back as data have been examined. Rapid employment suburbanization occurred during the prosperous 1920s, and population has been suburbanizing rapidly for as far back as the 1880s. The data provide no evidence that suburbanization has been of a different character since World War II than in earlier periods.

DISCUSSION QUESTIONS

1. Do you think it likely that suburbanization will proceed to the point where density is about uniform within each metropolitan area? Might density eventually be greater in suburbs than in city centers?
2. What are the implications for congestion in central business districts of continued employment suburbanization?
3. Do you think that the rapid growth of circumferential transportation (e.g., on beltways) since World War II is related to the convergence of population and employment density gradients? If so, what does it suggest about likely future metropolitan transportation patterns?
4. What would be the effect on suburbanization of population and employment of building radial subway lines?

REFERENCES AND FURTHER READING

Benjamin Chinitz, *City and Suburb*, 1965.

Colin Clark, "Urban Population Densities," *Journal of the Royal Statistical Society*, Series A, Vol. 114 (1957), 490–496.

Edwin S. Mills, *Studies in the Structure of the Urban Economy*, 1972.

Richard Muth, *Cities and Housing*, 1969.

John Niedercorn and John Kain, *Suburbanization of Employment and Population 1948–1975*, Rand Corporation, P-2641, January 1963.

Chapter 7
The Size Distributions of Urban Areas

Many factors interact in subtle and complex ways to determine the size of a particular urban area. Among the most important, with the direction in which they probably affect size, are the following: Some natural conditions, such as topography, climate, and availability of natural resources, provide comparative advantage to certain regions in the production of certain commodities. The stronger a region's comparative advantage in producing a group of commodities, the larger are the urban areas it is likely to contain. Natural conditions affect the cost of trading with other urban areas, regions, or countries. Other things being equal, an urban area with a good natural harbor will be larger than one with a poor harbor. Natural conditions also affect the desirability of an area to households. The greater the amenity resources of a region, the larger its urban areas are likely to be. The total population of a country affects the sizes of its urban areas. Generally, countries with large population densities have large urban areas. The demand for exports affects urban size. The stronger the demand in other places for goods in which an urban area has a comparative advantage, the larger the urban area will be. Finally, technology affects urban area size. An urban area has relatively rapid growth if it has a comparative advantage in producing goods for which technological progress is rapid.

Although little is known about the effective magnitudes of most of these factors, nothing said so far in this book suggests that they should result in any particular pattern of urban area sizes. It would seem that some sets of conditions might result in urban areas of nearly equal size, whereas other sets of conditions might result in urban areas of unequal sizes. It would be remarkable—and call for an explanation—if a particular pattern of urban area sizes were found to be common to many countries, or to persist through time. Nevertheless, a large literature has appeared through the years claiming to provide evidence or explanation of a particular pattern of urban area sizes across space and through time. In this chapter, major contributions to this literature are surveyed and criticized.

THE NATURE OF URBAN AREA SIZE DISTRIBUTIONS

A distribution function $f(x)$ shows the frequency with which the variable X takes the value x in a given population or sample of observations. (If X is continuous, it is more precise to say that $f(x)dx$ shows the frequency of observations within an interval dx centered on x.) Related to every distribution function $f(x)$ is a cumulative distribution $F(x)$ which shows the number of observations not greater than x in the population or sample. $F(x)$ is a sum or integral of $f(x)$. For some reason, writers on urban area size distributions follow the slightly confusing tradition of working with a function which shows the number of observations greater than x. The two functions are of course related in a simple way. If $G(x)$ is the number of observations greater than x, and N is the total number of observations, then

$$G(x) = N - F(x)$$

since the sum of $F(x)$ and $G(x)$ must be N.

The most important of all distribution functions is the normal or Gaussian distribution. It is symmetrical and fully specified by two parameters, mean and variance. The importance of the normal distribution stems partly from the fact that it closely approximates the frequencies of many natural phenomena, such as the various heights of people. But even more important is the fact that many sample statistics, such as the means of large random samples, are approximately normal even if the population variable is not.

It has long been observed that many economic phenomena systematically follow nonnormal distributions. (This does not mean that the normal distribution is unimportant to economics; it is as relevant to sample theory in economics as in other subjects.) To take the most prominent example, personal incomes follow a characteristically skewed distribution in which the upper tail is much longer than the lower tail, and the arithmetic mean of incomes exceeds modal and median incomes. Indeed, Pareto and many others have used the cumulative distribution which bears Pareto's name to describe the upper tail of personal-income distributions. The Pareto distribution is usually written

$$G(x) = Ax^{-a} \qquad (7\text{-}1)$$

where $G(x)$ is the number of incomes greater than x, and A and a are constants to be determined from the data. A depends on the total number of income recipients, but a has been found to be about 1.5 in many studies. Firm sizes also follow a skewed distribution in which there are a large number of rather small firms and a small number of very large firms.

Many scholars in different disciplines have studied urban area sizes and concluded that they are highly skewed, and follow either the Pareto or a closely related distribution. (Consult Berry and Garrison for an excellent survey of this subject, and for references to many of the studies.) In particular, George Zipf has claimed, on the basis of urban area size data in the United States and in other countries, that urban area size distributions follow a special case of the Pareto distribution, called the *rank-size rule*. It can be written as

$$G(x) = Ax^{-1} \qquad (7\text{-}2)$$

where $G(x)$ is the number of urban areas with at least x inhabitants. Thus Equation 7-2 is the special case of the Pareto distribution in which $a = 1$. The rank-size rule stems from the observation that $G(x)$ is the rank of the urban area with x inhabitants. For example, if there are five urban areas with at least 3.5 million people, then an urban area with 3.5 million is said to have rank 5. If both sides of Equation 7-2 are multiplied by x, the result is

$$xG(x) = A \qquad (7\text{-}3)$$

which says that the product of an urban area's size and rank is a constant. If $G(x) = 1$, Equation 7-3 says that $x = A$; that is, A is the size of the largest urban area. The rank-size rule, Equation 7-2, then has the easy implication that the second largest urban area has half the population of the largest, the third largest has one third the population of the largest, and, generally, an urban area of rank n has 1 nth the population of the largest urban area.

If the rank-size rule is an accurate description of urban area sizes, it is certainly one of the world's remarkable statistical regularities. Thus, the first question is whether the rank-size rule fits the facts.

THE EVIDENCE

The size distribution of urban areas has been studied, not only for every U.S. decennial census, but also for censuses in virtually every country that publishes the requisite data. Almost every study has concluded that the rank-size rule provides a remarkably close fit to the data. No one who looks at the graphs and tables presented in such studies can fail to be impressed by the persistence of the relationship, at least as a rough approximation.

But it is also true that most empirical studies of urban area size distributions employ remarkably unsophisticated statistical methods. The usual procedure is to present tables and graphs showing city sizes and ranks, and to conclude by inspection that the data approximately obey the rank-size rule. Few studies employ even elementary methods of curve fitting and significance testing.

Studies of urban area size distribution employ a large number of urban concepts, with almost no discussion of which might be most relevant. Madden uses urban places as his basic unit. But it was shown in Chapter 1 that large urban areas consist of many urban places, and that urban places are of little interest in the study of urban areas. Other writers use the legal city or the SMSA as their basic unit, but without discussion of its relevance to the hypothesis.

A final criticism of studies of urban area size distributions is that they rarely discuss the geographical area in which the rank-size rule is expected to apply. The rank-size rule has been fitted to data from states, provinces, regions, and countries. But it is obvious that the rule cannot hold for all levels of geographical aggregation. Suppose it holds exactly for two countries with identical city size distributions. Then it cannot hold for the two countries taken together. The rule requires that the second largest urban area be half as large as the largest, whereas in the two countries together, the two largest urban areas would be the same size.

These criticisms result from the fact that most writers have treated the rank-size rule as something of a statistical curiosity. In that case, it may be just as interesting for one definition of urban area as another, or on one level of geographical aggregation as another. But a more satisfactory approach would formulate a mechanism by which the rank-size rule is generated. Then the mechanism would suggest the appropriate unit of observation. Most plausible mechanisms (certainly the two discussed in the next section) indicate that urbanized areas in an economically integrated region or country are the appropriate observations.

A detailed examination of a small sample of evidence might be helpful at this point. Table 7-1 shows the population and rank of every tenth entry in the list by size or urbanized areas in the 1960 U.S. census of population. The right-hand column shows the product of rank and population. Do these data confirm or refute the rank-size rule? Of course, no theory in the social sciences is exactly confirmed by any significant body of evidence. The

Table 7-1   Population and Rank of a Sample of U.S. Urbanized Areas,
1960

Urbanized Area	Rank	Population (000)	Rank X Population
New York/northeastern New Jersey	1	14,115	14,115
St. Louis	11	1,668	18,348
Miami	21	853	17,913
Louisville	31	607	18,817
Albany/Schenectady/Troy	41	455	18,655
Bridgeport	51	367	18,717
Grand Rapids	61	294	17,934
Des Moines	71	241	17,111
Scranton	81	211	17,091
Pomona/Ontario	91	187	17,017
Charleston, W. Va.	101	170	17,170
Madison	111	158	17,538
Lincoln	121	136	16,456
Augusta, Ga.	131	124	16,244
Kalamazoo	141	116	16,356
Wichita Falls	151	102	15,402
Eugene	161	96	15,456
Lake Charles	171	89	15,219
Champaign/Urbana	181	78	14,118
Reno	191	70	13,370
Harlington/San Benito	201	62	12,462
Texarkana	211	53	11,183

Source: U.S. census of population, 1960.

most that can be hoped is that deviations from the theory are small and random.

There is clearly some tendency for the product of rank and population of urbanized areas to cluster, and the average product in the sample is 16,213. But there are also some substantial and apparently systematic departures. The smallest entries are at the top and bottom of the table. The largest entry is the fourth, and they fall quite smoothly toward the bottom of the table. The best way to test the rank-size rule is to go back to the Pareto distribution of Equation 7-1. Taking logs of both sides yields

$$\log G(x) = \log A - a \log x \qquad (7\text{-}4)$$

The accuracy of the Pareto distribution in describing the relationship between rank and urban area size can be tested by computing the least-squares regression[1] of Equation 7-4 using the data in Table 7-1. If the co-

---

1. The least squares regression simply means using as estimates of A and a the numbers that minimize the sum of the squared deviations between values of log G(x) calculated from Equation 7–4, and those calculated from the data in Table 7–1. For further discussion of this and related matters, consult any good textbook on statistical methods, such as Fraser.

efficient of log x is about -1, it can be said that the rank-size rule is confirmed by the sample data. The result is

$$\log G(x) = 9.4540 - 0.9573 \log x \qquad (7\text{-}5)$$
$$(0.1238) \quad (0.0223)$$

The numbers in parentheses are the estimated standard deviations of the coefficients, and they indicate the likely difference between the true and estimated coefficients. In a sample the size of this one (twenty-two urbanized areas) the probability is about 0.05 that the true and estimated coefficients will differ by as much as twice the standard deviation. It is unlikely that the true coefficient of log x is larger than 1.0019. Thus, the sample data are consistent with the possibility that the rank-size rule holds, but the best guess is that the true exponent in the Pareto distribution of urban area sizes is nearer -0.95 than -1.0. It should also be reported that the squared correlation coefficient between log $G(x)$ and log x is 0.989. This means that the log of city size explains almost 99 percent of the variance of the log of rank in the sample.

The conclusion is that the relationship between rank and urban area size is extremely close in the sample examined here, but that the rank-size rule is unlikely to hold with precision. Many studies support the conclusion. It is safe to say that the relationship between urban area size and rank is one of the most remarkable in all the social sciences. Intuition tells us that some powerful mechanism must be at work.

THEORIES OF URBAN AREA SIZE DISTRIBUTION

The evidence is strong that urban sizes in a particular country follow the Pareto distribution, although not necessarily the special case implied by the rank-size rule. As social and demographic regularities go, the Pareto distribution seems remarkably persistent through time and across very different kinds of societies. Why should urban area sizes follow this particular distribution? Two quite different hypotheses were put forward by Martin Beckmann and Herbert Simon in the 1950s to explain the Pareto distribution of city sizes. Each must be considered in some detail.

The Beckmann Model

Beckmann's model comes from a line of thought that goes back to Christaller, Zipf, Rashevsky, and, most importantly, Lösch. Beckmann's important contribution was to extract the crucial features from a diffuse literature and to show that they entail a simple formal model.

The model rests on two apparently simple, but powerful, assumptions. Suppose each urban area performs certain functions for its own residents and for the residents of a set of smaller urban areas. The first crucial assumption is that each person can perform the functions for a limited number of people. The term k is a parameter whose reciprocal is the number of people for whom one worker can perform the functions. Then k is the fraction of a worker it takes to perform the functions for one person, and k must be between zero and 1. If the functions performed by cities are the production of commodities, and if the unit in which to measure output is chosen such that one unit of the commodity is consumed by each customer, k is the labor input required per unit of output of the commodity.

Let p_1 be the population of an urban area of the smallest size, and P_1 the population served by the smallest urban area. The population of and the population served by an urban area of the second smallest size are p_2 and P_2. Generally, p_m and P_m are the population of and population served by an urban area of the mth smallest size. Then the first assumption can be expressed as follows:

$$p_m = k\,P_m \qquad (7\text{-}6)$$

which simply says that each urban worker produces enough to satisfy the needs of k people. A subsidiary assumption is that workers in the smallest urban areas serve themselves and some rural residents. It is assumed that only a limited number, say r, of rural residents can be served by an urban area of the smallest size. Then $P_1 = r + p_1$, and Equation 7-6 implies that

$$p_1 = k(r + p_1)$$

or

$$p_1 = \frac{kr}{1 - k} \qquad (7\text{-}7)$$

It easily follows that

$$P_1 = \frac{r}{1 - k} \qquad (7\text{-}8)$$

Equation 7-6 limits the number of people that one person can serve. The second basic assumption limits the number of urban areas of the next smallest size that can be served by an urban area of a given size. Specifically, it is assumed that an urban area of a given size can serve s urban areas of the next smallest size. Then

$$P_m = p_m + sP_{m-1} \qquad (7\text{-}9)$$

which says that the total number of people served by an urban area of size m is the population of the urban area plus the population served by s urban areas of the next smallest size. The s must exceed 1.

The r and s play similar roles in the model, and can be understood only within the context of the spatial pattern of urban areas that Lösch developed. If the rural landscape has a uniform population density, r is determined by the distance that rural residents can or will go for the goods provided in the smallest urban areas. Likewise, Lösch envisaged a spatial pattern in which urban areas of a certain size were located in a certain way. For example, one urban area of a certain size might be located at each point of a hexagon, with an urban area of the next larger size located in the center of the hexagon. Such a pattern would determine the value of s.

The assumptions of Equations 7-6, 7-7, and 7-9 have a remarkable implication. If the right-hand side of Equation 7-6 is substituted for p_m Equation 7-9, the result is

$$P_m = kP_m + sP_{m-1} \quad \text{or} \quad P_m = \frac{s}{1-k}P_{m-1}$$

This is called a difference equation, relating P_m to P_{m-1}. It implies that P_m can be expressed as an explicit function of m, which can be found as follows: P_{m-1} is related to P_{m-2} exactly as P_m is related to P_{m-1}. Thus

$$P_m = \frac{s}{1-k}\left(\frac{s}{1-k}P_{m-2}\right) = \left(\frac{s}{1-k}\right)^2 P_{m-2}$$

Likewise, the population served by an urban area of any size is similarly related to the population served by an urban area of the next smaller size. So

$$P_m = \left(\frac{s}{1-k}\right)^3 P_{m-3} = \ldots = \left(\frac{s}{1-k}\right)^{m-1} P_1$$

But the value of P_1 is known from Equation 7-8. So

$$P_m = \frac{rs^{m-1}}{(1-k)^m}$$

This is the solution of the difference equation for P_m. Using Equation 7-6, p_m is related to m by

$$p_m = \frac{krs^{m-1}}{(1-k)^m} = \frac{kr}{s}\left(\frac{s}{1-k}\right)^m \tag{7-10}$$

Since $s > 1$, and k is between zero and 1, it follows that $s/(1-k) > 1$. Therefore, Equation 7-10 says that urban area size increases geometrically with m. Dividing p_m by p_{m-1} gives

$$\frac{p_m}{p_{m-1}} = \frac{s}{1-k}$$

which says that an urban area of any size is $100\,[s/(1-k)]$ percent as big as urban areas of the next smaller size. For example, if $s = 2$ and $k = 0.2$, $s/(1-k)$ would be about 2.2. Of course, if $m = 1$ in Equation 7-10, the result is the value of p_1 given by Equation 7-7.

The final step in Beckmann's argument is to show how urban area sizes governed by Equation 7-10 are related to the rank-size rule. In this model there is one largest urban area, s urban areas of rank 2, s^2 urban areas of rank 3, and generally s^{n-1} urban areas of rank n. Taken literally, the model implies that all urban areas of rank n are the same size. Suppose, more realistically, that there is a small random effect on urban area size, and that populations of urban areas in a given size class are distributed evenly between the population of the largest urban area in the next smaller class and that of the smallest urban area in the next larger class. Then, using the rule for the sum of a geometric series, the middle urban area in the nth class will have the rank

$$1 + s + s^2 + \ldots + s^{n-1} + \frac{s^n}{2} = \frac{1-s^n}{1-s} + \frac{s^n}{2}$$

If n is fairly large, s^n is much larger than $1/(s-1)$, and the above expression can be approximated by

$$s^n\left(\frac{1}{s-1} + \frac{1}{2}\right) \tag{7-11}$$

Recall that Equation 7-10 gave the population of an urban area in the middle of the mth *smallest* size class, whereas Equation 7-11 gives the rank of an urban area in the middle of the nth *largest* size class. If there are N size classes altogether, Equations 7-10 and 7-11 refer to the same urban area if we put $m = N - n$. Then the product of rank and population for an urban area in the middle of the mth smallest or nth largest size class is

$$\frac{kr}{s}\left(\frac{s}{1-k}\right)^{N-n} s^n\left(\frac{1}{s-1} + \frac{1}{2}\right)$$
$$= \frac{kr}{s}\left(\frac{1}{s-1} + \frac{1}{2}\right)\left(\frac{s}{1-k}\right)^N (1-k)^n = C(1-k)^n \tag{7-12}$$

which says that the product of rank and size is a constant C times $(1-k)^n$. If, as seems reasonable, k is close to zero, $(1-k)^n$ will be close to 1, and rank times size will be nearly constant, which is the rank-size rule. As a matter of fact, Equation 7-12 suggests that the product of rank and size should decrease somewhat as n increases. That pattern was observed in the data presented in Table 7-1.

Despite the use of a certain amount of algebra in the derivation, the Beckmann model is an extraordinarily simple rationalization of what appears to be a complex phenomenon. The model includes almost none of the complex factors summarized at the beginning of this chapter as determinants of urban area sizes. First, it assumes a simple production function in which cost curves are L-shaped, labor is the only input, and input/output ratios are constant above the minimum output.

Second, the entire model is built on the foundation of the number of rural residents that can be served by cities of the smallest size. That determines the spatial distribution of urban areas of smallest size, which in turn determines the spatial distribution of urban areas of the next smaller size, and so on. This hardly seems an adequate foundation for a theory of urban area size in an economy in which two thirds of the population is urban. It is probably not accidental that the best empirical confirmation of the spatial pattern of urban areas of different sizes obtained by Lösch was in predominantly rural areas.

Third, the model ignores all geographical irregularities, natural resource availability, amenity resources, availability of harbors and other discrete transportation modes, and climatic differences. In short, it ignores all the natural factors that contribute to the comparative advantage of particular areas. Fourth, the model treats urban areas as points, without regard for spatial phenomena within urban areas. It ignores the possibility that urban area size may be partly limited by diminishing returns of the kind discussed in Chapter 1.

The Simon Model

Beckmann's theory shows that a very simple economic mechanism can generate a distribution of urban sizes that is similar to the Pareto distribution; Simon's theory shows that an equally simple statistical mechanism can generate the same size distribution. The basis of Simon's theory is the law of proportionate effect, which can be explained as follows: Suppose that z is a weighted sum of random variables $z_1, \ldots z_n$; that is,

$$z = \sum_{i=1}^{n} w_i z_i \qquad (7\text{-}13)$$

Then the central limit theorem in statistics tells us that z will be approximately normally distributed if only n is sufficiently large and the x_i terms are well-behaved random variables. The theorem has many applications in statistics, including the fact that arithmetic means of large samples are approximately normally distributed. But it also suggests that many natural phenomena will be approximately normal.

Suppose, for example, that yield per acre of a certain crop depends on soil fertility, pest infestation, rainfall, seed type, fertilizer, and other factors. If the number of such factors is large and the effects are additive, crop-yield distributions will be approximately normal. Now suppose a variable x which depends on the product of n random variables; that is,

$$x = x_1{}^{w_1} x_2{}^{w_2} \ldots x_n{}^{w_n} \tag{7-14}$$

Taking logs of both sides gives

$$\log x = \sum_{i-1}^{n} w_i \log x_i \tag{7-15}$$

If the x_i terms are positive and well-behaved random variables, the central limit theorem applies equally as well to $\log x$ in Equation 7-15 as to z in Equation 7-13. It then tells us that $\log x$ will be approximately normally distributed if n is sufficiently large. A variable x whose logarithm is normally distributed is said to obey the *lognormal distribution*, the properties of which have been extensively studied (see Aitcheson and Brown). The lognormal distribution, shown in Figure 7-1a, is quite different from the Pareto distribution, shown in Figure 7-1b. Both are skewed to the right, but the lognormal has a positive mode, whereas the mode of the Pareto distribution is zero. However, if one considers only the part of the lognormal distribution above a value of x, such as x_o, called *truncating* the distribution at

Figure 7-1

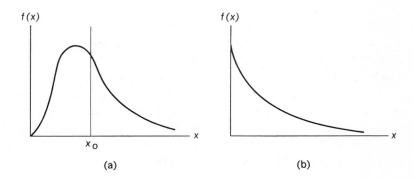

(a)   (b)

x_o, it and the Pareto distribution are similar. In fact, all the data on urban area sizes are truncated, because only settlements above a certain size, such as 2500 people, are included. In such data, that is, above a value like x_o, the lognormal and Pareto distributions may approximate each other.

Equation 7-14 expresses the law of proportionate effect. Applied to urban area sizes, it assumes that an urban area size is determined by a large number of random factors whose effects are multiplicative. Suppose, in addition to the law of proportionate effect, a certain probability of urban areas being born, that is, of settlements reaching the value x_o at which they are counted. Simon has shown that these assumptions lead to a class of urban area size distributions, of which the Pareto is a special case and a good approximation.

Simon and others have suggested that the law of proportionate effect is a pervasive fact about social phenomena. Why should urban area sizes be subject to the law of proportionate effect? It is easy to think of several factors that suggest that the law might be operative. The simplest has to do with human birth and death rates. Many of the factors that change birth and death rates affect large segments of society at once. Birth rates might be lowered by a depression or by the adoption of new methods of birth control. Death rates might be lowered by progress in medical knowledge. A significant change in birth or death rates would affect each city's size about proportionately to its existing population. Births and deaths are factors in which the law of proportionate effect is clearly operative.

Another possibility has to do with rural-urban migration. Suppose that each year a given number of people migrate from rural areas to urban areas. Suppose further that migrants tend to go to urban areas in which they have friends. Then a migrant is more likely to have a friend in a large urban area than in a small one simply because there are more people in the large one. The number of migrants going to each urban area therefore tends to be proportionate to its size.

The two sets of factors just mentioned are somewhat more demographic than economic. Although they are probably significant influences, it is unlikely that they tell the entire story. The analysis in earlier chapters suggests that, during particular periods of time, some urban areas offer unusually good or poor income and employment opportunities, or unusually attractive or unattractive amenities, and that these factors affect urban area size. It seems likely that some specifically economic factors may lead to proportionate effects on urban area size, but no very suggestive analysis has yet appeared in the literature. One obvious example is pollution (discussed in detail in Chapter 13). Suppose that all urban areas above some small size become subject to air pollution. Suppose further that pollution affects a certain percentage of people and that, of those, a certain percentage leave the urban areas or, conceivably, die. Then it is not hard to imagine that pollution might cause a loss of population roughly proportionate to urban size. But much more study is needed to know whether there are many such factors, and if so, which are important.

EVALUATION

It is an interesting coincidence that Beckmann and Simon published their two fairly simple but apparently quite general models at about the same time. Although the mechanisms in the two models are very different, they lead to roughly the same conclusions about the distributions of urban area sizes. A substantial body of evidence exists which is broadly consistent with both models. This situation is in striking contrast with the usual situation in economics, in which competing theories tend to be rather involved and often little data exist which can be used to test the theories.

Ideally, this chapter would conclude with a demonstration that one theory is definitely right and the other definitely wrong. But the world is not so simple, and knowledge is not so far advanced. First, both mechanisms may be at work and both may have a substantial effect on urban area sizes. No theory exists which combines both mechanisms, and there is no guarantee that such a theory would yield a Pareto distribution—although this is not unlikely. Second, since the two theories have virtually identical implications for urban area size distributions, there is little hope of testing one against the other. But the theories are not identical in all their implications. Lösch's work, on which Beckmann's model is based, has strong implications about the spatial distribution of urban areas, although they have not been emphasized here. It is likely that these implications accord rather poorly with the facts, although they can be tested. Likewise, if Simon's theory is correct, it should be possible to identify and measure some of the important factors that give rise to the law of proportionate effect.

To what extent are the Beckmann and Simon theories consistent with the determinants of urban area size summarized at the beginning of this chapter? Again, the conclusions must be speculative. The factors that affect regional comparative advantage are absent from the models of Lösch and Beckmann. Research is needed to reformulate the models, using more realistic production functions and allowing for heterogeneity in natural conditions. One conjecture is that, although such a reformulation would be much more accurate in explaining the sizes of particular urban areas, it would have much the same implications for their overall distribution. If the conjecture is correct, there is little conflict between Beckmann's model and more detailed models of the determinants of urban sizes.

Much the same is true of Simon's model. It may be that exogenous factors are important in affecting the sizes of particular urban areas, but that the distribution and effects of these factors lead to a Pareto distribution. It could happen in two ways. Urban area size might be proportionate to relevant measures of exogenous factors, and the factors themselves might follow the Pareto distribution. Or, exogenous factors might follow other distributions, but their effect on urban area size might be in accord with the law of proportionate effect. Only further study of the determinants of urban area size can provide better answers.

SUMMARY

Many studies have shown that the size distribution of urban areas in all countries tends to be highly skewed, with a small number of very large urban areas and larger numbers of small areas. Two quite different kinds of theories have been advanced to explain this predominant distribution.

The Beckmann model builds on the view of Lösch and others that the urban areas of a country form an integrated system. In such a system, urban areas of different sizes serve different functions. A very simple model generates a distribution similar to those that have been shown to fit much of the observed data.

Simon's model is statistical, and uses a simple stochastic process to generate the size distribution of urban areas. A class of skewed distributions results, depending on the precise assumptions about births and deaths of minimum-size urban areas.

Work remains to be done to understand how the Beckmann and Simon mechanisms might be combined into a single model, and to test the relative importance of various forces on urban sizes.

DISCUSSION QUESTIONS

1. Much has been written in recent years to the effect that economic forces tend to produce a few urban areas that are too big. Do you think that the urban areas generated by Beckmann's or Simon's model might be too big?

2. It is sometimes claimed that small urban areas need government assistance so that they can reach minimum efficient sizes. Evaluate that argument within the context of Beckmann's and Simon's models.
3. Would you expect the distribution of urban sizes to differ systematically between underdeveloped and developed countries?

REFERENCES AND FURTHER READING

J. Aitcheson and J. A. C. Brown, *The Lognormal Distribution*, 1957.

Martin J. Beckmann, "City Hierarchies and the Distribution of City Size," *Economic Development and Cultural Change*, Vol. 6 (1958), 243–248.

———— and John McPherson, "City Size Distributions in a Central Place Hierarchy: An Alternative Approach," *Journal of Regional Science*, Vol. 10 (1970), 25–33.

Brian Berry and William Garrison, "Alternative Explanations of Urban Rank-Size Relationships," *Annals, Association of American Geographers*, Vol. 48 (1958), 83–91.

W. Christaller, *Die Zentralen Orte in Süddeutschland*, 1933.

B. Fraser, *Statistics: An Introduction*, 1958.

August Lösch, *The Economics of Location*, 1954.

Carl Madden, "On Some Indications of Stability in the Growth of Cities in the U.S.," *Economic Development and Cultural Change*, Vol. 14, No. 3 (April 1956), 236–252.

N. Rashevsky, *Mathematical Theory of Human Relations*, 1947.

Herbert Simon, "On a Class of Skew Distribution Functions," *Biometrika*, Vol. 42 (1955), 425–440.

George Zipf, *Human Behavior and the Principle of Least Effort*, 1949.

Chapter 8
Welfare Economics and Urban Problems

The preceding chapters have built a theoretical and empirical framework within which to analyze urban processes and trends. In Part II, attention is turned to the analysis of urban problems and of alternatives open to society to solve them. Welfare economics is the link between the positive analyses and the normative or policy analyses. A brief presentation is included here to emphasize certain topics that are of great importance in urban policy analysis. Fuller treatment can be found in a good intermediate price-theory text, such as Scitovsky.

WHAT IS WELFARE ECONOMICS?

Welfare economics is a branch of economic theory concerned with evaluating the performance of the economic system. In order to decide whether the system is performing well, and whether a change in public policy would improve its performance, a yardstick is needed by which to measure performance. Such a yardstick is called a "value judgment." Some people feel that economics becomes unscientific, or at least less scientific, when value judgments are introduced into analysis, but the feeling is misplaced. Economic theory is the deduction of implications from assumptions or axioms. There is no reason for economists not to include value judgments among their assumptions, and hence judgments about the performance of the economy among their conclusions. It is important that economists make their value judgments as clear and explicit as possible, so that others can decide whether to accept the value judgment and hence the concluding evaluation of performance. A major element of progress in welfare economics during recent decades has been to make value judgments explicit rather than implicit in the analysis. This has been part of an important trend in economics to make all assumptions as explicit as possible.

The other side of the coin is that it is not possible to judge the performance of the economy without value judgments. An earlier generation of economists was confused on this issue. They thought that at least some judgments about good performance could be made without subjective assessments or value judgments. But it is now clear that they were wrong. Whenever someone judges that an economy is performing well or badly, he is explicitly or implicitly using a value judgment as to what constitutes good or bad performance. The implication is that if economics did not involve value judgments it would be an entirely academic discipline, incapable of advising society on solutions to economic problems.

What value judgments should economists use in evaluating the economy's performance? In a free society, each person can make whatever value judgments he wishes. Economists have spent enormous amounts of time and effort discussing and clarifying value judgments that would be interesting and acceptable to many people, or at least to many thoughtful people. The value judgments underlying modern welfare economics are the result of decades of thought and analysis. But they nevertheless are value judgments, and the conclusions of analysis can be no more persuasive than the value judgments and other assumptions from which they follow.

Welfare economics begins with the idea that the purpose of economic activity is to produce goods and services for people to use. It leads to the broad judgment that the economic system should be evaluated by the efficiency with which it produces goods and services, and by the efficiency and equity with which it distributes them for people's use. For many purposes, goods and services can be defined narrowly as inputs and outputs traded on markets. But for some purposes it is desirable to broaden the definition. To take the most important example, suppose that the production and consumption of traded goods and services damage the environment in undesirable ways. Then one can broaden the definition of goods and services to include the quality of the environment, and include it in the analysis. Of course, the broader definition may require somewhat different and more complex analysis than the narrow definition.

The foregoing value judgment is not sufficiently precise for purposes of analysis. A crucial step toward precision is the assumption that each individual has a set of preferences for goods and services that lead to indifference curves, with the properties postulated in consumer behavior theory, and that a person's welfare is measured by the indifference or utility level he attains. This value judgment is usually expressed by the assumption that each individual is the best judge of his own welfare. Nobody accepts that value judgment without qualification. We all make mistakes, and a few people are persistently incapable of judging their own self-interest. But for many people, the attractiveness of this value judgment as a broad guide to public policy is clinched by the following consideration. People make mistakes in choosing cars to buy, plays to see, and someone to marry. But who among humanity is qualified to make such decisions for us? The value judgment that each person is the best judge of his own welfare underlies all the subsequent analysis in this book.

CRITERIA OF ECONOMIC PERFORMANCE

The foregoing consideration leads economists to two specific criteria for evaluating the performance of an economy. The economy is said to perform well if, given the productive resources and technology available to it, (1) no reallocation of inputs and outputs can improve the welfare of some without worsening the welfare of others, and (2) income and wealth are equitably distributed. Criterion 1 is known as the efficiency criterion, or sometimes the Pareto efficiency criterion, after its founder; and criterion 2 is known as the equity criterion.

Most people find these criteria easy to accept. Objections come from the fact that 2 does not specify what distribution of income and wealth is equitable. Utilitarian economists of the nineteenth century believed that a society's welfare was the sum of the utilities of its members. Add the assumptions that all people have the same utility functions and that marginal utility decreases with income, and it is easy to derive the utilitarian conclusion that social welfare is maximized if income is equally distributed. But modern theory of consumer behavior does not attach any meaning to the sum of people's utilities. Specifically, if a utility function can be found that represents a person's preferences, any utility function that is an increasing function of the first one will represent his preferences equally well. In particular, one can make the sum of all people's utilities any number one likes by choosing appropriate individual utility functions.

Despite this, all of us have strong feelings about the distribution of income. But at the present, economics is able to provide very little help in forming or evaluating such feelings. About all that can be said is that each person's evaluation of public policy proposals should depend on the effect of the proposals on income distribution. Of course, a citizen can unhesitatingly support a policy proposal that improves the economy's efficiency without worsening its income distribution, given the citizen's feelings about income distribution. Likewise, he can support a proposal that improves the income distribution without worsening efficiency. The difficult choices involve proposals that would improve efficiency at the expense of equity, or improve equity at the expense of efficiency. Although these distinctions are important, they do not go beyond a classification of possibilities. However, there is an elaborate body of analysis concerning the efficiency criterion.

CONDITIONS FOR ECONOMIC EFFICIENCY

The efficiency criterion has implications for the allocation of both outputs and inputs. The basic ideas are most easily understood by considering the simplest situation in which a problem of resource allocation can be posed, a model of pure consumption.

A Pure Consumption Model

Suppose a society must allocate fixed amounts of two consumption goods per unit of time between two members. Shortly, it will be assumed that the commodities are produced with scarce inputs, but for the moment it is assumed that they simply appear in fixed amounts. X units of one good are available and Y units of the other. Designate the two people A and B, and the amounts of the two goods allocated to each by X_A, X_B, Y_A, and Y_B. The allocation of the goods must satisfy the conditions

$$X_A + X_B = X \qquad Y_A + Y_B = Y$$

and all of the allocations must be non-negative.

Individuals A and B have indifference maps representing their tastes for the two goods, as shown in Figure 8-1. Society's allocation problem is

Figure 8-1

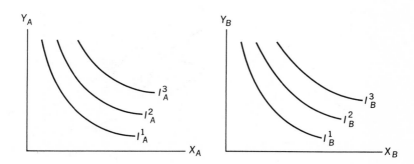

usually represented as in Figure 8-2. The horizontal and vertical axes of the indifference diagrams in Figure 8-1 have been extended to lengths X and Y, and the indifference diagram for B has been rotated so that its origin is in the upper right-hand corner of the rectangle. Each point in Figure 8-2 corresponds exactly to one of the possible allocations of X and Y between A and B. Society's problem is therefore to choose a point in the rectangle which satisfies the efficiency criterion.

Unless the tastes of A and B differ greatly, there will be some allocations at which the indifference curves for A and B have the same slope. Assume that such allocations exist and can be represented by a continuous curve, designated cc in Figure 8-2. The cc curve represents all of the allocations such that

$$MRS_A(X_A, Y_A) = MRS_B(X_B, Y_B) \qquad (8\text{-}1)$$

where MRS stands for one person's marginal rate of substitution between the two goods. The basic welfare theorem in the pure consumption model is that the set of allocations that satisfies the efficiency criterion is precisely the set that satisfies Equation 8-1.

To prove the theorem, consider an allocation P_1, not on cc in Figure 8-2. There must be exactly one of the indifference curves for A and one for B passing through P_1, but they cannot be tangent. Then any reallocation from P_1 to a point like P_2, which lies between the indifference curves passing through P_1, must place each individual on a higher indifference curve than he was on at P_1. Thus, each person is better off at P_2 than at P_1. Repeating the argument shows that reallocation from P_2 to a point between the two indifference curves passing through P_2 makes both individuals still better

Figure 8-2

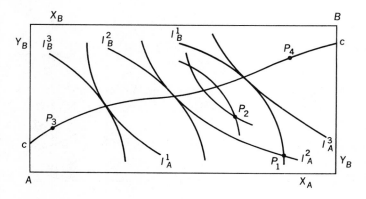

off. The argument can be repeated until an allocation is reached on cc. This proves the theorem.

Note that nothing in the argument rests on the assumptions that there are only two people and only two goods in the society. If it consists of any finite number of people, and the problem is to allocate among them amounts of any finite number of goods, an efficient allocation must satisfy Equation 8-1 for every pair of goods and every pair of people.

All of the points on cc are efficient, but they are by no means all equitable. At allocation P_4, A has practically all of both goods and B has almost nothing, whereas at P_3 the opposite is true. Thus, a person who felt that A was relatively deserving would prefer P_4 to P_3, whereas a person who felt that B was relatively deserving would prefer P_3 to P_4. The efficiency criterion narrows society's choice from the set of points in the rectangle in Figure 8-2 to the set of point on cc. The equity criterion narrows the choice from the set of points on cc to one or a few of those points.

What kinds of institutions might society develop to solve its allocation problem? If someone knew each person's indifference map, he could compute the set of efficient allocations. But of course no one has the required information. Recall from price theory that if goods are allocated on markets, and if the price each person pays for each good is independent of the amount he buys, each individual maximizes his welfare by buying amounts of goods that equate his marginal rates of substitution to the price ratios of pairs of goods. Thus all buyers who face the same prices will choose amounts of goods that equate to each other every person's MRS for a particular pair of goods. Competitive markets, in particular, will allocate goods to satisfy Equation 8-1 and hence allocate efficiently. In the pure consumption model, monopoly is also efficient, but it will be shown that only competitive markets, among all market allocations, satisfy the efficiency conditions when input allocations are included in the model.

Are competitive markets equitable as well as efficient? Obviously not, since competitive markets ensure only that the allocation will be on cc, and not that it will be at any particular point on cc. Equity depends on how much purchasing power or income A and B bring to the market. Suppose, for example, that A and B each inherit amounts of the two commodities. Their inheritances put them at a point like P_1, and they then trade the commodities on competitive markets and end up on cc between I_A^2 and I_B^1. The point P_1 is entirely determined by the legacies, and the amounts A and B inherit determine where on cc they end up after trading. Thus, competitive markets can only guarantee to get the society to cc, not to an equitable point on cc. In this simple example, society could insure equity as well as efficiency by creating inheritance laws that reallocated purchasing power in an equitable way and then letting individuals trade on competitive markets.

A Production-Consumption Model

The model can now be enriched by recognizing that X and Y are produced with scarce inputs. Suppose two inputs, labor and land, and fixed amounts of each available to society. There are N units of labor and L units of land. Both inputs are needed to produce each output. The amounts of the goods produced are related to the amounts of the inputs used by two production functions

$$X = F(N_X, L_X) \qquad Y = G(N_Y, L_Y)$$

Subscripts indicate the amounts of the inputs used to produce the commodity indicated, so the use of inputs is limited by

$$L_X + L_Y = L \qquad N_X + N_Y = N$$

Society now has two problems. First, it must allocate the inputs to production of the two commodities. Second, it must allocate the commodities to the two individuals. The production functions can be represented by their isoquants, as shown in Figure 8-3. A representation of the input allocation problem can be formed from Figure 8-3 in precisely the same way that Figure 8-2 was formed from Figure 8-1. The result is Figure 8-4, where the horizontal sides of the rectangle have length L and the vertical sides have length N. The origin for the production of Y is at the upper right-hand corner of the rectangle.

Given an understanding of the proof of the theorem in the pure con-

Figure 8-3

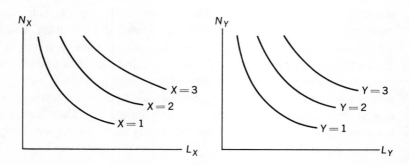

Figure 8-4

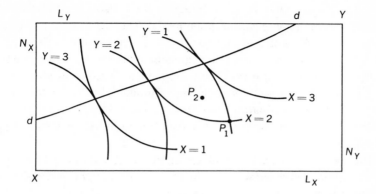

sumption model, it is easy to see how inputs must be allocated in the production-consumption model to satisfy the efficiency criterion. Any allocation of the two inputs between X and Y corresponds to a point in Figure 8-4. The curve dd connects all the points of tangency between pairs of isoquants. It is shown in price-theory texts that the slope of an isoquant is the ratio of the marginal products of the two inputs. Thus, dd is the set of input allocations such that the ratio of the marginal products of the two inputs is the same for the production of both commodities at a given point; that is, dd is the set of input allocations such that

$$\frac{MP_{L_X}}{MP_{N_X}} = \frac{MP_{L_Y}}{MP_{N_Y}} \tag{8-2}$$

The basic efficiency theorem in the production-consumption model is that the set of input and output allocations that satisfies the efficiency criterion is precisely the set that satisfies Equations 8-1 and 8-2. The theorem and its proof are analogous to those in the pure consumption model. Suppose that the input allocation is at a point like P_1 in Figure 8-4, not on dd. Then the same amounts of the two inputs can be reallocated so as to produce more of both X and Y by moving from P_1 to a point like P_2, which is between the isoquants passing through P_1. Clearly, P_2 represents more output of both X and Y than P_1 does. Thus, it is possible to improve the welfare of both individuals (A and B) by moving from P_1 to P_2, since each can receive more of both goods. Repeating the argument shows that reallocations of inputs can improve the welfare of both individuals as long as the input allocation is not on dd.

The set of efficient input allocations is the set on *dd*. But given the total outputs of X and Y, efficiency also requires that the outputs be allocated efficiently between A and B. Thus, Equation 8-1 is also a condition for efficiency, just as in the pure consumption model. Therefore, input and output allocations are efficient only if Equations 8-1 and 8-2 are both satisfied. Once again, it is easy to see that the argument applies if there are more than two inputs or outputs. If more than two inputs are used to produce X and Y, Equation 8-2 must hold for each pair of inputs taken separately. There would then be many equations like Equation 8-2. If there are more than two outputs, input allocations must satisfy Equation 8-2 for those outputs as well as for X and Y.

The conditions for efficient allocation of inputs and outputs have been derived without reference to social institutions that might undertake production and distribution. It can now be shown that allocations of inputs and outputs by competitive markets do satisfy the efficiency conditions. It is shown in price-theory textbooks and was shown in Chapter 3 that the necessary conditions for profit maximization for producers who deal in competitive input and output markets are

$$MP_{L_X} \cdot p_X = R \qquad MP_{N_X} \cdot p_X = w \qquad (8\text{-}3)$$

for an X producer, and

$$MP_{L_Y} \cdot p_Y = R \qquad MP_{N_Y} \cdot p_Y = w \qquad (8\text{-}4)$$

for a Y producer. MP is the marginal product of each of the two inputs in producing the two outputs; p_X and p_Y are the prices of X and Y; R is the rental rate of land; and w is the wage rate.

It only remains now to show that Equations 8-3 and 8-4 imply Equation 8-2. Divide the first equation by the second in Equations 8-3 and 8-4. The result is

$$\frac{MP_{L_X}}{MP_{N_X}} = \frac{R}{w} \qquad \frac{MP_{L_Y}}{MP_{N_Y}} = \frac{R}{w}$$

Thus, the two ratios of marginal products are equal to the same factor price ratio, and hence to each other. This shows that competitive profit-maximizing firms employ inputs in amounts that satisfy the efficiency criterion of Equation 8-2. It was shown in the pure consumption model that competitive output markets satisfy Equation 8-1. Thus, competitive input and output markets satisfy both sets of efficiency conditions.

A corollary to the foregoing discussion is that efficiency requires outputs of X and Y to be such that their marginal costs are equal to their respective prices. This condition is of course satisfied by competitive (but not by monopoly) markets.

The efficiency criterion tells society that, among all the points in Figures 8-2 and 8-4, it should choose input and output allocations on cc and dd. As in the pure consumption model, there are many efficient input and output allocations, but not all of them are equitable. Suppose (to stay within the two-input model) that every worker is equally productive, and thus in competitive markets receives the same earned income. Suppose further that ownership of land is determined by inheritance. Then each unit of land receives the same rental rate, but the overall distribution of income or purchasing power is affected by the distribution of land ownership. In this model, society can obtain efficient and equitable input and output allocations by using an inheritance tax to produce an equitable distribution of land ownership, and by using competitive markets to allocate inputs and outputs.

A Variable Input/Output Model

The pure consumption model assumed that the amounts of the two consumer goods available to society were fixed. The assumption was relaxed in the consumption-production model, and replaced by the assumption that the amounts of inputs were fixed. In the model here, the assumption of fixed input quantities is relaxed. It is replaced by the assumption that workers can vary their supplies of labor freely, at least within limits.

This assumption is of course an approximation, since many jobs require more or less rigid hours of work. But hours of work are more flexible than is sometimes realized. Over a period of a decade or two, hours of work change substantially, falling as incomes rise. But even within short periods of time, there are many ways to vary hours of work. Moonlighting, overtime, and part-time jobs are available. Many professional and self-employed workers have flexible hours of work. So, to some extent, do many commission and piece-rate workers.

Leisure, a euphemism for whatever is done during nonwork hours, is valuable, just as consumer goods are valuable. Assume that each individual has a set of indifference curves between leisure and each commodity, as illustrated in Figure 8-5. $\bar{N}_A$ represents hours of leisure for A per unit of time, just as X_A represents the amount of X consumed by A per unit time. If N_A is hours of work for A,

Figure 8-5

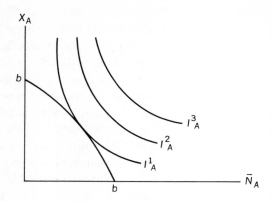

is the total hours available to A for work and leisure. The indifference curves in Figure 8-5 depend only on the tastes of individual A. Now introduce the production side by supposing that A produces X at work. His output of X depends on his hours of work, and therefore varies inversely with the amount of leisure he takes. The relationship is shown by bb in Figure 8-5. Since bb shows how the production of X by A varies with his hours of leisure, its slope is minus the marginal product of an extra hour of work by A in producing X. If bb is concave, as shown in Figure 8-5, it means that the marginal product of A falls as he works more hours producing X.

The final criterion for efficient resource allocation can now be derived. It says that the hours of work by A should equate his marginal rate of substitution between X and leisure to his marginal product in producing X; that is,

$$MRS_A(X_A, \bar{N}_A) = MP_{AX} \qquad (8\text{-}5)$$

The curve bb is like a budget constraint for A, showing the combinations of leisure and X available to him. He achieves the highest possible indifference curve by choosing a combination of X and leisure that places him at the point of tangency between bb and an indifference curve. Since the movement of A to the point of tangency from another point on bb does not affect the welfare of other members of society, the move satisfies the efficiency criterion; that is, it makes him better off without making anyone else worse off.

It only remains to show that competitive markets satisfy this efficiency criterion, as well as those already discussed. If A sells his labor and buys X and Y on markets, his budget constraint is

$$p_X X_A + p_Y Y_A = w(N_T - \bar{N}_A) \qquad (8\text{-}6)$$

where $N_T - \bar{N}_A$ is the number of hours A chooses to work, and w is the hourly wage rate. If the labor market is competitive,

$$w = MP_{AX} \cdot p_X$$

Substituting for w in Equation 8-6 and rearranging terms, the budget constraint can be written as

$$X_A = \left(MP_{AX} N_T - \frac{p_Y}{p_X} Y_A \right) - MP_{AX} \bar{N}_A \qquad (8\text{-}7)$$

Thus, in a competitive labor market, the slope of the budget constraint of A is the same as that of bb. It follows that the market choice by A will lead him to the tangency point in Figure 8-5 that has been shown to satisfy the efficiency criterion.

In the consumption-production model, it was shown that society could obtain an efficient and equitable allocation of resources by choosing an appropriate initial distribution of input ownership, and permitting exchange of inputs and outputs on competitive markets. In the model, input supplies were fixed and therefore redistribution of their ownership did not affect resource allocation decisions. But matters are more complicated in the model with variable input. In this model, only a wage rate equal to the value of the worker's marginal product results in an efficient allocation of labor resources. If there are many workers, with a variety of skills and abilities, the wage of each must be equal to the value of his marginal product. Thus, in the variable input model, the efficiency conditions imply a distribution of earned income, which will be referred to as an efficient distribution of income.

Is an efficient distribution of income also equitable? The competitive market values of worker skills vary enormously. Many people have no saleable skills at all because of physical or mental disabilities, whereas some have skills worth hundreds of thousands of dollars per year. It is likely that most people's sense of equity requires a distribution of income less unequal than the efficient distribution. As a result, societies have long had policies of reducing income inequality through government tax-transfer systems. In every society, resolution of the conflict between efficiency and equity and between the various income groups is one of the most important and controversial tasks of government.

SOME CAUSES OF RESOURCE MISALLOCATION

Succeeding chapters will analyze specific problems of efficiency and equity in the urban economy. Each problem requires facts and analysis specific to that problem, and they are presented in the appropriate chapters. This chapter concludes with a general classification and analysis of reasons for resource misallocation.

Monopoly and Monopsony

It is easy to show that monopolists and monopsonists misallocate resources. A monopolist maximizes profits by employing input quantities that satisfy equations similar to 8-3 and 8-4, but with product prices replaced by marginal revenues. Since a monopolist's marginal revenue is less than price, Equations 8-3 and 8-4 require that marginal products be greater for the monopolist than for the competitive firm for given input prices, and the monopolist therefore employs smaller input quantities and produces less output than is efficient from society's point of view. Similar reasoning shows that Equation 8-7 is also violated if the employer is a monopoly, and therefore inefficient amounts of labor are supplied. (As an exercise, it should be possible to show that monopsony power also leads to inefficient resource allocation.)

The quantitative importance of resource misallocation from monopoly monopsony is a subject of debate among specialists in industrial organization economics. If misallocation is substantial, it must be substantial in urban areas, since most economic activity occurs there. But it is claimed in following chapters that monopoly is unimportant in understanding most serious urban problems; poverty, poor housing, congestion, pollution, and inadequate public services result only to a minor extent from monopoly power. They would be serious problems even if all markets were perfectly competitive. Many people resist this conclusion, in part because they use the term "monopoly" more broadly than economists do, and in part because of the human tendency to search for villains to blame for causing problems.

External Economies and Diseconomies

For decades, economists have analyzed a closely related set of considerations that entail resource misallocation, even in competitive markets. Despite important recent progress in clarifying the concept, there is still considerable disagreement among economists about the causes and effects of externalities. The result is that the term tends to be used somewhat loosely in applied studies. Especially in urban economics, the term is badly overused and abused.

The basic idea behind the notion of an external effect is that the actions of one person or institution may affect the welfare of another in ways that are difficult to regulate by private agreements among the affected parties. As has been discussed, if a firm buys and sells on competitive markets in certain assumed circumstances, market prices and profit maximization induce the firm to behave efficiently from society's point of view. It employs just the inputs and produces just the output that are in society's interest. Now suppose that one of the firm's activities affects people's welfare in a way not based on agreement or market transaction. The classical example, used by generations of writers, is smoke emission. Suppose that a certain fuel is among the firm's inputs, and that burning the fuel creates smoke which spreads over the neighborhood and reduces residents' welfare. If the fuel is an important input, and its smoke is not too harmful, some smoke may be worth its cost to the firm and to the public. But there is no market on which to register the advantages of smoke production to the firm and its disadvantages to the neighbors. If the firm maximizes profits, it fails to take into account the cost that its smoke imposes on others. Even though some smoke may be worth the cost, too much is produced. The smoke is then said to be an *external diseconomy*. The resulting resource misallocation, too much smoke, is no less serious just because the firm buys inputs and sells outputs in competitive markets.

In fact, smoke is a less serious problem than it used to be, but practically all economists would agree that air pollution is a serious public problem because of its external effects. In a general way, practically everyone would agree on the underlying explanation that private agreements cannot allocate resources to abate air pollution efficiently. Disagreement comes when we try to establish exactly why private agreements do not work.

The basic reason why private agreements do not work is that private transactions costs sometimes exceed the potential gain from the agreement. The reason is not hard to understand in the smoke example. Many people suffer more or less harm from the smoke, and many sources may be more or less responsible for the smoke damage to each person and his property. Thus, a private agreement to abate smoke discharges would require negotiations among large numbers of people and factories, and the public would have complex and poorly understood interests in abatement by particular sources. Obviously, a private agreement on such an issue would be extremely difficult and costly to specify and negotiate. That is the meaning of the statement that the transaction cost of such an agreement is high.

Exactly what circumstances entail transaction costs so high as to prevent otherwise desirable agreements? There is no satisfactory answer at present, and the result is that many studies of externalities are merely anecdotal. About all that can be said is that transaction costs may be high regarding agreement about an activity if the activity affects large numbers of people in complex ways. But any study of an apparent externality should include a careful investigation of the kinds and amounts of transaction costs that prevent agreement.

Once an important externality has been identified, the next question is what to do about it. The usual answer is that the government should tax or subsidize so as to create an appropriate market, or it should regulate so that private activity will approximate the missing market. In the smoke example, the government can tax emissions, subsidize abatement, or regulate emissions. But the first question that needs to be asked is whether transaction costs will be lower if the government intervenes than if private parties try to reach agreement. If not, the transaction costs are unavoidable and the agreement is not worth having. In the smoke example, the disadvantage of the smoke is less than the cost of doing something about it. In many cases, however, the government can adopt policies that at least approximate the results of private agreements, and with relatively small transaction costs. But in each case, the facts must decide the issue. Sometimes government programs become cumbersome because the government must bear exactly the transaction costs that prevented the private sector from undertaking the transactions in the first place.

If transaction costs are low enough that government intervention is justified, the appropriate policy is easy to specify in principle. In the smoke example, the efficient amount of smoke is the amount such that the cost to the neighbors of a little more equals the cost to the factory of a little more abatement. Another way to put it is to say that the amount of smoke should be such that marginal costs and marginal benefits of abatement are equal. The goal might be achieved by an appropriate tax on smoke, a subsidy for abatement, or regulation of smoke discharges. Which policy should be chosen depends on the transaction costs of the policies and on the extent to which they approximate efficient resource allocation. Of course in practice, the benefits of abatement may be difficult to estimate.

Taxes

Governments must raise large amounts of money by taxes on citizens to finance the public services and transfers demanded of them. An important goal of tax policy should be to employ taxes that cause as little misallocation of resources as possible.

Price-theory texts show that a change in the price of a consumer good has an income effect and a substitution effect. Almost all taxes are directly or indirectly taxes on particular kinds of goods and services. They therefore alter the prices of the taxed items relative to untaxed items. The income effect is the desired effect of the tax, and represents no misallocation of resources. The purpose of a tax is to transfer resources from the private to the public sector, and the income effect measures the value of the resources transferred. If the resources are less valuable in the public sector than in the private sector, there should be no tax and no transfer. But if the resources are more valuable in the public sector, the transfer should be made, and the income effect of the tax is the desired reduction of private purchasing power. The income effect may reduce demands for private goods and services by varying amounts, but it represents the least costly way of transferring the purchasing power represented by the tax.

The substitution effect of a tax on the demand for the taxed goods and services represents a loss of welfare to consumers beyond that which is necessary to transfer purchasing power. The substitution effect leads to what is called the excess burden of the tax, that is, the excess loss of welfare over that necessary to transfer the purchasing power to the public sector. Among all the taxes that have a given income effect in transferring given resources to the public sector, the best is the one with the smallest excess burden, or substitution effect.

These ideas can be illustrated with the property tax (discussed in detail in Chapters 10 and 12). Here it is only necessary to note that the property tax is a high sales tax on housing services. Figure 8-6 shows a household's set of indifference curves between housing services x_1 and another commodity x_2 for a given amount of a public service provided by the government. Suppose that x_1 and x_2 are produced by competitive firms, and that aa would be the household's budget line in the absence of any tax. Then P_1 would be the household's equilibrium, and it would be efficient. But P_1 is not available because it does not provide resources to the government necessary to produce the public service. Suppose then that the government finances the public service with a property tax, and that the entire tax is

Figure 8-6

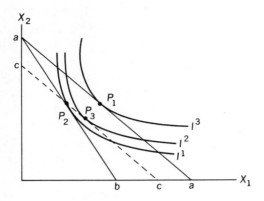

paid by the consumer of housing services. The household's budget line is shifted to *ab*. Its new equilibrium is P_2. Budget line *cc* is drawn parallel to *aa* and passes through P_2. P_3 is the household's equilibrium position for budget line *cc*. The movement from P_1 to P_3 is the income effect of the tax; that is, it represents the household's loss of welfare if the government had taken the resources it needs without affecting the relative prices of x_1 and x_2. The movement from P_3 to P_2 represents the substitution effect of the tax. The fact that the property tax has a substitution effect causes an excess burden of the tax on the household that reduces its welfare from I^2 to I^1.

What kinds of taxes would have no excess burdens? In principle, the answer is that the only taxes with no excess burdens are those that do not affect relative prices. A "head" tax, which simply charges the same amount of tax to each person, is probably the only tax that has no excess burden. The property tax is presumed to have a large excess burden, since it is a high tax on a narrow range of activities, namely, housing consumption. A broadly based sales tax is probably somewhat better. A sales tax that taxed all consumer goods and services at the same rate would be a flat-rate consumption tax. It would leave unaffected the relative prices of goods and services. But most sales taxes fall far short of this ideal. Most are levied on a narrow set of consumer goods, excluding almost all services and some commodities. Some are also levied on a few intermediate goods, which entails double taxation of the final goods they are used to produce.

An income tax, like a broadly based sales tax, leaves relative prices of goods and services unchanged, which accounts in part for the strong preference of most economists for income taxes over other taxes. But an income tax and a broadly based sales tax do have an excess burden. An income tax is a tax on the result of hours spent working, but not on hours of leisure. In Figure 8-5, an income tax changes the relative prices of goods and leisure, and therefore, the slope of the budget line *bb*. The substitution effect of an income tax is an inefficiently large amount of leisure. The total effect of an income tax on hours of work and leisure depends on the relative sizes of the income and substitution effects.

Is the excess burden of an income tax large? The best study on the subject, by Harberger, concludes that it is substantial, but probably small relative to the excess burdens of existing sales and property taxes. Sales and property taxes, like income taxes, affect the relative prices of goods and leisure. But, unlike income taxes, they also affect the relative prices of goods and services.

It should be emphasized that the entire discussion here has been about the efficiency aspects of taxes. Taxes, like other public policies, also have important equity effects. A major goal of government tax policy is to redistribute income, specifically to reduce income inequality. That goal requires progressive taxes or transfer payments, and the income tax is almost the only tax that can be made to be progressive. Thus, if equity considerations require progressive taxes, they are an important reason for the use of income rather than other taxes. It is also possible that equity considerations indicate the desirability of one kind of tax, and efficiency considerations indicate the desirability of another. In such cases, a compromise between the desires for equity and efficiency is necessary.

SUMMARY

Welfare economics is a branch of economic theory concerned with evaluating the performance of the economic system. Economists evaluate the system's performance by its efficiency and equity in meeting people's economic wants.

An elaborate system of conditions for economic efficiency has been worked out by economists during recent decades. A major result obtained in welfare economics is that competitive markets allocate resources so as to satisfy the efficiency conditions if fairly strong assumptions are made. But competitive markets may not produce distributions of income and wealth that meet people's senses of equity.

Monopoly and monopsony misallocate resources, although neither is likely to be an important source of urban problems. External economies and diseconomies imply that even competitive markets will misallocate resources. Congestion and pollution are good examples of external diseconomies in urban areas.

Governments must raise large amounts of money by taxes to finance public services and transfers. Taxes for revenue purposes should be equitable and should involve as little resource misallocation as possible. Most economists believe that sales and property taxes are both less efficient and less equitable than income taxes. But there may well be conflict in tax policy between equity and efficiency.

DISCUSSION QUESTIONS

1. Economists tend to urge that poor people be provided transfers of money, whereas public officials prefer to provide them with goods and services such as housing and medical care. Evaluate the two strategies on the grounds of efficiency and equity.
2. Show that price discrimination violates the requirements for efficient resource allocation.
3. Economists tend to urge that activities causing external diseconomies be taxed, whereas public officials tend to regulate such activities. Which strategy is better on the grounds of equity and efficiency?
4. The do-it-yourself movement, in which people repair and maintain their own houses instead of hiring craftsmen, has blossomed since World War II. Do-it-yourself labor is not subject to income tax, whereas a craftsman's wages are. Do you think the do-it-yourself movement is a distortion resulting from high income tax rates?

REFERENCES AND FURTHER READING

Francis Bator, "The Simple Analytics of Welfare Maximization," *American Economic Review*, Vol. 47 (March 1957), 22–59.

———, "The Anatomy of Market Failure," *Quarterly Journal of Economics*, Vol. 72 (August 1958), 351–379.

Arnold Harberger, "Taxation, Resource Allocation, and Welfare," in *The Role of Direct and Indirect Taxes in the Federal Revenue System*, 1964.

Tibor Scitovsky, *Welfare and Competition*, 1971.

Part Two
Urban Problems and the Public Sector

Chapter 9

The Problem
of Poverty

Poverty is the most urgent and widely discussed domestic problem of our time. The 1960s witnessed a vast outpouring of literature on the subject, much of it written as though poverty had been invented or discovered about 1960. Although the subject has not been, and should not be, the exclusive preserve of economists, they have made their share of contributions to the subject. Many of the great nineteenth-century economists were deeply concerned with the most fundamental issues related to poverty. Beginning about 1900, some of the best applied economic research was on demand and family budget studies, motivated by concern with poverty and related nutritional problems. During the 1930s, much of the profession's effort was devoted to public and private measures to alleviate poverty, especially as caused by the massive unemployment that dominated the decade.

Nevertheless, there was a rapid growth of concern with poverty during the 1960s among economists, public officials, and the general public. Both a cause and an effect was a rapid improvement in the data available about poverty. It is now possible to identify the numbers and characteristics of poor people.

THE CULTURE OF POVERTY

Economists are practically unanimous in defining poverty as an inadequate standard of living, and in believing that the overwhelming cause of poverty is lack of access to income and assets that permit an adequate standard of living. But many other social scientists disagree. Sociologists and anthropologists often write about poverty as a way of life, and about the culture of poverty.[1] Several distinct conceptions are covered by the term.

---

1. The best-known writer on this subject is the late anthropologist Oscar Lewis, who wrote books about the family life of poor people in several societies. Although their scientific merits are in dispute among his professional colleagues, Lewis' books are extraordinarily well-written and interesting. For references and an interesting survey of the subject, see Valentine.

In part, the literature on the culture of poverty simply shows that sociologists and anthropologists share the growing concern with poverty, and are making their own contribution to understanding how poor people live. In part, however, literature on the culture of poverty suggests that there is a more fundamental kind of impoverishment, characterized more by disorganization and misery than by a low standard of living. It is probably fruitless to argue whether one kind of misery is more fundamental than another. But it is indisputable that economic poverty is only one cause of misery, and other causes certainly ought to be studied. It is also indisputable that sufficient poverty is a guarantee of misery. Thus, there seems to be no conflict between this conception and economists' views on poverty.

Finally, and most important, literature on the culture of poverty sometimes suggests that one set of causes of poverty may be attitudes toward family life, religion, economic activity, and life in general. Research on this subject is extremely difficult to conduct because cause and effect are hard to separate. Poverty certainly causes people to feel hopeless and helpless. The issue is whether causation also runs the other way. Sociological and anthropological research has not yet produced results that are useful in the context of poverty in the United States. It is likely that research results in this area will be most valuable in the context of international economic development. Certainly, it is an admissible hypothesis that international differences in social organization and attitudes are among the causes of the vast differences in levels of economic development among the world's societies.

The issues raised above are extremely important, and it is unfortunate that good answers are not available. The purpose of including the discussion here is to warn that some economists are too ready to dismiss out of hand noneconomic explanations of poverty.

MEASURES OF POVERTY

Personal income is by far the best simple measure of standard of living. But several cautions are in order. First, income fluctuates from year to year. If a family had a low income in 1970, but a much higher income in the preceding and succeeding years, it would be of much less concern than if its low income persisted from year to year. Some Americans do have temporarily low incomes, mainly because of disability or unemployment. But the vast majority of those with low incomes are persistently in low-income categories year after year.

Second, we must consider assets. If a low-income family has assets, it can temporarily maintain a high standard of living by drawing on its assets. But assets are more unequally distributed than income in the United States, and few poor people posses substantial assets. The only important exception is homes owned and occupied by old people with low incomes.

Third, income must be defined properly. Some poor people receive goods and services directly, either from governments or from employers. The major examples in the United States are food received by poorly paid agricultural workers from their employers, and government medicare, medicaid, and food-stamp programs for which some poor people are eligible. Official poverty statistics include estimates of income-in-kind paid to agricultural workers, but exclude goods and services provided by government programs. The result is an understatement of incomes for those who benefit from the programs. But the understatement is typically less than the market value of the goods and services provided, since the value of the goods and services is greater than the amount the recipients would have spent on them if they had been given the money instead of the goods and services. The distortion is probably greatest in the case of the medicaid program.

Judged on the basis of income as a good approximation of standard of living, poverty becomes a matter of degree. A family with a $4000 annual income is better off than one with an annual income of $3000, and one with $3000 is better off than one with $2000. There has been a great deal of debate in recent years on where the poverty line should be drawn. The answer depends on the purpose for which poverty is to be measured. For research purposes, it is desirable to have data on the numbers and characteristics of people below a variety of income levels.

But a major reason for urging a certain official poverty line on the government is that there is inevitable pressure on the government to adopt programs that will raise everybody's income to at least the poverty line. Thus, those who want the government to undertake large programs to assist low-income people urge that the official poverty level be set high, and those who want little or no government assistance to low-income people urge that the poverty level be set low.

In the early 1960s, the federal government adopted an official poverty measure, and raising low incomes to at least that level became a quasi-official goal for the rest of the decade. The 1964 Economic Report of the President's Council of Economic Advisers defined the broad outlines of the federal government's policy, and succeeding reports had sections on poverty which traced progress in the reduction of poverty and proposed measures for further progress.

The official poverty income level is computed in a relatively simple way. The Department of Agriculture computes the annual cost of a nutritious diet for low-income families of various sizes. The food budget is then multiplied by three because surveys have shown that low-income families spend about one-third of their incomes on food. As food prices change, the poverty income is adjusted accordingly. In 1963, the poverty income for a family of four was $3104. In 1967, it was $3388.

The official poverty measure is subject to the criticism that the standard of living it represents changes if the relative price of food changes. If food prices rise more slowly than prices of other items in the low-income family's budget, the standard of living represented by the poverty measure declines. But little bias has been introduced, since, at least during the 1960s, food prices rose about as fast as the general price level.

The U.S. poverty income is about one third of the country's median income. By a realistic worldwide standard it is very high, nearly ten times the average income of many of the most populous Asian countries. But Americans can take little comfort from the fact that their poverty problem is small in comparison with those of countries whose standard of living is a small fraction of U.S. living standards. A more relevant comparison is with countries in northern Europe, where per capita incomes are mostly at least half as large as in the United States. Although exact comparisons are difficult, informal evidence indicates that the poorest people in several northern European countries have higher standards of living than the poorest people in the United States. By this or any other realistic standard, the United States does have a poverty problem.

THE DEMOGRAPHY OF POVERTY

How many Americans are poor? The numbers below the official poverty line have been computed only back to 1959, as shown in Table 9-1. But it is possible to find approximate measures of poverty for much earlier years. Allowing for changes in the price level since then, 1929 income per capita was about the same as the current poverty level. Thus, about half the country was poor in 1929 by the current poverty standard. Using a similar but slightly cruder measure than the current official one, the Council of Economic Advisers in its 1964 Economic Report estimated that about one third of all Americans were poor in 1947. Table 9-1 indicates that the number of poor decreased from 22.4 percent of the population in 1959 to 12.8 percent in 1968.

Table 9-1   Poverty in the United States, 1959–1968

Year	Poor Population Number (millions)	Percent
1959	39.5	22.4
1960	39.9	22.2
1961	39.6	21.9
1962	38.6	21.0
1963	36.4	19.5
1964	36.1	19.0
1965	33.2	17.3
1966	28.5	14.7
1967	27.8	14.2
1968	25.4	12.8

Source: U.S. Census Bureau, *Revision of Poverty Statistics, 1959 to 1968*, August 1969.

Not only the percentage, but also the number, of poor has decreased during the forty years between 1929 and 1968. Fifty percent of the 1929 population was about 60 million people, and one third of the 1947 population was 48 million people. Table 9-1 shows that the number of poor decreased from about 40 million to about 25 million between 1959 and 1968.

These data represent a remarkably persistent trend in the reduction of poverty. During the 1929–1968 period, the percentage of poor decreased about 0.9 per year. Table 9-1 shows that the long-term rate of decrease has persisted during the most recent decade. Of course, the 0.9 percent average annual decrease has not occurred each year; poverty increased enormously during the early 1930s, and the rate of decrease was lower in the early years covered by Table 9-1, when unemployment was high. Nevertheless, if we are to believe projections by simple extrapolation, we can predict that poverty will be eliminated in the United States by about 1982.

Who are the poor? Table 9-2 presents basic demographic data concerning poverty. The column headed "Incidence of Poverty" shows the percentages of the people in the groups in each row who are poor. It is important to distinguish incidence from percentages of poor in each group. For example, the first column of the table shows that about 61 percent (19.0 million out of 27.8 million) of the poor were white, but the incidence of poverty among whites was less than one third of its incidence among non-whites (11 percent compared with 37 percent). Table 9-2 also shows the remarkably uneven incidence of poverty among various demographic groups.

The data under family status show that 16 percent of all children are in poor families. Why is the incidence of poverty among children greater than among the entire population? In part, it may be because low-income

Table 9-2   Numbers of Poor and the Incidence of Poverty in the United
States, 1967

Characteristic	Number of Poor (millions)	Incidence of Poverty (percent)
Total	27.8	14%
Family status		
Family head	5.7	11
Family members under 18	11.4	16
Other family members	5.7	9
Unrelated individuals	5.0	38
Race		
White	19.0	11
Nonwhite	8.8	37
Residence		
SMSA central city	9.4	16
SMSA suburb	6.0	9
NonSMSA	12.4	18

Sources: U.S. Council of Economic Advisors, *Economic Report of the President, 1969*;
and U.S. Census Bureau, *Revision of Poverty Statistics, 1959 to 1968.*

parents tend to have more children than do high-income parents. But it is
also because mothers tend to return to work as children grow up, and family incomes thus rise; and because it takes less income to escape poverty
after children have grown up and moved out than when they are small. The
38-percent incidence of poverty among unrelated individuals is strongly
affected by the high incidence of poverty among the elderly, many of whom
are widowed and live alone. In 1967, 53 percent of unrelated individuals 65
and over were poor.

The data under race show the crushing burden of poverty borne by
nonwhites in the United States. In addition to blacks, Indians, Eskimos,
and some Orientals are included in the nonwhite category. Although the
incidence of poverty is extremely high among these small minorities, blacks
are more than 90 percent of the nonwhite population, and the data therefore
mainly reflect their situation. Although there are nearly twice as many poor
whites as poor nonwhites, the incidence of poverty is more than three times
as high among nonwhites as among whites.

The data on residence show that, contrary to some popular writing,
poverty is by no means entirely a phenomenon of large cities. Both the
numbers of poor and the incidence of poverty are greater outside SMSAs
than in SMSA central cities. Table 9-2 shows that about 55 percent of the
poor live in SMSAs. Table 2-3 of Chapter 2 showed that about 64 percent
of the entire population live in SMSAs. Thus, metropolitan areas have

somewhat less, rather than more, than their share of the poor. Most of the places where the incidence of poverty is extremely high are rural. No SMSA central city has an incidence of poverty as high as those in parts of Appalachia and the rural south. Furthermore, much of the nation's most destitute poverty is in rural areas. Most of the evidence of severe malnutrition that shocked the nation in 1969 was from rural areas. Nevertheless, there are pockets of destitute poverty in the slums of every large city.

For reasons that are probably not rational, many people are especially concerned with urban poverty these days. The nation should of course be deeply concerned about poverty, but many people are disturbed that the poor are increasingly found in large metropolitan areas. Some almost seem to believe that the cities create poverty. In fact, the opposite is true. In recent decades, the poor, like others, have migrated to metropolitan areas in large numbers. And they have come for much the same reasons: to seek improved income and employment opportunities. The large numbers of blacks who have migrated to metropolitan areas have an additional incentive: to escape intolerable oppression in the rural south. However bad conditions are in urban slums, the migration has been successful. Real incomes and employment opportunities are better in urban than rural areas, and the incidence of poverty is lower despite the immigration of poor.

Some people are concerned about the growing concentration of welfare cases in metropolitan areas. In fact, surveys suggest that poor people come to urban areas mainly because they hope to find employment, and they seek welfare only after an unsuccessful job search. But it should not be a cause for concern that some people migrate to urban areas because welfare benefits there are more nearly adequate. The provision of welfare for the needy has been national policy for decades. And it may be more economical to provide welfare in large cities than in rural areas for precisely the economies of scale and agglomeration that make it more economical to undertake other activities in urban areas. For this and other reasons, welfare is so inadequate in many rural areas that residents are often effectively deprived of access to benefits for which they are eligible. Only if urban residence made migrants less able to provide for themselves than they could in rural areas would the urbanization of poverty be genuine cause for concern. But the evidence is to the contrary.

Legitimate concern with the urbanization of poverty comes from the concentration of the poor in segregated parts of central cities. Metropolitan areas do not have a disproportionate share of the poor, but central cities do. Most importantly, enforced segregation in urban ghettos, especially of blacks, violates their human rights, even if, as was suggested in Chapter 4, large numbers of poor people would choose to live there in the absence of coercion. Second, as was also suggested in Chapter 4, enforced segregation of the poor in central cities lessens their employment opportunities because it impairs their access to suburban jobs. Third, as is discussed in Chapter 10, enforced segregation raises the cost and lowers the quality of ghetto housing. Finally, as is discussed in Chapter 12, concentration of the poor in central cities worsens the problems of financing urban government.

RACE AND POVERTY

In his 1944 classic, Gunnar Myrdal described race relations in the United States as "an American dilemma." It is not much exaggeration to say that race relations became "the American trauma" during the succeeding quarter century. The subject extends far beyond the bounds of a textbook on urban economics. But the elemental and brutal fact is that American blacks have been forced into demeaning and subservient status by legal and extra-legal means since they arrived in the holds of slave ships. No subject can place greater stress on the endemic optimism of textbook writers.

Income is the best single measure of the status of blacks. Table 9-2 shows that the incidence of poverty is more than three times as great among nonwhites as among whites. Table 9-3 shows the trend of nonwhite incomes in relation to those of whites since 1950, and of blacks in relation to whites for recent years. The table shows that incomes of nonwhites have been little more than half those of whites for most of the postwar period.

Table 9-3   Median Family Income of Nonwhites as a Percent of White Family Income, Alternate Years, 1950–1968

Year	Nonwhites	Blacks
1950	54	NA
1952	57	NA
1954	56	NA
1956	53	NA
1958	51	NA
1960	55	NA
1962	53	NA
1964	56	54
1966	60	58
1968	63	60

NA = not available.

Source: U.S. Census Bureau, *The Social and Economic Status of Negroes in the United States, 1969.*

The table also shows some improvement in the relative position of non-whites during the 1960s, after deterioration during the latter part of the 1950s. It indicates that the relative position of nonwhites is worst during periods of high unemployment. It has been estimated that the income of nonwhites was little more than a third that of whites during the late 1930s. A striking implication of Table 9-3 is that incomes of blacks were lower than those of other nonwhites between 1964 and 1968.

The final comparison between white and nonwhite incomes is in Table 9-4. It shows that the disparity between white and nonwhite family incomes pervades the entire distribution. For example, in 1968, the percentage of white families with incomes of at least $10,000 was twice the percentage of nonwhite families. But once again, the data indicate that the disparity has decreased somewhat since World War II. In 1947, the percentage of white families with incomes of a purchasing power at least $10,000 in 1968 prices was more than three times the percentage of nonwhite families having the same income.

Most other social and economic statistics tell about the same story: there are large gaps between the positions of whites and nonwhites; non-whites have made substantial absolute and small relative gains since World War II. Life expectancy at birth is more than six years greater for whites than for nonwhites. The discrepancy has hardly changed since about 1950, but was more than ten years before World War II. Median years of educational attainment of nonwhites increased from 5.8 in 1940 to 8.2 in 1968. But the gap between educational attainment of whites and nonwhites fell only from 2.9 years to 2.7 years during the same period. It follows that the gap is substantially smaller between younger than older age groups. Unemployment rates of nonwhites were about 2.1 times those of whites during the 1960s. The ratio had been about 2.2 during the late 1950s, but it was

Table 9-4 Percent Distribution of Families by Income, 1947 and 1968 (in 1968 dollars)

	1947		1968	
	White	Nonwhite	White	Nonwhite
Under $3000	23	60	9	23
$3000 to $4999	28	23	11	22
$5000 to $6999	23	9	14	17
$7000 to $9999	15	5	24	18
$10,000 and over	11	3	42	21

Source: U.S. Census Bureau, The Social and Economic Status of Negroes in the United States, 1969.

Table 9-5 Racial Composition of Metropolitan and nonmetropolitan Areas, 1950, 1960, and 1969 (in millions)

	1950		1960		1969	
	Black	White	Black	White	Black	White
Metropolitan areas	8.3 55%	80.2 60%	12.2 65%	99.7 63%	15.6 70%	111.7 64%
Central cities	6.4 43	45.3 34	9.7 52	47.5 30	12.3 55	45.3 26
Suburbs	1.9 13	34.9 26	2.5 13	52.3 33	3.3 15	66.4 38
Nonmetropolitan areas	6.6 44	54.2 40	6.6 35	58.3 37	6.7 30	63.6 36
Totals	15.0 100%	134.4 100%	18.8 100%	158.1 100%	22.3 100%	175.3 100%

Sources: 1969 Statistical Abstract of the United States; and U.S. Census Bureau, The Social and Economic Status of Negroes in the United States, 1969.

Table 9-6   Black Families Below the Poverty Level, by Residence, 1968

	Number (millions)	Incidence (percent)
Inside metropolitan areas	0.779	23
Central cities	0.620	23
Suburbs	0.159	24
Outside metropolitan areas	0.589	47
Totals	1.366	29

Source: U.S. Census Bureau, *The Social and Economic Status of Negroes in the United States, 1969.*

below 2.0 during the early 1950s. Prewar data would undoubtedly show higher ratios.

It is well known that there has been a massive migration of blacks from the rural south to metropolitan areas since World War II. Table 9-5 shows that 55 percent of blacks and 60 percent of whites lived in SMSAs in 1950. By 1969, the percentages were 70 and 64. By this measure, blacks are now substantially more urbanized than whites. Blacks are of course heavily concentrated in central cities. In 1950, 77 percent of the blacks in metropolitan areas lived in central cities. In 1969, the percentage was 78. Nevertheless, the percentage of all blacks who were living in SMSA suburbs rose slightly from thirteen in 1950 to fifteen in 1969. In the late 1960s, there was some evidence that blacks were at last making progress in acquiring suburban housing in at least a few areas.

Table 9-6 shows that the incidence of poverty among black families was considerably lower in metropolitan areas than elsewhere: 23 percent of the black families living in SMSAs were below the poverty line in 1968, whereas 47 percent of the black families living outside SMSAs were poor. Urbanization has been even more important for blacks than for whites in improving income and employment opportunities.

PUBLIC POLICIES FOR REDUCING POVERTY

Macroeconomic Policies

By far the most important factor in the gradual reduction of poverty in the United States has been the overall growth of the economy. The percentage distribution of income has changed little since World War II. Thus, all income classes have shared about proportionally in the rapid rise in real incomes during the postwar period. As real incomes rise, people gradually rise above the poverty level. The most obvious beneficiaries of economic growth are employed people and their families. But economic growth also reduces poverty among the retired and others not in the labor force, in that it is easier to save for retirement and other contingencies during the working years if income is high than if it is low. Finally, economic growth increases revenues received by governments at fixed tax rates. Thus governments have more money to finance such public services as education, and such transfers as unemployment compensation, welfare, and social security, all of which help to reduce poverty.

Closely related to economic growth is level of unemployment. The incidence of poverty has fallen much more rapidly during periods of full employment than at other times. During periods of severe unemployment, the incidence of poverty rises. Poorly paid workers in general, and blacks in particular, tend to be the last to be hired and the first to be fired.

Macroeconomic fiscal and monetary policies to promote full employment and rapid economic growth have been by far the most important of government antipoverty programs since World War II. (These policies are discussed in macroeconomics textbooks, and are beyond the scope of this book.)

Income Maintenance Policies

Government expenditures are either purchases of goods and services or transfer payments. Many goods and services, such as national defense and highway construction, are provided for the general public, and it would be meaningless to estimate the extent to which they benefit the poor. But transfer payments, such as veterans' benefits and unemployment compensation, and some goods and services, such as public housing, are provided for identifiable groups of people. In principle, it is possible to estimate the income classes of beneficiaries of such programs.

In practice, the number and complexity of the programs make accurate estimation extremely difficult. Some of the programs, such as welfare payments, were designed to aid particular groups of needy people. But others, such as veterans' benefits, were designed to aid groups thought to be worthy, regardless of need. In a remarkable set of tables, the Council of Economic Advisers estimated the number of poor beneficiaries in fiscal year 1969 for a large number of federal, state, and local government programs classified under the heading of income maintenance. The term "income maintenance" indicates that the programs contribute directly to the income, or in some cases to the consumption, of the beneficiaries. These estimates are summarized in Table 9-7.

Table 9-7   Major Income Maintenance Programs, Fiscal Year 1969

Program	Total Outlays (millions of dollars)	Percent of Beneficiaries in Households with Income <$3300
All programs	58,679	NA
Aid to families with dependent children	3,206	100
Unemployment insurance		
Federal-State unemployment compensation	2,300	20
Federal employees and ex-servicemen	111	10
Railroad	52	NA
Disability programs		
Workmen's compensation	1,686	NA
Federal employees	57	15
Veterans' compensation	2,611	24
Railroad	77	NA
Social Security	2,691	39
Aid to the blind	92	100
Aid to permanently and totally disabled	726	100
Assistance to those 65 and over		
Social Security	24,681	31
Old-age assistance	1,833	100
Military retirement	2,265	NA
Civil service retirement	2,364	NA
Railroad retirement	1,542	34
Veterans' pensions	2,127	80
General assistance	32	100
Assistance-in-kind	10,226	
Food programs	665	
Food stamps	273	100
Child nutrition	128	100
Special supplementary package	9	100
Other direct distribution	255	100
Housing programs	484	
Public housing	456	57
Rent supplements	28	67
Health-service programs	9,077	
Medicare	6,222	36
Medicaid	2,384	75
Maternity and infant care	193	70
Public Health Service medical programs		
Neighborhood health centers	103	75
Other	175	55

Source: U.S. Council of Economic Advisors, *Economic Report of the President, 1969.*

Some of the estimates are subject to considerable error, and some include only federal outlays on programs to which state governments also contribute. Nevertheless, the data in Table 9-7 indicate that government income-maintenance programs in the United States certainly exceed $60 billion, and must be nearly 10 percent of national income. Although comparable figures are not available for earlier years, they would undoubtedly show that income maintenance expenditures grew rapidly during the 1960s. Some of the programs, such as Medicare and Medicaid, were begun during the 1960s. Others, such as Social Security benefits and aid to families with dependent children, were begun during the 1930s, but expenditures for them increased rapidly during the 1960s.

It should also be noted that some of the largest programs have a relatively small proportion of beneficiaries who are poor. Social Security benefits for the aged, for example, are $25 billion per year. Benefits depend mainly on Social Security taxes paid during working life, and not on need. To take a second example, federal-state unemployment compensation is paid to the unemployed who are covered by unemployment insurance, and not according to need. A small proportion of unemployment compensation went to the poor because most of the beneficiaries were unemployed only a short time and earned enough while employed to remain above the poverty line. As a third example, Medicare finances health care for the aged, not all of whom are needy.

In contrast, aid to families with dependent children, aid to the blind, aid to the permanently and totally disabled, old-age assistance, and general assistance constitute the country's welfare programs and are administered with a means test. Medicaid finances health care for the medically indigent, and is also administered with a means test. Food programs mainly benefit those on welfare. Some health programs, such as neighborhood health centers, are in principle available to the general public but are used almost entirely by the poor.

In addition to those listed in Table 9-7, a variety of federal government programs is intended to help the poor in somewhat indirect ways. The most important, and certainly the most controversial, are those authorized by the Economic Opportunity Act of 1964, the legislative basis of the "war on poverty." Many of the important provisions of the act establish educational and training programs to improve marketable skills, or to provide direct employment for poorly educated people. The Job Corps, the work-training program, and the work-study program provide training for young people. Headstart provides nursery schools for preschool-age children in poor communities. There is also a program of adult education. The act also authorized VISTA, the domestic analog to the Peace Corps.

The most controversial section of the act provides for community action programs. Under this provision, communities with large concentrations of poor can apply to the federal government for funds to support organizations in which the poor participate. The act provides great latitude for the activities that can be supported, but the goal is to help the poor organize, to help themselves and to obtain better local public services.

In 1962, the Manpower Development and Training Program was established to provide job training for both young people and adults. In its early years, the program concentrated on retraining adults whose skills had been made obsolete by technical change. As national unemployment fell during the 1960s, its focus changed to the provision of literacy and other basic educational training, and of on-the-job training for poorly educated, hard-core unemployed.

The final programs to be mentioned authorize the federal government to finance assistance to public and private organizations in depressed areas. The first such program was established by the Area Redevelopment Act of 1961, one of the first programs of the Kennedy administration. In 1965, the Appalachian Regional Development Act and the Public Works and Economic Development Act were passed. The former provides for federal government assistance in Appalachia, and the latter provides similar assistance in other depressed areas designated by the government.

To what extent have government policies affected the distribution of income? Recently, two Census Bureau scholars (Herriot and Miller) prepared a remarkable study that sheds light on the issue. Their results, which are for 1968, are shown in Table 9-8. They started with the family-income intervals shown in the left-hand column of the table. From the incomes in each interval, they subtracted the federal, state, and local taxes they estimated were paid by families in the interval. They then added to incomes in each interval the transfers paid to people with incomes in the interval by the three levels of government. The results are estimates of the effects on incomes in each interval of all government taxes and transfers.

It should be noted that the figures in Table 9-8 take account only of transfers, and not of public services. The authors made no attempt to identify the beneficiaries of public services by income class. Thus, the 24.6 percent of total taxes minus transfers in the top row of the table means that taxes equal to 24.6 percent of incomes were used to finance public services in 1968.

The third column of Table 9-8 summarizes the results. Those with pre-tax-transfer incomes below $2000 in 1968 received an excess of transfer payments over taxes paid equal to more than half of their incomes. Those in the highest income class, over $50,000, had an excess of taxes paid over transfers received equal to nearly 45 percent of their incomes. Taxes paid minus transfers received, as a percentage of income, rise rapidly moving up

Table 9-8   Government Tax and Transfer Rates as a Percent of Total Income, 1968

Adjusted Money Income Levels	Total			Federal Taxes				State and Local Taxes		
	Taxes	Gov Transfer Payments	Taxes minus Transfer Payments	Total	Income Tax	Corporate Profit Tax	Social Security Tax	Total	Property Tax	Sales Tax
Under $2000	50.0	106.5	−56.5	22.7	1.2	6.0	7.6	27.2	16.2	6.6
2000–4000	34.6	48.5	−13.9	18.7	3.5	4.3	6.5	15.7	7.5	4.9
4000–6000	31.0	19.6	11.4	19.0	5.3	3.6	6.7	12.1	4.8	4.1
6000–8000	30.1	8.6	21.5	19.4	6.5	3.2	6.8	10.7	3.8	3.6
8000–10,000	29.2	5.5	23.7	19.1	7.4	2.9	6.2	10.1	3.6	3.3
10,000–15,000	29.8	3.9	25.9	19.9	8.7	2.9	5.8	9.9	3.6	2.9
15,000–25,000	30.0	3.0	27.0	20.7	9.9	3.9	4.6	9.4	3.6	2.4
25,000–50,000	32.8	2.1	30.7	25.0	12.9	7.5	2.5	7.8	2.7	1.8
50,000 and over	45.0	0.4	44.7	38.4	19.8	15.4	1.0	6.7	2.0	1.1
Total tax and transfer rates	31.6	6.9	24.6	21.7	9.5	4.7	5.1	9.9	3.7	2.8

Source: Roger Herriot and Herman Miller, "Who Paid the Taxes in 1968?"

the income scale in the table. The data indicate that the government tax-transfer system in the United States is much more substantial and egalitarian than is widely appreciated.

The reason for widespread misunderstanding is easily seen in the first column of Table 9-8. The lowest income group pays half of its incomes in taxes, a larger percentage than any other income group in the table. Not until well above the median family income, which was about $8000 in 1968, do total taxes paid begin to increase as a percentage of income. The last columns of the table show that total state and local taxes are regressive throughout the income distribution, and that property taxes are a crushing burden on the lowest income groups. (More is said about the burden of property tax in Chapters 10 and 12.) Of all the taxes listed in the table, only the federal income tax is progressive throughout the income distribution.

What is not widely appreciated about the data of Table 9-8 is the magnitude of the transfer payments received by the lowest income groups. Those with incomes below $2000 received transfers in excess of their incomes in 1968. Even those with incomes in the $2000–$4000 interval received transfers equal to nearly half their incomes.

The data in Table 9-8 are not necessarily grounds for complacency. As was seen in Chapter 8, there is no objective criterion by which the adequacy of government income redistribution can be judged. Although the roughly 50 percent by which the tax-transfer system raises the incomes of the poorest group is impressive, it must be remembered that they start from extremely low incomes. The group in the $2000–$4000 interval, many of whom are below the poverty level, nevertheless pays more than one third of its income in taxes, and receives a net addition of only about 14 percent of its income by the tax-transfer system.

FURTHER POSSIBLE STEPS FOR REDUCING POVERTY

Reform of Income Maintenance Policies

Where do we stand in the national effort to eliminate poverty? How should we judge the programs listed above? And what further steps should be taken by the public sector? These are very difficult questions to answer. The variety and complexity of the programs listed above are enormous. Some are federal-state programs in which the federal government provides part of the money, and the state governments administer the program. In some such programs, fifty separate evaluations are needed. Some programs are not primarily intended to benefit the poor, and evaluation of such programs depends on personal opinion as to the desirability of providing certain kinds of assistance to certain groups of people. Although specific evaluation of programs cannot be attempted here, several general comments can be made.

First, the amount of money spent on income-maintenance and anti-poverty programs is substantial. Each person must judge for himself whether it is too much or too little. But 10 percent of national income is by no means an insignificant amount to spend on such programs.

Second, programs vary greatly in the extent to which they provide the intended assistance. Two examples will illustrate. Veterans' educational benefits have been quite large since World War II. Practically an entire generation of male college students was financed following World War II. Payments have been made either to the veteran or to the educational institution of his choice, with only minimal control over the kinds of education that could be financed. Despite the enormous sums involved, there has been little misuse of funds, and hardly any claims of federal interference with colleges and universities. The key to the success of the program seems to be that students were financed rather than educational institutions, and that the purposes of the benefits were well-defined. In contrast, the criteria for funding community action programs are ill-defined, and it is difficult to say what constitutes misuse of funds. The result is that the program has been embroiled in controversy, with claims and counterclaims about misuse of funds, unwarranted interference, and so on.

Third, many of the programs, especially some older ones, have become complex and cumbersome. Successive sessions of Congress tend to modify programs to improve the benefits for some deserving group. In some cases, the programs have become so complex that specialized legal assistance is required to establish eligibility. An excessive burden is placed on prospective beneficiaries, especially those who are poorly educated. Administrative costs are too high, and the door is opened to manipulation of programs by people expert on particular programs, both within the administrative agency and within groups of potential beneficiaries. Someone ought to ask of each program exactly what group it is intended to help and in what way, and what is the simplest set of procedures that will do the job.

What about programs specifically designed to aid the poor? An overall judgment is that progress has been considerable in reducing poverty, but that most of it has come from the general growth of the economy, and during the 1960s, from reductions in the unemployment rate. Specific government programs to raise the standard of living of poor people have been substantial, but have been offset in part by high taxes paid by poor people. Additional public programs to aid the poor have been suggested, but these proposals cannot be catalogued here.

Self-help is at the center of traditional ways to reduce poverty in the United States. Yet the white majority has used discriminatory obstacles to block the efforts of the black minority to lift themselves from poverty. It is painfully obvious that one of the most important antipoverty measures is for whites to accelerate their progress in getting out of blacks' way. Serious discrimination still exists at every step: the provision of public services such as education, police protection, and refuse collection; union membership; employment; housing; and many other areas. The civil rights bills of the 1960s were intended to reduce the unequal treatment of blacks. A great deal remains to be done.

But there would still be some poverty even if there were no discrimination. In considering proposals to reform or extend programs to aid the poor, several criteria should be kept in mind. First, programs should concentrate on increasing the purchasing power of the poor rather than on planning their lives for them. Many existing programs are excessively detailed and paternalistic. Welfare programs entail unwarranted intrusion into recipients' lives and control over the use of benefits. Assistance-in-kind programs impose artificial consumption patterns on recipients.

The situation stems from a traditional view that the poor cannot be trusted to spend money wisely. But evidence on this point is notably lacking. Certainly, the ability to waste money is by no means exclusive to people with low incomes. Even if there were evidence that poor people were less skillful than others in managing money, experience and responsibility with money would improve their skills. In any case, it would be better for government to provide advice and training in money management than to coerce the poor by providing predetermined amounts of goods and services. Many people reject the recommendation that consumer sovereignty be given to the poor. Some who accept it in principle balk at the implication that it is better to give the poor money rather than food stamps, even if some decide to spend less on food and more on cars and color television sets.

Second, a given amount of resources will provide the most aid to the poor if poverty is the criterion for assistance. A major reason that antipoverty programs are so expensive is that criteria other than poverty are used to determine eligibility. The motivation for Medicare, for example, was the worthy one that old people require a great deal of medical care which many of them can ill-afford. But age was made the only criterion for eligibility, and so only just over one third of the benefits go to poor people.

The Council of Economic Advisers estimated that only $10 billion was needed to put all poor people above the poverty line in 1967. It is not a large amount even in comparison with existing income-maintenance programs. But poverty can be eliminated with such a small sum only if poverty is the sole criterion for eligibility.

Third, programs should provide beneficiaries with at least some incentive to help themselves. To the extent feasible, antipoverty programs should encourage people to be self-supporting and not to depend on public transfers. Of course, some groups are not and should not be in the labor force, and many of the programs in Table 9-7 are intended to benefit such groups. Aid to the disabled and Social Security programs are prominent examples. A popular concern is that liberal welfare benefits will discourage recipients from seeking jobs. It is unlikely to be a serious problem with present welfare levels and eligibility requirements, but sufficiently high benefits would certainly discourage large numbers of people from working. And there probably are at least a few welfare families, eligible for food stamps and Medicaid only if they remain on welfare, whose incomes would fall if the family head took a full-time job at the legal minimum wage rate.

Negative Income Taxes

Unfortunately, there is no unique antipoverty program that is best by all three criteria discussed above. But it is useful to conclude this chapter by using them to judge the most prominent and one of the most far-reaching proposals that has been made in recent years to reform antipoverty programs, the negative income tax. The basic idea of the negative income tax is suggested by its name. Just as the government collects a positive income tax on incomes above a certain level, so it would collect a negative tax from (i.e., pay a subsidy to) those with incomes below a certain amount. As with an ordinary income tax, the cutoff point and the tax rate must be set. Many economists have advocated a negative income tax, though with a variety of schedules and other conditions.

A conservative proposal would pay poor people a proportion, say 50 percent, of unused parts of personal exemptions on federal income-tax schedules. Suppose the personal exemption is $700, so that a family of four has exemptions of $2800. If the family had no income, it would receive $1400, or half of $2800. Each dollar of income would be "taxed" at 50 percent, that is, the subsidy would go down by fifty cents, so that the subsidy would vanish at an income of $2800.

A liberal proposal would use the negative income tax to eliminate poverty. Assume a poverty income level of $3300 for a family of four, and use the 50-percent negative income-tax rate. To eliminate poverty, the cutoff would be $6600. For each dollar by which income fell short of $6600, the family would receive a fifty-cent subsidy. Thus, if income were zero, the subsidy would be $3300, or half of $6600, just at the poverty line. The higher the cutoff, the higher the minimum income the proposal would guarantee, and the more expensive the plan would be. The higher the tax rate, the less the government expense of providing a given minimum income. But high tax rates defeat the basic purpose of the proposal, to reduce the penalty to poor families if they increase their income, thus providing them with incentive to accept even poorly paid jobs.

The negative income tax is attractive under the first two criteria discussed above. It provides the poor with money which they can spend as they please, and entails no intrusion into their affairs other than that imposed on all taxpayers. It is relatively easy to administer, in that the bureaucracy already exists to collect income taxes, and the tax form for low incomes is already simple. It seems likely that a 50-percent tax rate would provide considerable incentive to accept paid employment.

The problem with the negative income tax comes with the third criterion. If the cutoff is set low, it does not eliminate poverty. If it is set high, the expense becomes great because large sums are paid to those who are not poor. The Council of Economic Advisers has computed that the liberal proposal outlined above would have cost the government $20 billion in 1967, which means that half the money would have gone to those who were not poor. Under the liberal propooal, a family of four with an income of $5000 would receive a negative tax of $800, or one half of $6600 minus $5000. Although the subsidy per family is small at this income level, there are many more families with incomes of about $5000 than of about $2000. Liberal negative income-tax schemes are costly, partly because no positive income tax can be collected from those with incomes below the cutoff. If it were, those people would have a marginal tax rate in excess of 50 percent.

It has been proposed that the negative income tax be supplemented with some conventional programs. Indeed, if the federal government adopted the proposal, it could hardly object if state and local governments supplemented the benefits. That would reduce the total cost of eliminating poverty, since it would permit a low cutoff to be used. But it would also impair the incentive effect, since it would raise the tax rate above 50 percent for some groups. If a family's income rose from a level at which it qualified for a conventional program to one at which it did not, its total purchasing power might fall.

The foregoing discussion by no means shows that the negative income tax is a bad idea. But it does show that there is a conflict between the desire to incorporate incentives into an antipoverty program and the desire to restrict benefits to the poor. Judgment must be used to weigh the relative importance of the three criteria.

SUMMARY

Poverty is a matter of degree. Although there are almost no Americans who are poor by worldwide standards, we have many poor people for a country with such a high average standard of living. The incidence of poverty is especially high among blacks, the elderly, and the poorly educated. Poverty has decreased steadily since World War II, mainly because of the economy's rapid overall growth and low unemployment rate. Urbanization has been an important factor in the reduction of poverty among blacks.

The United States has a large variety of income maintenance programs which absorb about 10 percent of national incomes. Some are directed at poor people, but much of the money goes to groups—such as veterans and the elderly—who are regarded as worthy of public help although they are not poor.

An important controversy regarding income maintenance programs is whether money or goods and services should be given to the poor. A second controversy is the extent to which income maintenance programs can be focused specifically on poor people. A third controversy is the extent to which antipoverty measures can provide the poor with incentives to help themselves.

DISCUSSION QUESTIONS

1. People concerned with poverty sometimes advocate a system of family allowances under which each family would receive a monthly payment for each child in the family. Evaluate this proposal under each of the three criteria for antipoverty measures discussed in this chapter.

2. Referring to Table 9-8, what changes would you advocate if you wanted to reduce the tax burden on low-income people?
3. To what extent do you think the poor would benefit from a wage-price freeze that curtailed inflation without raising the unemployment rate?
4. President Nixon has said, "The concentration of population growth in already crowded areas is not a trend we wish to perpetuate. This administration would prefer a more balanced growth pattern—and we are taking a number of steps to encourage more development and settlement in the less densely populated areas of our country." Keeping in mind the data in Table 9-6, what effect do you think this policy will have on poverty?

REFERENCES AND FURTHER READING

Roger Herriot and Herman Miller, "Who Paid the Taxes in 1968?," unpublished.

John Kain (editor), *Race and Poverty*, 1969.

Oscar Lewis, *The Children of Sanchez*, 1961.

Gunnar Myrdal, *An American Dilemma*, 1944.

———, *Asian Drama* (three volumes), 1968.

Lester Thurow, *Poverty and Discrimination*, 1969.

United States Council of Economic Advisers, *Economic Report of the President, 1969*.

United States Census Bureau, *Revision of Poverty Statistics, 1959 to 1968*, Current Population Reports, Series P-23, August, 1969.

———, *The Social and Economic Status of Negroes in the United States, 1969*, Current Population Reports, Series P-23, No. 29, 1969.

Charles Valentine, *Culture and Poverty*, 1968.

Chapter 10

Housing, Slums, and Urban Renewal

Housing, like food, satisfies a fundamental human need. Except for food, no commodity is more important than dwelling place in determining standard and style of living. Indeed, if housing costs are taken to include the cost of operating as well as of owning or renting a dwelling, the average American spends about the same part (20 percent) of his disposable income on housing as on food. In poor countries, larger parts of income are spent on both commodities. On the supply side, the two industries are similar in that, in contrast with manufactured goods, food and housing are produced by small, competitive firms. A further similarity is that housing and food production are among the most land-intensive of industries. More than half of the land in urban areas is devoted to housing. But a crucial difference between the two industries is that housing is the most durable of capital goods, whereas food is the least durable of commodities.

Housing, especially in urban areas, is the subject of controversy, and of public policies of great variety and complexity. Slums are rightly at the head of the list of controversial housing topics, and rank just behind poverty as the most serious contemporary urban problem. Americans are now clearly aware that many people, especially blacks, live in abominable housing in the central cities of metropolitan areas. A great deal of public effort has been devoted to the design of policies that will improve or eliminate slums. And a great deal of public and private controversy has been devoted to the merits of alternative slum improvement proposals.

The literature on urban housing and slums is enormous. As with poverty, the study of housing and slums is by no means the preserve of economists. Yet housing and real estate has been a recognized specialty among economists for decades. Nevertheless, the quality of the literature was surprisingly low until the 1960s, considering the importance of the subject. No studies of housing demand appeared before 1960 that matched the quality of prewar studies of food demand. And a careful study of the construction industry has yet to appear.

STRUCTURE OF THE HOUSING INDUSTRY

Expenditure on housing services, as on any product or service, equals price times quantity purchased. A major stumbling block to research on any service industry is the difficulty of measuring the output. It is hard to know whether one doctor produces more or higher quality medical services than another. The problem is no less serious in the study of housing. The quality and quantity of housing services depend, in complex and poorly understood ways, on many variables. The kinds, sizes, and arrangements of rooms, the kinds and conditions of materials in the structure, and the condition of utilities, style, and decoration are among the important variables.

Expenditure on housing services is relatively easy to observe. But for many purposes, expenditure comparisons must be separated into price and quantity components. For example, expenditure on housing was greater in 1960 than in 1940. To what extent was there an increase in housing consumption and to what extent an increase in housing prices? To take another example, housing expenditure is greater among blacks than among others with similar incomes in central cities. To what extent do blacks consume more housing and to what extent do they pay higher prices? (Although the problem is real, it should not be exaggerated. No one would question that a run-down slum tenement yields less and poorer quality housing services than a well-maintained single-family house in the suburbs.) Much ingenuity has been used in housing studies to learn something from the data despite the measurement problem.

Supply

The supply side of the housing industry is easy to describe in broad outline. Housing is supplied from the stock of used housing and by construction of new housing. The durability of housing implies that the former is large relative to the latter. A typical house may last fifty years, which means, in a growing economy, that somewhat less than 2 percent of the stock must be replaced per year. If population grows by about 1.5 percent per year, new construction may increase the stock of housing by somewhat more than 2 percent per year. Adding replacement and expansion, construction probably provides a supply of housing of less than 5 percent of the housing stock per year. But the average family in the United States moves about once in five years, which means that 20 percent of the housing stock comes on the market per year. Thus, the supply of used housing may be four times as large as the supply of new housing.

The supply of both new and used housing is competitive. There are twice as many construction as manufacturing firms, despite the fact that the value added in manufacturing is more than five times that in construction. Construction is of course more localized than manufacturing, and the firms that build houses tend to be different from those that build roads and commercial buildings. But housing construction firms tend to be smaller than other construction firms. Furthermore, house building is an industry in which entry and exit are easy and frequent.

There is no substantial concentration of ownership of used housing. More than 60 percent of all dwellings in the United States are owner-occupied, and ownership is, by definition, unconcentrated. Comprehensive data are not available on the ownership of rental housing, but there is no evidence of monopoly power in urban areas. Since there is free entry in housing construction, monopoly power in used housing would require ownership not only of a substantial part of the housing stock in an urban area but also of a substantial part of the land available for development. Contrary to some popular opinion, there seems to be little monopoly control, even of slum housing. A survey of slum landlords in Newark, New Jersey, for example (Sternlieb), showed that only 25 percent of the slum dwellings were owned by landlords who owned more than six slum dwellings.

Demand

Considerable uncertainty surrounds the parameters of the housing demand function. It was once accepted that the income elasticity of demand for housing was 1.0, or somewhat less. But recent, more sophisticated research (Reid) has indicated that it may be 1.5 or more. Likewise, early studies suggested that housing demand was inelastic with respect to its own price, whereas more recent research (Muth) suggests that the price elasticity may be about 1.0. (Of course, the demand curve slopes downward.) There is of course no guarantee that the elasticities are constants. For example, it may be that the income elasticity of demand for housing is very high at low incomes and small at very high incomes.

A study by the National Bureau of Economic Research (Grebler *et al.*) has established that during the first half of the twentieth century, housing prices rose about twice as fast as average consumer prices, and that the stock of housing per capita rose very little. The reasons for the rapid rise in housing prices are not well understood, but the trend is shared with other capital goods. It seems likely that rising real incomes and a fairly high income-elasticity of demand for housing have stimulated housing demand, but that the effect has been largely offset by the rapid increase in housing prices.

Housing demand-and-supply studies frequently require cost comparisons between rental and owner-occupied housing. The costs of rental are clear enough. They include contract rental payments, and any utility and other operating costs not included in the contract rents. A practical difficulty is that utilities may or may not be included in rents, and some data sources do not make it clear to what extent they are included.

But what are the costs of home ownership? Obviously, utility and other operating costs must be included. So must real estate taxes, insurance, maintenance, and repairs. But the items that cause confusion are interest costs. Of the monthly mortgage payment, interest is a cost of ownership, but the principal payment is a form of saving. In addition to interest paid, interest forgone on the owner's equity is a cost of ownership. If the owner rented instead of buying, he could invest the equity in bonds or other income-producing assets. The interest he could have earned, but did not, is a cost of ownership. A rule of thumb in real estate is that the monthly rental of a dwelling should be about 1 percent of its sales value. If the annual rental is 12 percent of market value, about 3 percent might be real-estate taxes, 6 percent interest on the mortgage and on the owner's equity, and the rest insurance, depreciation, and maintenance. These are rough figures and they depend somewhat on tax considerations, discussed later in this chapter.

TRENDS IN SLUM HOUSING

Housing experts debate the proper definition of "slum." The basic point, however, is that slums, like poverty, are a matter of degree. Housing of any given quality is better than housing of lower quality. The housing quality to which a family or a nation aspires should depend on its income, and on the costs of housing and other things it wants. And the fact that many residents of poor countries live in housing of worse quality than almost any Americans do is hardly grounds for complacency.

There is a tendency to identify slums with high density, but it is not a useful definition. Many high-income high-rise apartment areas in large cities have extremely high population densities, but they are certainly not slums. Even more important, there is much poor housing in rural areas, although density is low, and it is now common to use the term "rural slum."

Ideally, the entire frequency distribution of housing qualities, like the frequency distribution of incomes, would be available. Each person could then choose his own cutoff and refer to housing of lesser quality as "slums." But housing quality is much harder to measure than income, and we know correspondingly less about its distribution. The only comprehensive data available on housing quality are collected by the Census Bureau. The census employs two concepts of substandard housing. First, housing is said to lack basic plumbing facilities if it lacks one or more of the following: hot running water in the structure, flush toilet for private use of the household, and bathtub or shower for private use of the household. Second, housing is said to be dilapidated if it does not provide safe and adequate shelter and endangers the health, safety, or well-being of its occupants. Dilapidated housing has defects that mean it should be torn down, extensively repaired, or rebuilt. These definitions and their elaboration appear in the first few pages of every volume of the census of housing. Housing that either lacks basic plumbing facilities or is dilapidated is described as "not meeting specified criteria." In this book, the less cumbersome term "substandard" will be used.

The plumbing facilities criterion is objective, but the dilapidation criterion is somewhat subjective. The Census Bureau tries hard to ensure that the criteria are uniformly applied, and private studies have confirmed the census findings. If there is a bias, it is probably that successive censuses use more stringent criteria as the standard of tolerable housing rises.

Most people are aware that large numbers of Americans live in substandard housing. But many people are not aware of the extent to which substandard housing has become less common since World War II. In 1950, the Census Bureau found that about 35 percent of housing was substandard. By the 1960 census, the percentage had fallen to 19. By 1968, it had fallen to 8.

Table 10-1 presents detailed data for recent years. The incidence of substandard housing is much greater among nonwhites than among whites. In 1968, the precentage of nonwhites living in substandard housing was four times that of whites. Substandard housing decreased rapidly among both groups during the eight-year period. But progress was greater among whites than among nonwhites, the incidence of substandard housing having fallen by somewhat more than half for whites and by somewhat less than half for nonwhites.

Table 10-1 shows that substandard housing is much less common in metropolitan areas than elsewhere. More than half of the nonwhites and more than 10 percent of the whites living outside metropolitan areas lived in substandard dwellings in 1968. Furthermore, progress in reducing the in-

Table 10-1   Incidence of Substandard Housing, 1960 and 1968

	Nonwhite		White	
	1960	*1968*	*1960*	*1968*
United States	44	24	13	6
Metropolitan areas				
Central cities	25	9	8	3
Suburbs	43	16	7	3
Nonmetropolitan areas	77	55	23	11

Source: U.S. Census Bureau, *Social and Economic Status of Negroes in the United States, 1969.*

cidence of substandard housing has been much less outside metropolitan areas than in. The incidence of substandard housing among nonwhites fell by almost two thirds in metropolitan areas, but by less than one third elsewhere. Table 10-1 strongly indicates that migration of nonwhites to metropolitan areas has enabled them to make massive improvements in their housing conditions.

Substandard housing and poverty are two sides of the same coin. Although the data do not tell us how many poor live in substandard housing, and how many living in substandard housing are poor, the correlation must be very high. Comparison between Table 10-1 and Table 9-6 of Chapter 9 indicates that, among nonwhites, the incidence of poverty exceeds that of substandard housing. Within central cities of SMSAs, more than twice as many nonwhites are poor as live in substandard housing. Outside metropolitan areas, the incidence of substandard housing exceeds that of poverty. The suggestion in these figures is that migration of nonwhites to metropolitan areas has been even more important in eliminating poor housing than in eliminating poverty.

CAUSES OF SLUMS

City planners and social reformers have long speculated about the causes of slums, but much of the literature[1] is of remarkably low analytical quality. For example, it was once common to attribute slums, at least in part, to the neglect of structures by greedy landlords. Presumably "greed" means the aggressive pursuit of profit, but neglect of profit-making assets is hardly the way to achieve that goal. More important, no matter how greedy landlords

---

1. An extensive critique of this literature is in Muth.

may be, they need monopoly power to be able to affect resource allocation, and evidence indicates they have none. In any case, the most reasonable assumption would seem to be the one that has been made throughout the analysis in this book: that owners of all kinds of assets typically seek the highest return possible on their assets. The strength and persistence of the greed theory probably stems from the fact that collecting rent from tenants who can ill afford to pay it can hardly be the world's most pleasant occupation. Thus, it would not be surprising if it attracted rather insensitive people. But that is a far cry from being an explanation of slums. If "nice guys" were a requirement for efficient resource allocation, the entire economy would be in bad shape.

A recent reincarnation of the greed theory places the blame for slum housing, especially among blacks in central cities, on villains in the real-estate and mortgage industries. A forceful exposition of this view can be found in "The Ghetto Makers," by Jack Rothman (see Kain). But to blame housing segregation on realtors and mortgage lenders is like blaming bad news on the journalist. To the extent that racial segregation causes slums, the villains are the whites who are unwilling to sell to, rent to, or live near blacks. Without such seller/buyer attitudes, racist realtors and mortgage lenders would have to look for other work.

Serious discussion of the causes of slums must start by distinguishing between demand and supply considerations. The most important considerations on the demand side are easy to understand, although sophisticated analysis is required for some causes there that may be important. But it is the supply side that people find most mysterious.

Demand for Housing

By far the most important cause of slums is that there is a large demand for poor-quality housing by poor people who can afford no better. Given that the average family spends about 20 percent of its income on housing, even a low estimate of the income elasticity of demand for housing implies that low-income families spend only about 25 percent of their income on housing. Surveys confirm the figure. For a family with a $3000 annual income, it comes to less than $15 per week for rent and utilities. Assume for the moment that markets work perfectly, so that poor people have no barrier other than income in competing for housing. Nevertheless, $15 per week would buy only a small amount of very low-quality housing. To put the point somewhat differently, practically no families with incomes in the middle range spend so little on housing, for the simple reason that no decent housing can be supplied at that price.

Housing markets, especially in low-income areas, probably do not work very well. Some public intervention is undoubtedly justified to improve their functioning. Although such policies might substantially reduce the amount of very poor quality housing, the discussion above indicates that there are stringent limits to the benefits of improved market performance. If public policy is to make much difference to the housing of low-income people, it must lower housing costs (for example by stimulating new technology), subsidize low-income housing, or raise the incomes of the poor.

Many writers claim that slum housing markets work very poorly. The factors for which a substantial case can be made can be classified under three headings: racial discrimination, the "neighborhood effect," and flattening of rent-distance functions.

Racial Discrimination

The conventional view is that, especially in northern cities, whites discriminate against blacks in the sale and rental of housing, and the result is higher housing costs for blacks than for whites. This conventional view has been challenged by several writers.[2] The argument goes as follows: Assume that whites have a greater aversion to living among blacks than blacks have to living among whites. Then the two groups will be segregated, and there will be a frontier between the two communities. The assumptions about racial aversion imply that whites are less willing than blacks to live near the frontier on the white side. Housing prices will be lower there than in the interiors of the two communities. Blacks will move in and whites will move out, add the frontier will move toward the white community. Movement will stop only when the supply of housing in the black community is so large that housing is cheaper there than across the frontier. Thus, the argument concludes, racial aversion may make housing less rather than more expensive for blacks relative to whites.

The model is naive. A more realistic model is as follows: Assume that the races are segregated, and that the frontier is a circle around the city center. Blacks are within the circle and whites outside it. Assume that whites are averse, not only to living near, but also to selling or renting to blacks in

---

2. See Muth for a review of the relevant literature.

the white community. Now suppose that housing demand increases in the black community because incomes rise or because blacks migrate there from rural areas. Then pressure develops to move the frontier outward because excess demand raises housing prices in the black community above those across the frontier. Eventually, prices become high enough that some whites near the frontier sell or rent to blacks. The magnitude of the excess of housing prices in the black community over those in the white community that it takes to move the frontier depends on the strength of whites' aversion to dealing with blacks. Note that the argument is unaffected by increasing housing demand in the white community. Unlike blacks, whites can expand outward at the edge of the urban area.

The model outlined above is a restatement of the conventional view. The crucial element in the model is the assumption that whites are unwilling to rent or sell to blacks on the white side of the frontier except at premium prices. Ample evidence exists in the files of every fair-housing agency.

Housing prices in the black community might (but need not) tend to equal those in the white community if black housing demand were stationary. But this does not matter. Rising black income is, hopefully, a permanent trend, and migration of blacks to metropolitan areas is clearly a long-term phenomenon. Both factors cause black housing demand to rise in metropolitan areas.

Economists can propound many theories on the subject, but the facts should settle the matter. As often happens, the facts are subject to several interpretations. The most comprehensive data on the subject are from the 1960 census of housing, presented in Table 10-2. The data refer to all rental housing in SMSAs. Owner-occupied housing is excluded because costs, especially forgone interest on the owner's equity, are hard to compare.

Table 10-2 classifies households by rent paid. The first columns show median rent/income ratios for households in each rent class. Since rent/income ratios are higher for nonwhites than for whites, it means that nonwhites spend more on rent than whites in comparable income classes. These data are the subject of lively debate. They constitute a *prima facie* case for discrimination against nonwhites. But several writers have claimed that they may be explained by other factors.

Some rents include payment for some or all utilities and for furniture rental, and it has been suggested that inclusion of these items in rents may be more common among nonwhites than among whites. It is hard to imagine why it should be more common among nonwhites than whites at given income levels. But if so, it is a subject for serious study. It has also been suggested that mobility may be greater among nonwhites, and that the result-

Table 10-2 Characteristics of SMSA Rental Housing, 1960

Monthly Gross Rent	Median Rent/ Income Ratio		Percent Substandard		Median Number of Rooms		Percent with More than One Person per Room	
	Total	Nonwhite	Total	Nonwhite	Total	Nonwhite	Total	Nonwhite
Less than $30	19.8	22.3	50.3	62.1	2.4	2.2	17.3	25.8
$30–$39	20.8	24.2	42.9	56.3	2.7	2.4	16.5	28.5
$40–$49	19.6	24.3	36.8	50.9	3.1	2.6	17.3	29.2
$50–$59	19.0	23.9	29.3	44.5	3.4	3.0	17.0	30.0
$60–$69	19.2	24.8	23.2	39.1	3.6	3.2	16.5	29.9
$70–$79	19.8	24.8	17.8	33.9	3.8	3.4	14.5	28.3
$80–$99	20.4	26.2	12.9	30.6	4.1	3.7	12.7	27.9
$100–$119	21.8	28.1	8.6	27.4	4.3	4.1	11.2	27.9
$120 and over	22.1	29.4	4.5	23.9	4.6	4.7	7.8	25.7
Totals	20.0	26.1	20.7	41.2	3.8	3.2	14.0	28.5

Source: "Price Discrimination Against Negroes in the Rental Housing Market," by Chester Rapkin, in Kain. Compiled from 1960 census of housing.

ing frequent vacancies in nonwhite areas make costs higher than in white neighborhoods. Again, reasons for greater mobility of nonwhites at given income levels are not clear, and should be studied if mobility is indeed greater.

It is hard to imagine that the factors above are important. Also, the data in Table 10-2 suggest strongly that nonwhites do not buy more or higher quality housing than whites with comparable incomes. In every rent class there is more substandard housing among nonwhites than among whites. And in every rent class nonwhite dwellings contain fewer rooms.

Only two factors seem to be serious competitors with the discrimination hypothesis as explanations of the data in Table 10-2. The last columns in Table 10-2 show that nonwhites average more people per room in every rent class. This is to be expected, since nonwhite families are larger than white families on the average, and a given family income therefore means less income per capita and consequently less housing per capita. But the larger number of occupants per room means also that utility costs and depreciation are likely to be somewhat greater than among white families. The former is relevant only to the extent that utilities are included in rents. But both factors would raise housing costs and therefore rents.

The most important issue has to do with elasticity of demand for housing. Rent is price per unit times quantity bought. Elementary price theory tells us that total expenditure increases with price only if demand is inelastic. Therefore price discrimination against nonwhites would imply more expenditure on housing by nonwhites only if demand were inelastic. If demand were elastic, greater expenditure would imply lower price. If demand had unitary elasticity, price discrimination could not explain expenditure differences, since expenditure would not depend on price. Therefore, knowing the demand elasticity is crucial in evaluating the discrimination hypothesis. It has been stated that recent research suggests that the elasticity might be about 1.0. But the precise magnitude makes a great deal of difference to the issue. Suppose that price and income elasticities are constant, so that housing demand can be represented by Equation 5-4 of Chapter 5. Suppose, realistically, that the income elasticity is about 1.5. If the price elasticity were slightly below 1.0, the data in Table 10-2 would imply that housing prices for nonwhites were many times those for whites. No corrections for extra depreciation or utilities would substantially alter the picture. If the elasticity were as small as 0.25, the data would be consistent with a price about twice as high for nonwhites as for whites. If the elasticity were slightly above 1.0, the data would suggest that housing prices for whites were many times those for nonwhites.

The sophisticated study of housing demand by Muth concludes that most, but not all, variation in housing prices can be explained by factors other than race. But hardly anyone who has studied the data would conclude that nonwhites pay less than 5 to 15 percent more for given amounts and qualities of housing than whites, only because of racial considerations. More research is needed on this very important issue.

The Neighborhood Effect

In recent years, several writers[3] have analyzed an external diseconomy of the kind defined in Chapter 8, the "neighborhood effect," which impairs the functioning of urban housing markets. The market value and desirability of a dwelling depend not only on expenditures in constructing and maintaining it, but also on expenditures for neighboring structures. Most people prefer to live in neighborhoods where the houses are attractive and well-maintained. The implication, however, is that some of the benefits or returns from expenditure by an owner on his house are realized by owners of neighboring homes. In other words, only part of the return to housing investment accrues to the owner or, more succinctly, the social value of housing investment exceeds the private value. But the owner of a dwelling takes account only of the return he realizes in deciding how much to invest in his house. He invests the amount which makes the marginal return to him of an additional dollar invested equal to the opportunity cost of funds. But social return exceeds private return, so the owner therefore invests less than is needed to equate marginal social returns to opportunity cost. Thus, competitive markets induce too little investment in urban housing.

This is an important theoretical argument, and provides a major justification for urban-renewal programs and other public policies (discussed below). But its value as a guide to public policy depends not only on its theoretical validity but also on its quantitative importance. The analysis above suggested that poverty is by far the most important cause of slums. If that is correct, the neighborhood effect cannot be a primary explanation of slums. It is unfortunate that so little empirical work has been done on the issue, even though imaginative research should go a long way toward establishing orders of magnitude. But two theoretical considerations confirm the suggestion that it is not of primary importance.

---

3. See Rothenberg for a survey and references.

First, it appears that the argument applies as much to suburban as to central city housing. Clearly, the strength of the external diseconomy is affected by the distance between dwellings. If my nearest neighbor lives five miles away, the condition of his house is of little interest to me. But by how much is the effect diminished by intervals of 50 or 100 feet between houses, as are typical in suburban developments? A widely held and probably correct belief about the views of suburbanites is that the quality of the neighborhood is of great importance to them. If so, the external effect must be about as important in the suburbs as in the slums. And real-estate advertisements to the effect that "when you buy in Clearview Estates you buy a neighborhood, not just a home," point to the same conclusion. The suggestion here is that the neighborhood effect is either important in both slum and suburb or unimportant in both places, with the odds on the later.

Second, if the neighborhood effect were important, it would provide incentive for common ownership of large numbers of proximate properties. If a single person or firm owns a large part of a neighborhood, the external effect is internalized. Returns on investment that accrue to neighboring properties then accrue to the person or firm that makes the investment decision. In the suburbs, the income-tax advantages to high-income owner-occupants (discussed below) make common ownership not feasible. But low-income residents have practically no incentive to own their homes, and owner-occupancy is uncommon in very low income areas. Unfortunately, not much is known about the extent to which neighboring slum properties are under common ownership, but available evidence suggests that ownership is fragmented.

It is sometimes suggested that the difficulty in assembling proximate properties impedes common ownership. Once a single owner has acquired several properties in a neighborhood, owners of remaining properties acquire some monopoly power and may be able to extract the benefits of common ownership in sales to the common owner. This is unlikely to be a major consideration. It is not necessary to own all the properties in a neighborhood to internalize most of the neighborhood effect. Property is frequently acquired through "straw man" sales and in other ways that hide the true purchaser. It is also sometimes suggested that unavailability of capital limits the extent of common ownership. But with a highly organized mortgage market, the capital requirements for even a large suburban development are small compared with the capital that is assembled by relatively small firms in manufacturing.

The tentative judgment here is that the neighborhood effect is unlikely to be a major cause of slums.

Flattening of Rent-Distance Functions

In Chapter 4 it was shown that there are strong theoretical reasons to expect urban land rent and population and employment density functions to flatten through time. In Chapter 6 evidence was surveyed that showed such flattening to be a pervasive characteristic of urban areas.

There are typically two influences on land values near the city center. The growth of the metropolitan areas raises the rent-distance function at each distance from the center. But flattening of the function lowers land values near the center and raises them in the suburbs. The net effect on land values near the center depends on the net effect of growth and decentralization.

For fifteen to twenty years after World War II, it was widely reported that land values near city centers were falling either absolutely or at least relative to the general price level. Although adequate data are lacking, this seems likely, since it was the period of most rapid postwar suburbanization. Falling land-rent and density-distance functions require slow, painful, and costly adjustments. Large capital losses may occur. And the kinds and sizes of structures that are appropriate near the city center may change. Major adjustments undoubtedly require decades to complete.

Shortly after World War II, loud cries for federal help went out from city-center business interests, central city governments, and concerned citizens. The plea was to stem and reverse the tide of blight and decay. The response was the federal urban renewal program (discussed later in this chapter). Here the issue is the role of shifting land rent and density functions in slum creation.

It is doubtful whether public policy can or should halt the decentralization process in metropolitan areas. But there is no strong reason to believe that the speed at which the market adjusts from one equilibrium to another is optimum. Disinvestment in city-center structures, when accomplished by private markets, entails long periods of low maintenance, followed by demolition and replacement. Although the analysis has not been worked out, it may be desirable for the public sector to intervene and speed up the process. There are of course many forms of intervention, so the statement above does not prejudge the evaluation of an urban renewal program.

If the rent-distance function flattens, the largest capital losses and the largest adjustments occur in the central business district (CBD). Commercial interests are the ones primarily affected, since few people live in CBDs of large cities. But some of the worst slum housing in metropolitan areas is

adjacent to CBDs, and it is likely that one reason for extremely poor maintenance of dwellings there has been the flattening of rent-distance functions.
Furthermore, racial discrimination has undoubtedly worsened the situation. In the absence of discrimination, residents would move out of extremely low quality housing near the CBD, thus reducing the profitability
of existing use and hastening the process of conversion or demolition. But
residents of such housing are mostly blacks, and the analysis earlier indicated that their outward movement is impaired by discriminatory practices
of the white community.

The discussion of the demand for housing in general and for slum
housing in particular can be summarized by the statement that poverty is by
far the major cause of slums, but that the situation is aggravated by racial
discrimination, the neighborhood effect, and the flattening of rent-distance
functions. It only remains to discuss the supply side.

Supply of Housing

Many people find the notion of slum housing supply confusing. After all,
nobody literally builds slum housing. So where does it come from? There is
an underlying suspicion that there must be something pernicious about
groups who would supply such poor-quality housing. But there is nothing
pernicious or confusing about the supply of slums. The basic point is that
the housing market will supply almost any kind of housing that people are
willing to pay for, whether it be suburban ranch houses, townhouses, or
slums.

Slum housing is produced by the so-called "filtering-down" process.
New housing is produced for middle and upper-income groups, and old
housing filters down to low-income groups. Housing loses value partly because it depreciates as a function of time. As time passes, housing preferences and the technology of construction change. More important, materials deteriorate from weather and use. Thus, older housing tends to be
cheaper and lower in quality than newer housing. Since cities are built from
the center outward, older housing is mostly near the city center, which is an
additional reason to the fundamental one discussed in Chapter 4 that low-
income residents are concentrated there. More important than depreciation
to the supply of slum housing are conversion and maintenance. Suppose, as
is true in many cities, that there is a section of townhouses near the city center. Suppose that the demand in the neighborhood for such housing falls as
high-income residents move to the suburbs, and that the demand for low-

income housing rises as poor people migrate to the city from rural areas. Conversion then decreases the supply of high-income townhouses and increases the supply of low-income apartments by breaking up the townhouses into apartments. Usually, the physical alterations are fairly simple and inexpensive.

Maintenance is relevant in that it takes considerable amounts of resources to maintain a dwelling in good condition. Inevitably, more maintenance is required to keep an old house high in quality than a new house. If high-income families are replaced in a neighborhood by low-income families, maintenance is reduced to the level that can be supported by the low-income group. Owner-occupiers do some maintenance themselves, and there is evidence that owner-occupied houses are somewhat better maintained than rental dwellings, even in low-income areas. But income, not ownership, is the key factor. Indeed, one reason for better maintenance of owner-occupied houses is that, even in poor areas, ownership is more common among those with high than with low incomes.

Anyone who has lived in a large city knows of neighborhoods that have gone downhill quickly as they changed from white to black. Whites blame deterioration on the slovenliness of black residents, and blacks blame it on pernicious landlords who fail to maintain their properties. Both groups miss the main point. Poverty is the culprit: the demand for high-income housing fell in the neighborhood and the demand for low-income housing rose. A family that can afford only $15 per week for housing cannot afford to live in a well-maintained house. And it is true whether they own or rent. (Low-income housing certainly could be produced by construction of new housing. But using the rule of thumb that monthly housing cost is about 1 percent of the sales price of the house, a $15 weekly housing budget requires a house worth no more than $6500. And houses that can be built for that price are much less satisfactory than houses that have filtered down.)

Since World War II, there has been a massive immigration of poor blacks and emigration of middle-income whites in northern central cities. The demand for low-income housing has risen and that for high-income housing has fallen. The market has responded by similar alterations in supply. Happily, the process also works in reverse. It was pointed out earlier in the chapter that there has been rapid upgrading of substandard housing since World War II. This has come about almost entirely by improved maintenance and renovation as the incomes of black residents have risen.

For some reason, city planners are often unwilling to admit that income is the chief determinant of housing quality. Their papers on slums often begin with the assertion that markets cannot renovate or rebuild slums. They then survey the evidence of rapid improvement in housing quality since World War II, and conclude by decrying the failure of the public sector to have done anything to help the process.

THE CONSEQUENCES OF SLUMS

There is an extensive literature on the alleged effects of slums on the people who live there. It is claimed that slums are dangerous because they are fire-traps and tend to cause accidents; that filth and poor sanitation cause disease and poor health; that slums breed crime; and that slums cause demoralization, despair, hopelessness, and alienation.

Some of these allegations must be taken with several grains of salt. A major school of nineteenth-century social thought claimed that rural life was superior to urban life, and regretted the rapid urbanization of the time. Cities were thought to breed crime, wickedness, depravity, and disorganization. This view is by no means absent from twentieth-century thought. Much of this writing can be dismissed as no more than fantasy concerning a nonexistent bucolic life back on the farm. At best, much of it is based on a false contrast between self-sufficient, hardworking yeoman farmers and the teeming urban poor. But most of the teeming urban poor never had the option to be yeoman farmers. The typical nineteenth-century slum resident in the United States had fled from unspeakable oppression and poverty in Europe, and his twentieth-century counterpart fled from almost equally bad conditions in the rural south.

It is easy enough to contrast life in poor slums with that in affluent suburbs. But what is relevant to slum residents is whether life is better or worse there than in rural areas and small towns. In this chapter and in Chapter 9, the overwhelming evidence shows that economic conditions are better in metropolitan areas. And studies are notably absent that show the contrary for other aspects of life. For example, it is extremely unlikely that rural poor have better physical or mental health than urban poor.

None of the above in any way denies that accidents, crime, poor health, and despair are worse in slums than elsewhere in metropolitan areas; they are. Life is shorter because death rates from disease and accidents are greater; health is poorer; crime is worse; and fire losses are greater.

Most of the above are direct or indirect results of poverty and would disappear with the disappearance of poverty. Others result from inadequate provision of public services in slum areas. Health and sanitation services and police protection are notoriously inadequate in slum neighborhoods.

Still others may be aggravated by the concentration of poor in small areas. For example, some writers believe that crime is made worse by large concentrations of poor. This is of doubtful importance since poverty is probably the major reason for high crime rates in slums. But to the extent that it is true, appropriate public policy should be aimed at discriminatory practices that prevent greater dispersion of the poor, and especially blacks, among other parts of the metropolitan area.

A CATALOG OF PUBLIC POLICIES

A great many policies exist that affect urban housing. Like other public policies that affect resource allocation, they often have unforeseen and unwanted effects. Careful and sophisticated economic analysis is needed to evaluate the likely effects of alternative policies for each set of problems. Unfortunately, most of the many public policies that affect urban housing have been formulated with practically no economic analysis as a basis. There is reason to believe that many policies have done more harm than good. Related as both cause and effect is the fact that economists have shown little interest in the study of local government policies that affect resource allocation. Thus, the effects of many public policies are matters of conjecture.

Fortunately, urban renewal, the most important public policy for urban housing, is an exception to the generalizations above. Several good studies, most notably that by Rothenberg, have appeared. (His study is discussed in greater detail under "Urban Renewal".)

Real-Estate Taxation

The purpose of real-estate taxation is of course to finance local government (a role discussed in Chapter 12). But it inevitably affects resource allocation in housing. Annual real-estate taxes in metropolitan areas are about 2 or 3 percent of the market value of land and structures. If, as was suggested early in this chapter, annual cost or value added of housing services is about 12 percent of asset value, a 3-percent real-estate tax is equivalent to a 25-percent sales tax on the market value of housing services. The only commodities taxed at similar rates are those, like cigarettes, whose consumption society wishes to discourage as a matter of public policy.[4] It is indeed ironic

---

4. Motor fuel is not really an exception, since the tax is properly viewed as a highway user fee. This is discussed in Chapter 11.

and paradoxical to levy a 25-percent sales tax on a commodity whose un-derconsumption is thought to cause the evils listed earlier. The irony is com-pounded by the fact that the highest real-estate taxes are in central cities where the problems of slums are much worse than elsewhere in metropoli-tan areas. Such a high tax must be a substantial deterrent to construction, maintenance, and improvement of housing. But how much? It is unfortu-nate that so little careful quantitative work has been done on this subject.

What is the alternative? The issue is the extent to which less distorting taxes can replace real-estate taxes to finance local government. (This is discussed in Chapter 12.)

Income Taxes on Owner-Occupied Housing

Federal income-tax provisions for owner-occupied housing are different than those for rental housing. Few owner-occupiers understand the tax break they receive, but an example will make it clear. Suppose my next door neighbor and I have identical incomes, and that we are owner-occupiers of identical homes. Suppose we both itemize deductions on the federal per-sonal income-tax return and are in the same marginal tax bracket T. We both pay the same interest rate r on our mortgages, which, in turn, is the rate we could make if we invested the equities in our homes in interest-earning assets, such as savings accounts. Then, to each of us, the oppor-tunity cost of home ownership is R_1, where

$$R_1 = t(1 - T)A + r(1 - T)A + dA$$

Here A is the market value of the house, t is annual real-estate taxes as a fraction of the house's market value, and d is the annual depreciation and maintenance cost, also as a fraction of market value. The cost of tA dollars of real-estate taxes to the owner-occupier is $t(1 - T)A$ dollars, because real-estate taxes are deductible, which means that Uncle Sam pays a per-centage T of the real-estate tax in the form of reduced income tax. I pay rM dollars of annual interest on my mortgage of M dollars, which is also de-ductible. I also forgo $r(1 - T)(A - M)$ dollars of after-tax income on my equity of $A - M$ dollars. The sum $r(1 - T)M + r(1 - T)(A - M)$ is the term $r(1 - T)A$ in R_1. If the house yields R_1 dollars worth of housing ser-vices to me, I earn the opportunity cost of my equity from ownership.

Now suppose my neighbor and I move into each other's houses and agree to pay rent to each other. What rent will we have to pay to yield the same after-tax return on equity? The rent must be

$$R_2 = dA + tA + rA$$

If the rent is R_2, each owner will have a before-tax return on his equity of $r(A - M)$, or an after-tax return equal to the opportunity cost $r(1 - T)$ $(A - M)$. Of course the owner of the rental housing pays income tax only on the amount left over after subtracting his depreciation and maintenance, real-estate tax, and mortgage interest expenses from the rent he receives.

If we subtract R_1 from R_2, we get

$$R_2 - R_1 = (t + r)TA \tag{10-1}$$

which is the extra cost to each of us of renting rather than owning identical houses. The reason for the difference between R_2 and R_1 is that income on the owner's equity is taxed if the house is rented, but not if it is owner-occupied.

It can be seen in Equation 10-1 that the tax break for ownership is larger, the larger are t, r, T, and A. In particular, the higher the income, the higher is the marginal tax bracket, and the greater is the tax break for owner occupancy. Typical values of t, r, and T might be 0.03, 0.06, and 0.25. Then the annual tax break for owner occupancy might be 0.0225 of the house's value. Using the rule of thumb that annual housing cost is about 12 percent of the house's value, the tax break reduces housing cost by nearly 20 percent.

The tax break has two effects. First, it increases the demand for housing by those in a position to take advantage of it. Second, it changes the mix of rental and owner-occupied housing. The percentage of housing that was owner-occupied changed little from 1890 to 1940, when it was 43.6. Since then, federal income-tax rates have become high and the ownership percentage had risen steadily, to 61.9 in 1960.

Accelerated Depreciation

Under certain circumstances, federal income-tax provisions permit landlords to depreciate during the first few years of ownership more than 1 nth of the fair market value of rental property with a life of n years. Later, they must deduct less, since only 100 percent can be deducted over the useful life of the structure. If the market value of the property decreases less rapidly than the allowable depreciation during the early years of ownership, it will pay to sell the property after only a few years of ownership. Thus, the tax provision encourages rapid turnover in the ownership of rental property.

Most writers believe that rapid turnover leads to poor maintenance since the owner has no long-term interest in the property. But the reasoning is faulty. The rent that can be charged tenants, and therefore the market value of the property, depends on how it is maintained. In fact the opposite argument is more plausible. An owner who expects to sell shortly may maintain the property better than one who plans to keep it for a long time, in order to protect the market value of the property.

Perhaps more important, accelerated depreciation is a favorable tax treatment for landlords, rather like the provision discussed for owner-occupiers. At given housing prices, it increases the return on rental property, thus inducing an increase in the supply and a decrease in the price of such property. Thus, the effect is to make rental housing cheaper than it would otherwise be. But there is no reason to think that accelerated depreciation creates slums.

Zoning

Zoning provides restriction on land use in urban areas. Local government creates a number—which may be large or small—of land-use categories. At the top of the list is a very stringent category, say single-family houses with no more than four families per acre. The second category might permit eight families per acre. The third would permit multiple-family dwellings. Further categories would permit various commercial and industrial activities. Each plot is placed in one of the categories, which means that uses in higher, but not lower, categories are permitted. A zoning map is drawn up and a commission established to hear requests for exceptions or changes in the zoning of particular plots or neighborhoods. Laws provide general guidelines for the commission's deliberations. The laws may stipulate that the zoning pattern be developed to promote the general welfare of the community, and that the commission may make a change only if the predominant character of the area has changed, or if a mistake has been made.

Zoning has a bad reputation because of widespread allegations of corruption and political influence on zoning commissions. It is potentially a powerful regulatory device. But no one has any idea how to determine in detail the optimum land-use pattern in an urban area. Thus, there are no good studies of whether zoning makes things better or worse. Serious study of zoning would have to start with a careful study of the advantages of clustering (subcenters) to commercial and industrial activities. It is likely that the advantages of clustering would produce about the same amount of segregation of various land uses that now exists under zoning provisions. If so, it suggests that zoning has had little effect on urban land use. But it does make adjustment of land use to changing conditions slow and cumbersome. Some wealthy suburban communities have zoning that requires very large minimum lot sizes, which are optimum for the predominant high-income residents, but which exclude low and middle-income, and especially black, families from the community. The result has been to slow down racial integration in suburban communities.

Mortgage Guarantees

The Federal Housing Administration and the Veterans' Administration insure or guarantee home mortgages in urban areas. There is a variety of programs, but the most important pertain to owner-occupied homes. The programs reduce the risk of loss to the lender from default, and thus make him willing to lend at lower rates and for larger fractions of market value than otherwise. The volume of insurance and guarantees has been large, especially on new suburban housing, and some writers have been led to believe that the programs have been mainly responsible for postwar suburbanization of population in urban areas.

That claim greatly exaggerates the effects of the programs. It was seen in Chapter 6 that suburbanization long predates the federal programs. In addition, mortgage interest cost is usually less than one half of the cost of home ownership, and insured loans are no more than 0.5 to 1 percentage point cheaper than conventional loans. Thus, the federal programs reduce housing costs by no more than about 10 percent and probably by less. With a price elasticity of demand as large as 1.0, housing demand would be increased by only 10 percent if all housing, rental and owner-occupied, were under the federal programs. But only part of owner-occupied, and little rental, housing is. It follows that only a small part of the postwar growth of urban housing can be explained by federal programs.

Although federal mortgage-insurance programs can hardly have had a major effect on suburbanization, they have probably been worthwhile. They make use of the public sector to reduce the risk of important and relatively risky private transactions. The subsidy element of the programs is small. In the FHA program, administration costs are paid by a fee charged to the borrower.

Building Codes

Local governments in urban areas have agencies established to compile and enforce standards which housing must meet. Codes typically specify kinds, amounts, and conditions of materials in the structure and are often extremely detailed. Their purpose is to protect the buyer or renter from fraud and from shoddy workmanship. A house is a complex product, and laymen are often unable to appraise the adequacy of materials and workmanship. In addition, some flaws are difficult to detect once the structure is completed.

The rationale is unexceptionable. Many products in our complex economy are difficult for laymen to evaluate, and protection of consumers is a proper function of government. Nevertheless, almost every writer on the subject of housing problems is critical of housing codes. In connection with slums, the most common criticism is that codes are not enforced there. Although it is a fact, the observation is superficial. The reasons for poor enforcement reveal the basic issues.

Codes are drawn up in close consultation with the local construction industry. Since housing is built almost exclusively for middle and upper-income residents, the construction industry naturally thinks in terms of code requirements appropriate to such housing. But we have seen that the basic characteristic of slums is that poor people cannot afford housing maintained at middle-income standards. Thus, the major problem with code enforcement in slums is that they force owners to undertake more maintenance than the slum housing market can support. The result is flagrant violation, poor enforcement, corruption of public officials, and widespread abandonment of structures on which codes have been enforced. The above is not to say that most standards required by codes are not desirable; they are. But it *is* to say that the poor are not helped by standards set so high that no one can meet them and still supply housing to poor people. Codes raise the cost and quality of slum housing, but they do not increase the ability of poor residents to pay for it.

Codes tend also to be poorly drawn. They stipulate kinds and amounts of materials in great detail. The result is that new and superior materials often cannot be used. Innovation is stifled in housing, an industry in which technical progress has been notoriously slow. Codes tend to exclude competition from construction firms or materials producers who do not have access to narrowly specified materials in the code. The remedy to the defect is to write codes that specify performance rather than materials. For example, flooring requirements should be in terms of load-carrying capacity and resistance to rot rather than of materials. However, a higher level of professional training is required to write performance codes than to write materials codes.

Almost all of the objections to building codes would be met if they emphasized disclosure rather than coercion. The government might inspect buildings and materials before, during, and after construction. It could then rate buildings in quality categories ranging from very high to very low, based more or less on technical considerations. Then it could require that the classification be shown to prospective buyers or renters. Buildings should be reinspected periodically so that classifications could be changed to reflect improved or worsened conditions. Low-income people could still occupy housing that was rated low if that was the best they could afford. And coercion regarding kinds and amounts of materials would be avoided.

Rent Control

Noneconomists often favor legal ceilings on rents that can be charged for housing in urban areas to protect renters, especially in low-income brackets, from price increases that would put decent housing beyond their means. Economists almost always oppose rent control except in wartime. Housing is a competitive industry, and the classical analysis of the effects of price control applies. If the controlled price is at least as high as the equilibrium price, controls have no effect. If it is below the equilibrium price, supply is less and demand more than in equilibrium. Thus, controls keep the price down, but at the cost of a reduced supply of housing, manifested by a low rate of construction of new housing and by reduced maintenance of old housing. In low-income areas, rent control means that housing is of poorer quality than it would have been without controls.

New York, the only large city in which rent control has been important throughout the post-World War II period, displays all the manifestations of such control. There is practically no private housing construction except for very high income families, there is excess demand for housing, and the city has fallen far behind the rest of the country in reducing the amount of substandard housing.

It is easy to be critical of rent control in New York. The best judgment is that it has hurt low-income people there more than it has helped them. But the judgment should be tempered by sympathy with the attempt to solve a very serious problem. New York has had an enormous influx of poor, mainly nonwhite, people since World War II. At the same time, a commercial construction boom has driven land values sky high, and demolished a large amount of low-income housing. The syndrome is completed by the classic unwillingness of suburbs to accept nonwhites displaced from Manhattan housing. The result is that the poor are caught in a vise that is, in some cases literally, squeezing them to death. City officials lack jurisdiction in the suburbs, sympathy in the state legislature, and money for costly remedial programs. Rent control was an attempt to do something that would have little budgetary impact on the city government.

Public Housing and Rent Supplements

In 1968, there were about 750,000 units of public housing in the United States. Most were constructed and owned by local governments under programs in which the federal government paid a large part of the cost. Public housing programs were begun during the Roosevelt and Truman administrations. Several new programs were begun during the Johnson administration in the mid-1960s.

Under the conventional programs, the local government acquires land, usually in slum areas, clears it, and lets contracts for the construction of new low-income housing. The new housing is managed by a local government agency. More recent programs provide a variety of alternative procedures. The local government may buy housing produced for the purpose by private enterprise. Or, housing produced privately for low-income families may be managed by private, nonprofit or limited-profit corporations. Finally, the federal government has a program under which it will pay fair rents in excess of 25 percent of incomes of low-income families in housing that meets certain standards.

The new programs were designed to improve the slow and cumbersome procedures for public housing construction. All the programs provide housing whose cost is beyond the means of low-income families. They therefore require substantial public subsidy. There is no reason to believe that the public sector can build faster, better, or cheaper low-income housing than can the private sector. Thus the major issue concerning public housing is whether it is a better way than the alternatives to subsidize the poor.

A goal of many public housing programs has been to remove the barriers of racial segregation that confine blacks to central cities. But it has been legally or politically impossible to build public housing in communities whose governments opposed the program. Public housing has been unsuccessful in furthering racial integration.

URBAN RENEWAL

The federal urban renewal program, begun in 1949 and greatly expanded during the 1960s, is by far the most ambitious program to eliminate central city slums and decay.[5] The most important goal of the program has been to improve slum housing conditions. In addition, it has attempted to trigger

---

5. This section draws heavily on the excellent study by Rothenberg.

the revival of decaying downtown business sections, to assist the expansion of nonprofit institutions such as universities and hospitals, to strengthen central city government, and to attract middle-class residents back to central cities.

Like many other urban programs, urban renewal is a cooperative federal-local program. A typical major project proceeds as follows: A local government draws up plans to renew a large part of its downtown area. Renewal usually consists of demolition of sium houses and decayed commercial buildings, and replacement by modern commercial structures, high-rise apartments, and buildings for schools, universities, museums, government offices, hospitals, and other nonprofit institutions. The plans are submitted to the federal government for approval. If the plans are approved, the local government acquires the real estate in the renewal area, clears the site, and sells the land to private developers to be used for the purposes in the plan. Normally, costs of acquisition and clearance exceed receipts from the sale of cleared sites. The federal government pays two thirds of the excess of costs over receipts, and the local government pays the rest.

The size of the program can be seen in almost every large city. Large parts of downtown areas have been cleared of decayed buildings, and large new structures have risen on the sites. By the mid-1960s, more than 1500 projects had been approved. Total expenditures on planning, acquisition, and clearance were estimated at more than $6 billion. It was anticipated that receipts from sale of cleared sites would be $1.5 billion, leaving a deficit of more than $4.5 billion to be paid by federal and local governments.

Urban renewal has been extraordinarily controversial. Critics claim it is a massive federal giveaway, an illicit federal invasion of local and private domains, and unconstitutional. Supporters claim it is the only hope of saving decaying downtown areas. Almost all partisans exaggerate.

One aspect for which the critics have the upper hand is slum housing. At least until the mid-1960s, urban renewal demolished about four times as many dwellings as it constructed. Most of the dwellings torn down were slums, and most were probably occupied by blacks. Most of the dwellings constructed were for middle and upper-income groups. Gradually, and in response to strong criticism, more consideration has been shown to displaced low-income families. Assistance in finding adequate alternative housing and moving expenses have been provided.

A good deal of debate has centered on the proportion of those displaced who have found standard alternative housing. But this is hardly relevant. Whatever alternative housing was found would have been available in the absence of renewal. The fact that the displaced poor did not move until coerced reveals that renewal made them worse off. It is hard to understand how anyone can claim with a straight face that the poor are helped by a program that demolishes their housing and replaces it by housing far beyond their means. In recent years, many urban renewal plans have included provision for low-income housing in renewal areas.

A second issue on which the critics come out ahead has to do with the goal of attracting middle-class residents back to central cities. The analysis in Chapter 4 indicated that there are strong reasons for relatively high income families to live further out than low-income families, and the goal is therefore unlikely to be achieved except at high cost. There are two arguments in favor of the attempt which must be taken seriously.

First, it is claimed that middle-class residents are an asset to the city in that they pay more in taxes than they consume in public services. But the program attempts to bribe them to move to the central city by providing them with public and publicly subsidized services (subsidized middle and upper-income housing and shopping and cultural facilities in renewal projects) which are large relative to the taxes they will pay. If renewal does not alter the proportion of public services and taxes, they will not come. But if it does alter the proportion enough to attract middle-income people, they will be a liability rather than an asset to the city government.

Second, it is claimed that metropolitan areas are excessively segregated, and that more heterogeneous communities are needed. The second argument is correct, but subsidization of middle-income people to move to the central city is a perverse response. Middle-class suburbanites already are able to live in any part of the metropolitan area they prefer. It is the low-income blacks in central cities who are coerced to live there. If somebody is to be subsidized to diversify communities, why not subsidize the poor to move out rather than the rich to move in?

Urban renewal must stand or fall on the success of its attempts to trigger the revival of downtown business activity. Earlier in this chapter an argument was made for public intervention to hasten the adjustment to a new equilibrium in response to flattened rent-distance functions. For that purpose, public assembly and clearance of downtown sites might be justified. But two questions must be answered.

First, why should the public sector decide the use to which cleared sites are to be put? The alternative is for the local government to sell the cleared land to the highest bidder, regardless of the use to be made of it. The issue is whether the local governments or the private sector are better at perceiving the nature and capital intensity of the new equilibrium land use. If the new use is to be public (e.g., for a school), the site should be retained in the public sector. But if it is to be private, it is hard to see why the public sector should decide the use. Any information the public sector has about desirable uses could be made available to all bidders for renewal sites. Selling sites to highest bidders would reduce the losses to the public sector on renewal projects. If it were felt that certain institutions, such as hospitals, deserve public subsidy, it should be given to them directly so they could use it either to bid on renewal sites or for other purposes, whichever best suits their needs.

Second, why do urban renewal projects lose money? One reason is that the public sector decides the uses to which cleared sites should be put. But even if cleared sites were sold to the highest bidder, losses would be substantial. The answer is that the social benefits of urban renewal may nevertheless exceed the costs to the public sector, if increases in the productivity of neighboring sites offset the public sector's losses.

The essence of the justification for public intervention to speed adjustment to new equilibrium uses of downtown land is that, if the public sector increases the productivity of land in renewal areas, it will increase the productivity of neighboring sites by increasing the jobs and other activities to which they are accessible. Increased productivity shows up in increased land values of areas near renewal sites. And there are many reports of increases in land values near renewal areas. If increased land values elsewhere offset public-sector losses in renewal areas, the total benefits of renewal exceed its total costs. Of course, renewal may decrease land values in some parts of the metropolitan area by transferring activities to the renewal site. Any decreases in land value must be subtracted in computing the net benefits of renewal.

A clear statement of the way the benefits and costs of urban renewal must be computed is the major contribution of the Rothenberg study. Unfortunately, there are not enough good quantitative studies of renewal projects to know how the balance sheet comes out. A guess is that even with all the benefits included, many renewal projects would still fail the benefit-cost test. In the absence of renewal, large capital losses on downtown properties would have been incurred since World War II. It seems likely that one of the unstated purposes of urban renewal has been to transfer these losses from property owners to the public sector and hence to the general taxpayer. This would account for allegations of overpayment by the public sector for renewal property. Whether one feels it is justified depends on his attitude toward the redistribution in question.

There are many alternative policies that could have been used to speed the transition to new uses of downtown land. There is no evidence that any

ry stop.

alternative policies were carefully analyzed in deliberations about the urban renewal program.

SUMMARY

Slums, like poverty, are a matter of degree. Available data show rapid progress in the reduction of slum housing since World War II, especially in metropolitan areas. By far, the most important cause of slums is the existence of large numbers of people whose low incomes do not enable them to purchase decent housing. The situation is exacerbated by racial discrimination, the neighborhood effect of poor housing, and disequilibrium resulting from rapidly flattening rent-distance functions. Slums are reputed to have a variety of bad effects, but it is difficult to separate poor housing from poverty as a cause of crime, alienation, despair, poor health, and other evils.

There is an enormous variety of public policies that have direct or indirect effects on slums. High central-city real estate taxes are a serious burden on poor residents. Some policies, such as income tax provisions for owner-occupied housing and mortgage guarantees, are designed to improve the housing stock, but help the poor only very indirectly. Zoning deprives the poor of access to low-cost suburban housing. Building codes often require housing standards the poor cannot afford. Accelerated depreciation on rental housing may provide some indirect help to poor renters. Publicly owned or subsidized housing has become much more important since the late 1960s.

Urban renewal is our largest and most controversial program to improve housing. It has subsidized large amounts of construction in urban areas in recent years, but its effects on the poor are extremely controversial. It seems clear that most of the large projects of the 1960s reduced the supply of housing available to the poor in central cities. It is too early to know whether more recent projects have provided benefits for the poor.

DISCUSSION QUESTIONS

1. Do you think the poor would be better or worse off if they were given the money spent on publicly owned and subsidized housing rather than the subsidies tied to housing?
2. On which of the following programs would a billion dollars of public ex-

penditure be most effective in reducing crime and drug abuse by slum dwellers: money transfers to the poor, improved housing, or dispersal of slum residents around metropolitan areas?

3. Keeping in mind the data in Table 10-1, what would be the effect on the housing conditions of black people of a national policy to discourage migration of the poor to metropolitan areas?

4. In the poor parts of some metropolitan areas, such as the near south side of Chicago and Bedford-Stuyvesant in New York, there are large amounts of unused land. What kind of public urban renewal program would you recommend for such places?

REFERENCES AND FURTHER READING

Frank De Leeuw, "Demand for Housing," *Review of Economics and Statistics*, Vol. 53, No. 1 (February 1971), 1–10.

Leo Grebler, David Blank, and Louis Winnick, *Capital Formation in Residential Real Estate*, 1956.

John Kain, editor, *Race and Poverty*, 1969.

Richard Muth, *Cities and Housing*, 1969.

Margaret Reid, *Income and Housing*, 1962.

Jerome Rothenberg, *Economic Evaluation of Urban Renewal*, 1967.

George Sternlieb, *The Tenement Landlord*, 1969.

United States Census Bureau, *Social and Economic Status of Negroes in the United States, 1969*, Current Population Reports, Series P-23, No. 29.

James Wilson, editor, *Urban Renewal*, 1966.

Chapter 11
Urban Transportation

The theoretical analysis in Part I showed that the function of an urban area is to facilitate the exchange of goods and services by proximate locations of diverse economic activities. Firms whose products are exported from the urban area have an incentive to locate near ports, railheads, highway interchanges, or other places from which intercity trade can be conducted economically. So also do households that provide the work force in export industries or consume goods imported into the urban area. Finally, so do firms that produce inputs for the export industries or consumer goods for local residents. Thus, an urban area consists of large numbers of specialized economic institutions, producing goods and services with large ratios of other inputs to land, that locate close to each other in order to facilitate exchange.

Exchange of goods and services entails the movement of goods and people. Thus, the size, structure, and efficiency of an urban area are influenced by the transportation system on which goods and people are moved. Commuting—that is, transportation of people for the exchange of labor services—is the single most important kind of urban transportation, and by far the most studied. Households also use the urban transportation system for noncommuting trips for shopping, recreation, and social activities. The movement of goods, or freight, within urban areas has been much less studied than the movement of people. Many writers assume explicitly or implicitly than an urban transportation system adequate for commuting is also adequate for all other demands made upon it. Although the assumption may be justified for analysis of an overall urban transportation system, it is not necessarily valid with respect to all the details of the system. Since little is known about the subject, practically nothing will be said in this chapter about the movement of freight in urban transportation systems.

Urban transportation is one of the most interesting examples of a mixed public-private sector in the U.S. economy. The supply side is clearly a public-sector responsibility. Streets and highways are constructed, maintained, and owned by governments. Public transit facilities such as buses, subways, and commuter trains are either owned or regulated by governments.

The demand side is more complex. Trucks and cars are privately owned, and pay to use the public streets with user fees, such as taxes on motor-vehicle fuel and tires, and vehicle registration fees. Public transit riders of course pay fares. To the extent that both are available, urban residents choose without coercion between private cars and public transit, depending on the combination of fares or fees and service they prefer. In contrast, public education (for example) is supplied with an important element of coercion. Children are forced to go to school, and public schools are financed by general tax revenues. Thus, parents cannot avoid paying for the public service, even if they refuse to consume it and instead send their children to private schools.

The difference is important. However bad public education is, large numbers of people will consume it just because they cannot afford to pay for both the public and the private service. But the use of private cars is almost always a viable alternative to the use of public transit systems. If the combination of fares and service is sufficiently bad in public transit systems, people simply refrain from buying the service and use their cars instead. Of course, governments can greatly influence the attractiveness of alternative modes of urban travel by the policies they follow. For example, public transit in the form of a subway system is relatively attractive if it provides frequent, economical service. Likewise, automobile travel is attractive if a system of urban expressways is available.

Thus, the basic decisions about the supply of urban transportation modes are the responsibility of the public sector. But consumers choose among available modes according to the terms on which modes are made available and according to their own needs and tastes. The public sector's task is to provide the urban transportation system that best serves the community. An important and beneficial constraint on the public sector is that transportation services are bought by the public, and they can register dissatisfaction with one mode by purchasing the services of another.

A Great Debate has been underway regarding urban transportation at least since the late 1950s. The issue is whether public policy should encourage the use of automobiles or public transit for urban commuting. One school of thought believes that only large public investment in mass-transit facilities can save central cities from strangulation by congestion and pollution. Another school of thought believes that the advantages of the automobile to relatively high income commuters are so great that no viable alternative exists to investment in urban expressways. A third school of thought advocates a balanced urban transportation system, normally interpreted to mean substantial investment in both public transit and urban expressways.

The issues are complex, and careful measurement of the benefits and costs of alternative urban transportation systems is an underdeveloped speciality. In part, the complexity results from the availability of several related alternatives. Streets and highways must be available in urban areas because there is no feasible alternative to the movement by motor vehicles of practically all intraurban freight and at least some intraurban passengers. To some extent, automobile commuters can share these facilities. So also can at least one major form of public transit, buses. The other important kinds of public transit, subways and commuter railroads, require their own right of way, which is practically unusable for intraurban freight movement. General railroad rights of way, however, can be shared among commuters, interurban freight, and interurban passengers.

The details of urban transportation investments must be tailored to the size, structure, and existing transportation facilities of each urban area. Transportation investments that are optimum for the Philadelphia metropolitan area may not be appropriate for Los Angeles or Albuquerque. This chapter therefore explores the implications for transportation policy of pervasive characteristics of U.S. urban areas, and surveys systematic procedures for evaluating the benefits and costs of alternative transportation systems.

TRENDS IN URBAN TRANSPORTATION

There can be no doubt that overall travel in U.S. urban areas has increased rapidly since World War II. Rapid increases in urban population, incomes, auto ownership, and suburbanization have inevitably led to rapid growth of both passenger and freight transportation in urban areas. But by far the most dramatic change in urban travel has been the changing mix of modes.

Table 11-1 summarizes data on urban travel modes since 1940. However, public transit and passenger-car figures cannot be added. The transit data refer to total passengers, whereas the automobile data refer to vehicle miles. The ideal figures to have would be passenger miles, but they are not available. Trip length per transit passenger and passengers per car have probably changed relatively little, so passenger miles are about proportionate to the figures shown. But the factors of proportionality differ among modes. A second caution is that the 1945 figures are badly distorted by the

Table 11·1   Urban Travel, 1940–1967

Year	Public Transit Passengers (millions)					Passenger Cars[b] (millions of vehicle miles)
	Railways	Subways[a]	Trolleys	Busses	Total	
1940	5943	2382	534	4239	13,098	129,060
1945	9426	2698	1244	9886	23,254	109,472
1950	3904	2264	1658	9420	17,246	182,518
1955	1207	1870	1202	7240	11,529	224,452
1960	463	1850	657	6425	9,395	284,800
1965	276	1858	305	5814	8,253	378,182
1967	263	1938	248	5723	8,172	410,779

a) Includes elevated railways.
b) Includes taxis and motorcycles.
Source: *Statistical Abstract of the United States*, 1962 and 1969.

effects of World War II. Auto production suspension and gasoline rationing caused many travelers to use public transit during the war. The 1940 figures are therefore a better base for postwar comparisons.

The stark message of the data in Table 11-1 is that urban auto travel in 1967 was more than three times its 1940 level, but public transit travel had fallen by more than one third. Thus, the postwar growth of urban travel has been accompanied by a massive shift from public transit to private cars. Data from metropolitan transportation studies suggest that there are about 1.5 occupants per car for an average urban passenger-car trip, and that the average transit trip is above five miles. If those averages are applied to the 1967 data in Table 11-1, they indicate that more than 90 percent of passenger miles traveled in urban areas were by private car. Thus, popular writers do not exaggerate when they emphasize the dominance of the automobile as the mode of urban travel.

The postwar decline of public transit travel has been accompanied by shifts in the mix of transit vehicles. Railroads and trolleys have nearly disappeared as modes of urban travel. Subway travel has declined only slightly since 1940, whereas bus travel has increased somewhat, although it is still far below its early postwar level.

Much of the urban transportation problem is a peak-load problem, resulting from the concentration of travel at morning and evening rush hours. Most rush-hour travelers are on their way to or from work, and much of the concern with urban transportation is therefore focused on work trips. In Chapter 6 it was shown that there has been rapid suburbanization of both employment and residences in the postwar period. We should therefore expect to find considerable diversity in the origins and destinations of work trips. Comprehensive data are presented in Table 11-2 for SMSAs with at least 100,000 population.

Despite suburbanization, the largest group in Table 11-2 are those who live and work in central cities, amounting to nearly one half of all SMSA workers. Only slightly more than one third of the workers who live in suburban rings commute into the central cities. Indeed, almost one third as many workers commute from central cities to suburbs as commute from suburbs to central cities. Many of those who live and work in suburbs, and some of those who live and work in central cities, commute crosstown (e.g., around circumferential highways) rather than toward or away from the central business district. The convergence of employment and population-density gradients observed in Chapter 6 probably means that origins and destinations have become more diverse since World War II, and will probably become even more diverse in the future.

Modal choices for work trips are systematically different from those for other kinds of urban travel. Some data are presented in Table 11-3. Less than one fifth of all SMSA workers commute via public transit, which is used by almost 30 percent of those who live and work in central cities, but by only 15 percent of those who commute from suburbs to central cities. It was assumed above that there are 1.5 occupants per car on an average urban trip, and that the average transit trip is five miles. If those assumptions are applied to the 1960 data in Table 11-1, it indicates that about 11 percent of urban passenger miles were traveled by public transit in 1960.

Thus, the percentage of urban work travel by public transit is nearly twice the percentage of all urban travel by public transit. Other evidence points to the same conclusion.

The above conclusion is consistent with evidence that the most drastic decline in public transit use has been for off-peak travel. It is not hard to guess the reasons. Destinations of nonwork trips are probably even more

Table 11-2   Places of Work and Residence in SMSAs with 100,000 or More Population, 1960

	Live in Central City			Live in Suburban Ring			
	Work in Central City	Work in Suburban Ring	Work Outside SMSA	Work in Central City	Work in Suburban Ring	Work Outside SMSA	Totals
Number (000)	18,301	2028	537	6491	11,325	1074	39,756
Percent	46.0	5.1	1.4	16.3	28.5	2.7	100.0

Source: United States census of population, 1960.

Table 11-3 Percent Using Public Transit for Work Trips in SMSAs With 100,000 or More Population, 1960

Live in Central City				Live in Suburban Ring				
Work in Central City	Work in Suburban Ring	Work Outside SMSA	Sub-total	Work in Central City	Work in Suburban Ring	Work Outside SMSA	Sub-total	Total
27.7	12.1	16.9	27.7	15.0	4.6	14.7	8.7	18.7

Source: United States census of population, 1960.

diverse than for work trips, thus making automobiles relatively convenient. Also, several family members may go together on nonwork trips, which adds practically nothing to the cost of auto travel but increases transit fares proportionately. Finally, many nonwork trips are for shopping, and autos are more convenient than public transit for transporting purchases. The decline in off-peak transit use has made the financial position of transit companies even worse than would be indicated by the overall decline in transit use. Vehicles and other facilities can be reduced proportionately only to peak use, but revenues fall proportionately to overall use.

In most metropolitan areas, the worst congestion is in central cities, and in many metropolitan areas the central cities contain the only serious congestion. Table 6-1 of Chapter 6 showed that total central-city employment has fallen slightly during the postwar period. Yet congestion has become worse, at least according to popular accounts. It seems paradoxical that central-city congestion should worsen during a period when its employment has been falling.

The resolution of the paradox is in the data in Table 11-1. To the extent that congestion has increased, the cause has been the massive switch from public transit to automobile travel in urban areas. Trains and subways do not use streets and highways, and trolleys and busses use them much more passenger-intensively than do cars. Thus, the switch from public transit to cars increases the total use of urban roads, and changes the use to a mode that generates more congestion.

The same data of Table 11-1 suggest that, even in the absence of dramatic shifts in public policy, urban road congestion may have passed its peak. With 90 percent of urban passenger travel already by car, it is hard to imagine that the percentage will increase much in coming years. If, in addition, central-city employment continues to decrease gradually, it seems likely that the demands placed on central-city streets and highways will fall gradually.

PRICING AND DEMAND FOR URBAN TRANSPORTATION

Pricing and demand are key aspects of all urban transportation problems. A major element in public-transportation investment decisions should be thorough studies of the demand for the various transportation modes. Until recently, the demand side has been badly neglected in urban transportation studies. For example, most studies of transportation problems in metropolitan areas have been done by engineering consultants who devote their major effort to comparing the costs of alternative transportation systems. They usually conclude that some form of mass transit is the most economical transportation system, mainly because mass transit systems have enormous passenger-carrying capacity and require only small amounts of land. The unwillingness of commuters to use the mass transit system at fares that cover its costs is attributed to the irrational attachment of Americans to automobile travel.

Recently, careful studies of transportation demand have begun to appear,[1] and there is now much more sympathy for the notion that consumers make transportation choices rationally. Indeed, the presumption should be that, of all the goods and services that people buy, transportation is among the most rationally chosen. Round-trip commuting decisions are made about 24 times a month, and the consumer therefore accumulates a great deal of evidence about the desirability of available alternatives. Furthermore, taking account of the value of travel time, transportation services are expensive, and people are thus motivated to choose carefully. A typical metropolitan commuter might earn $5.00 per hour and spend one hour a day driving the 20-mile round trip between home and work, Assume that his automobile operating costs are $0.10 per mile and that he values travel time at only half his hourly wage rate. Commuting thus costs him $4.50 per day, more than 10 percent of his money income.

Finally, transportation services are relatively easy for consumers to evaluate. The relevant dimensions of transportation services are cost, time, comfort, and convenience. Each is observed directly every time the service is consumed. Unlike medical services and many consumer durable goods, transportation services are relatively uncomplicated.

Most models of transportation demand are descendants of the "gravity" model, so-called because of its analogy with the law of gravity. The simplest gravity model of transportation demand can be written

$$T_{ij} = k \frac{N_i N_j}{d_{ij}} \tag{11-1}$$

---

1. Many of the best studies are collected in Quandt.

where T_{ij} is the number of trips between two places i and j; N_i and N_j are the numbers of residents at i and j; and d_{ij} is the distance between i and j. Equation 11-1 assumes that travel between two places is proportionate to the number of people in the two places, and inversely proportionate to the square of the distance between them. Although attempts have been made to apply gravity models to commuting trips, neither Equation 11-1 nor extensions of it are appropriate. The analysis in Part I showed that a worker's commuting is entirely determined by his residence and place of work. Thus, a model of commuting demand must determine places of residence or places of work, or both. Since places of residence and work are regarded as fixed in Equation 11-1, it can determine neither.

The Abstract-Mode Approach to Transportation Demand

Extensions of gravity models can be used to analyze commuters' choices of mode. The most useful extension for this purpose is the "abstract-mode" approach of Quandt and Baumol (see Quandt). It specifies the demand for modes of travel in terms of the characteristics of the modes that are of interest to the traveler. Suppose the locations of work and residence are fixed, and that N workers must commute between the two places. The basic assumption of the abstract-mode approach is that the number of workers who choose each mode depends on measurable characteristics of available modes. It was suggested above that cost, time, comfort, and convenience are the characteristics most likely to be of interest to commuters. If so, the demand for mode 1 can be written

$$N_1/N = f(p_1,p_2, t_1,t_2, C_1,C_2, S_1,S_2) \qquad (11\text{-}2)$$

which assumes that the commuter has two modes to choose between. The demand for mode 2 is $1 - N_1/N$. If there are more modes, additional variables for each mode must be included. N_1/N is the fraction of the workers making the trip that choose mode 1; p_i the price of mode i for the trip; t_i the time required; C_i its comfort; and S_i its convenience. Considerable care and ingenuity are needed in measuring each variable.

On public transit, p_i is the fare. If, as frequently happens, a car or other transit vehicle must be taken to the suburban station of the main transit vehicle, its fare must be included. Likewise, if another mode is required to complete the work end of the trip, its fare must be included. If the ith mode is a car, its operating cost and the cost of parking it while at work must be included. In principle, if the decision to commute by car requires the commuter to have a first or second car he would not otherwise have, p_i

should include the trip's share of the fixed costs of ownership. These costs include depreciation, licensing, and insurance. But transportation researchers normally have little information about the number of commuters who must have a car for commuting that they would not otherwise have. It is clear that the vast majority of American families would have at least one car even if it were not used for commuting.

The time required for the entire trip is t_i. In the case of automobile commuting, it includes time required to walk to and from the place the car is parked. In the case of public transit, it includes time needed to walk or ride to the transit stop, time spent changing modes and waiting for the transit vehicle, time spent on the transit vehicle, and time spent getting to the place of work after leaving the transit vehicle.

Comfort is hard to measure, but it is easy to indicate some factors that affect it. Comfort on transit vehicles is affected by noise, heating, crowding, condition of the vehicle, and the amount of walking or standing in bad weather. Comfort in cars is affected by temperature and traffic conditions.

Convenience is mainly affected by scheduling, hence its designation by S_i in Equation 11-2. A major advantage of automobile commuting is that it is self-scheduled, at least in the absence of car pools. An important element in the demand for public transit is the frequency of scheduling and the set of destinations that can be easily reached. If departures are few, the commuter must organize his life around transit departure times, and a missed vehicle causes great inconvenience. Likewise, public transit is at a disadvantage if many of the places workers want to go cannot be reached, or require changes of mode or vehicle.

The foregoing is a formidable list of considerations. But it seems likely that time costs are a dominant consideration in realistic choices. Return to our representative automobile commuter who takes 30 minutes for a 10-mile trip to work, values travel time at $2.50 per hour (half his hourly wage rate), and incurs operating costs of $0.10 per mile. The trip costs him $1.00 in operating costs and $1.25 in time costs, or $2.25.

Suppose the alternative to driving to work is to take the bus. Suburban collection and downtown distribution each require 10-minute walks. The bus trip takes 40 minutes and costs $0.25. Bus commuting costs $2.75 per trip, $2.50 in time costs, and $0.25 in fare. Suppose it costs him $1.00 to park his car downtown, but that this just offsets the added comfort and convenience of the car. The car trip is then $0.50 less than the bus trip. The importance of time is illustrated by the fact that the attempt to induce commuters to take the bus by cutting the fare to zero would still not make the bus worthwile for our commuter.

Suppose, as a second example, that a subway is built to replace the bus. Suppose the subway goes twice as fast as the bus so that the trip is cut from 40 to 20 minutes, but that collection and distribution times are unchanged. At the $0.25 fare, subway commuting costs $1.90 per trip and is cheaper than the $2.25 automobile trip. It would still be cheaper, even if the fare were raised from $0.25 to $0.50. If, on the other hand, the subway stops were further than the bus stops from home and work, so that the subway trip added five minutes each to collection and distribution times, the subway trip would take only 10 minutes less than the bus trip, and would not be competitive with the car even at the $0.25 fare.

These figures are not necessarily realistic, but they are meant to indicate that time costs are likely to be large relative to other factors in modal choices. The valuation of travel time is likely to be complex, depending on the alternatives available to the commuter. The time cost of travel certainly increases with income, and at least after a short time, the marginal time cost of the last minute of travel increases with the length of the trip. More careful empirical research is needed on this important topic, but the best work available[2] suggests that travel time is valued at between one third and one half of the wage rate, the fraction increasing with the wage rate. A fraction somewhat above one half would be consistent with U.S. wage levels. It is unlikely that travel time is valued at the wage rate, since wages are taxed, whereas travel time is not. A representative commuter might be in the 25-percent marginal income-tax bracket, which means that his forgone income for commuting can be no more than 75 percent of his wage rate.

Congestion

An important consideration omitted from Equation 11-2 and similar demand equations is congestion. Congestion means that the cost in time and comfort of travel depends, in addition to the variables in Equation 11-2, on the number of travelers using the mode in question. Although congestion is important for all modes of urban transportation, it has been studied carefully only for automobile travel (see Walters).

To take the simplest case, consider a stretch of road with no access between points A and B. Suppose cars enter the road at A at a uniform rate. Even if the number of cars entering at A is very small, there will be a maximum travel speed determined by legal speed limits and safety considera-

---

2. See the paper by Beesley in Quandt.

tions. Associated with the maximum speed will be a cost per vehicle mile of travel. It includes both time and operating cost, and depends on the maximum travel speed and on the characteristics of the vehicle. Now suppose that the rate at which vehicles enter point A increases. When the number of vehicles entering per hour becomes great enough, congestion begins to occur and travel speed falls.

The critical rate of entry at which congestion begins depends on characteristics of the road such as width, grade, curves, and surface. But on any road stretch, congestion occurs if the number of vehicles is great enough, because there are too many cars to permit the headway necessary for safety at high speeds, and cars must slow down to a speed consistent with the available headway. Automobile operating costs are relatively insensitive to speed, but time costs are inversely proportional to speed, Thus, slow travel caused by large numbers of cars entering at A increases the cost per vehicle mile of travel from A to B.

The foregoing ideas are illustrated in Figure 11-1. T is the number of vehicles entering per hour at point A, and $C(T)$ is the cost per vehicle mile of travel between A and B. $C(T)$ is constant for values of T up to T_o, which can be called the design capacity of the road. Beyond T_o, $C(T)$ rises rapidly with T. Several specific forms of $C(T)$ have been estimated by economists.

Now suppose, in the spirit of Equation 11-2, that the number of users of the road from A and B depends on the cost of travel. If travel is costly, people use a different route or mode, or alter their places of work or residence to avoid the trip. The number of people who make the trip as a func-

Figure 11-1

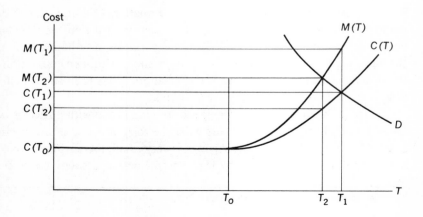

tion of the cost of travel is the demand curve for travel on the road from A to B, designated D in Figure 11-1. The equilibrium travel on the road is then T_1 vehicles per hour, the number of travelers willing to pay the cost of the trip. The equilibrium cost per vehicle is $C(T_1)$. $C(T_o)$ is the cost per vehicle in absence of congestion, and $C(T_1) - C(T_o)$ is congestion cost per vehicle.

With a constant rate of entry at A, all vehicles travel at the same speed, and incur the same cost $C(T_1)$. Thus, $C(T_1)$ is the total cost of travel for those making the trip divided by the number of travelers, or average cost per traveler. Elementary price-theory texts show that if an average cost curve is rising, the corresponding marginal cost curve must be above it. In the present context, marginal cost means the increase in travel cost to all travelers resulting from an increase in the number of vehicles using the road. In Figure 11-1, marginal cost is the curve designated $M(T)$. It is important to understand exactly why $M(T)$ is above $C(T)$. If T exceeds T_o, speed decreases with increases in T and $C(T)$ therefore exceeds $C(T - 1)$. But, since everybody travels at the same speed, everybody goes slower if T cars enter per hour than if $T - 1$ enter. Thus, the addition of a Tth user imposes costs on all T users because of the reduced speed. $M(T)$ exceeds $C(T)$ by the amount of the increased costs imposed on other travelers by the Tth entrant.

The excess of $M(T)$ over $C(T)$ is an external diseconomy of the type defined in Chapter 8. Each traveler perceives and bears the average cost $C(T)$. No traveler has any way of perceiving the cost his travel imposes on others. Therefore, the equilibrium number of travelers T_1 equates average cost to the price of the trip. As was shown in Chapter 8, the situation represents an inefficient allocation of resources in that too many people use the road and there is too much congestion. T_2 entrants per hour, which equates marginal cost to price, represents efficient use of the road. Of course, if D intersects $C(T)$ to the left of T_o in Figure 11-1, there is no congestion and no misallocation of resources.

The analysis above implies that a special method of rationing the use of the road is needed. If congestion were equally serious at all times and places in an urban area, a method such as special tax on gasoline sold in urban areas could be devised to induce travelers to take account of congestion costs. But congestion is concentrated at rush hours and on radial routes in most urban areas. If T_2 were known, it might be feasible to restrict entry to that rate during rush hours, at least on limited-access highways. But this is not feasible on city streets with many points of access. Perhaps more important, it is an arbitrary form of rationing in that it does not insure that the road is used by those to whom use is most valuable; that is, those to whom use is worth at least $C(T_2)$ in Figure 11-1.

Some economists and engineers believe that it would be feasible and economical to meter the use of all urban streets and highways by electronic means and charge congestion tolls appropriate to each use. In the situation depicted in Figure 11-1, the correct congestion toll is $M(T_2) - C(T_2)$. The congestion toll should equal the external diseconomy at the efficient use of the road, and should induce travelers to use the road in efficient numbers. Walters calculated that an appropriate congestion toll for large U.S. urban areas might have been about 2.2 cents per vehicle mile in 1959. It would have raised driving costs in metropolitan areas by about 20 percent in 1959. His procedure would undoubtedly indicate higher tolls today. Also, optimum tolls would be higher at heavily congested times and places.

It is unfortunate that we do not have studies of congestion costs for public transit facilities. The cost of travel increases with the number of passengers on transit vehicles, although its manifestation is somewhat different than that of automobile congestion. Congestion slows transit vehicles because it necessitates long and frequent stops, and the number of transit vehicles may congest the right of way. Congestion of transit facilities also adds to the waiting time and discomfort of travel, because of standing, for example. It would be useful to have estimates of appropriate congestion tolls for transit passengers, but they would presumably be less than for automobile commuting. Many economists believe that the decline in transit travel means that congestion is unimportant on public transit. But the fact that most of the decline has been in off-peak travel casts doubt on the belief.

It is important to note that the goal of public transportation policy should be efficient resource allocation, not the elimination of congestion. The efficient congestion toll in Figure 11-1 reduces but does not eliminate congestion. The appropriate amount of congestion depends on the cost of providing additional transportation facilities, whether for cars or for transit vehicles. Especially in downtown areas, such costs may be very high. Additional roads require land that can be used for other, extremely valuable purposes. Subways entail high construction costs in built-up areas. Thus transportation facilities should be used intensively in downtown areas because their opportunity cost is great. They are used intensively by having large numbers of cars or buses per lane-mile or large numbers of subway cars per track mile. All of these arrangements entail some congestion cost. Downtown transportation facilities should be used much more intensively that those in the suburbs for precisely the reasons that downtown land is used much more intensively than suburban land, evidenced by much taller buildings downtown than in the suburbs.

It can, however, be said that sufficiently large congestion costs justify additional investments in transportation facilities. The major benefit from investment in central-city transportation facilities is reduced travel time, and therefore congestion cost. If congestion costs are sufficiently large, they must be great enough to cover the opportunity cost of additional investments. But the fact that central-city streets are congested does not necessarily imply that the additional investments should be in streets or expressways. Whether the additional investments should be in the congested mode or in another mode depends on the benefits and costs of investments in all feasible modes.

Pricing Policy

The foregoing analysis suggests that underpricing of urban transportation is pervasive. No urban transportation fees include congestion charges. There is considerable dispute on whether some urban transportation charges even cover the capital and operating costs of the mode.

The vehicle operating costs of automobile travel are paid by the car owner. User fees in the form of gasoline and other taxes need cover only highway capital and maintenance costs. The best study on the subject, by Meyer *et al.*, concludes that urban automobile users pay in user fees somewhat more than the cost of urban streets and highways. Contrary to popular opinion, the evidence is strongest for urban expressways.

Popular writers are impressed by the fact that highway construction costs are much higher in urban than in rural areas. Not only are land values much higher in urban than in rural areas, urban highway construction requires the purchase and demolition of structures in the right of way. Since urban drivers pay about the same user fees per vehicle mile as do rural drivers, it is concluded that urban expressways are subsidized. The argument is fallacious, in that it ignores the fact that urban highways are used much more intensively than rural highways. In fact, the ratio of urban to rural highway use exceeds the ratio of urban to rural highway cost. Therefore urban user fees are actually somewhat greater than urban highway costs.

There are no comprehensive data on the costs of transit systems. Many public transit systems have practically no usable capital accounts, and many clearly do not cover their capital costs with operating revenues.

Netzer estimates that transit operating revenues cover about 80 percent of costs, on the average.

What is the correct pricing policy for urban transportation? It follows from the analysis in Chapter 8 that efficient long-run resource allocation requires that price equal long-run marginal cost, and the principle applies no less to urban transportation than to other goods and services. Long-run marginal cost in urban transportation includes vehicle operating costs, congestion costs, and in the case of commuting, the cost of extra lanes, roads, and transit lines required for peak-hour traffic. In the absence of congestion, it is likely that an urban transportation system as a whole would be subject to increasing returns, regardless of the mode used.

In that case, marginal cost would be less than average cost, and subsidy might be justified. But it has been shown that optimum congestion is substantial, especially in central cities, so it is unlikely that the optimum price is less than average cost.

The foregoing argument leads to the conclusion that urban transportation is generally underpriced. Transit fares should be higher and user fees for urban streets and highways should be greater. Charging higher transit fees presents political, but not technical, problems. It is not clear what is technically the best way to charge higher automobile user fees. The gasoline tax is an excellent user fee, and the case is strong for somewhat higher gasoline taxes in metropolitan than in other areas. In addition, there should be careful study of the feasibility of electronic metering of city streets. There should also be careful study of the feasibility of higher peak-load fares on transit facilities.

Many people reject the conclusion that urban transportation facilities, especially public transit systems, ought to pay their way. Some people do not believe that marginal cost would exceed average cost in an efficient system. The dispute hinges on matters of fact that can be settled, even though with considerable difficulty. Other people believe that, since urban automobile use is subsidized, the balance between public transit and automobile use can be righted only if transit systems are also subsidized. But it is not clear that automobile use is more heavily subsidized than transit travel; even if it were, transit subsidy would only compound the difficulty. A more appropriate policy would be to remove subsidies for automobiles. Furthermore, as so often happens, subsidy of transit facilities probably would have a perverse distributional effect.

Enormous pressure is now being applied to the federal government to promote construction of rail transit systems in middle-size metropolitan areas. Most proposals entail public subsidy of practically all of the capital costs of such systems. Yet it is quite clear from the designs that have been put forward for many metropolitan areas, which inevitably consist mainly of radial lines connecting suburbs and central business districts, that most benefits would go to middle-class suburban residents who work downtown It is doubtful whether transportation subsidies are a sensible means of re-distributing income, but it is hardly conceivable that subsidy of suburban commuters is appropriate public policy.

A final argument against subsidy of urban transportation is often over-looked by economists. A major part of the urban transportation debate has to do with the terms on which commuters would use public transit. Under what circumstances would the benefits of public transit exceed those of au-tomobile commuting? This question addresses itself to the properties of the demand curve of Equation 11-2. One reason so little is known about the benefits of alternative transportation systems is that the underpricing of most modes provides inadequate opportunity to observe the relevant part of the demand curve, and hence to compute benefits at prices that reflect costs. If all modes of urban transportation were appropriately priced, much more would be known about the relative benefits of additional investment in urban highways and in transit facilities.

Cost and Supply of Alternate Urban Transportation Systems

It is widely believed that public transit systems are subject to decreasing costs. Cost per passenger mile falls with the number of vehicles using an un-congested right of way, because indivisible capital and land costs are sig-nificant parts of total cost. Furthermore, most transit lines can carry many more passengers than can highways before congestion becomes substantial. For example, a subway with one track in each direction can easily carry 10,000 passengers per hour in each direction, whereas an urban expressway with two lanes in each direction requires a wider right of way than the sub-way, and can carry only about 3000 cars per hour of uncongested travel in each direction. But these data refer to the intensity of land use, not to cost. Furthermore, they refer only to line-haul or corridor travel, which is only one aspect of an urban transportation system.

A complete analysis of urban transportation costs must be of the costs of an entire system. Careful urban transportation analyses, such as that by Meyer *et al.*, divide each urban transportation system into residential col-lection, line haul, and downtown distribution. Residential collection con-sists of movement of passengers from their homes to the line-haul vehicle.

The line haul consists of the trip from the residential area to the vicinity of the workplace. Downtown distribution consists of movement of passengers from the line-haul vehicle to their workplaces. The terminology suggests that the major concern is with work trips from suburban areas to central-city workplaces.

The purpose of the analysis is to compare the costs of public transit systems with those of automobile travel. But it is not feasible to use public transit for nonwork trips in U.S. urban areas. All forms of public transit require large amounts of travel between particular pairs of origins and destinations to be economical. Nonwork trips and work trips to destinations other than central cities involve too much diversity of origins and destinations. Most actual and planned public transit systems are therefore based on radial travel between suburbs and a central business district.

Urban transportation systems are usually classified by their type of line-haul vehicle. The prominent alternatives in U.S. urban areas are rail, automobile, and bus systems. Rail systems may be surface, subway, or elevated. Modern rail commuting systems are usually below-ground in heavily built up areas and above-ground in suburbs. (Such systems are called "subways" here.) In automobile commuting, the car is used both for residential collection and for line haul, thus avoiding a change of mode in the residential area. Downtown distribution may, however, involve a substantial walk from the place where the car is parked to the place of work. Subway systems can be subclassified by the method of residential collection. The realistic alternatives are walking, traveling to the suburban station by car and leaving it there during the day ("park and ride"), being driven to the suburban station by a spouse, who then uses the car during the day ("kiss and ride"),[3] and traveling to the suburban station by bus. Subway systems may require a substantial walk from the downtown station to the place of work or, occasionally, a change to another subway or to a bus. Bus systems usually use the same vehicle for line haul as for residential collection, and may require a walk or another bus ride downtown.

There is of course no urban area in which everybody uses the same combination of commuting modes. In an urban area with the world's best expressways, some people would commute by bus. And in an urban area with an idyllic subway system, some people would commute by car. Furthermore, some subway commuters walk to suburban stations, some drive, and some take a bus. This obvious fact means that extreme solutions to urban transportation problems are almost never desirable. For example, ac-

---

3. The terms "park and ride" and "kiss and ride" are taken from Meyer et al.

ceptance of the frequent proposal to ban cars from central cities would impose great hardship on some commuters because no public transit system can serve all origin-destination pairs. Likewise, abolition of public transit would impose great hardship on those without access to cars. Thus, some automobile commuting and some transit commuting are desirable in almost all circumstances. The issue is the appropriate mix.

At any given time, an urban area has a legacy of land use and transportation facilities from the past. This is an initial condition which greatly affects the appropriate investment in additional facilities. For example, Los Angeles has an extraordinary diversity of origins and destinations. Whether its diversity is related to its freeway system as cause or effect is debatable, but the result is that it is impossible to construct a viable subway system there. At the other extreme, New York City has between one and two million workers in its Manhattan central business district. Lisco has estimated that they could not all commute by car even if all of Manhattan were paved over. In both of these large metropolitan areas, the existing pattern of land use and transportation has an overwhelming effect on the kinds of transportation investments that are desirable.

Mass Transit Systems

The choices of optimum transportation systems are complex, and each metropolitan area should have a transportation system that is appropriate for its particular circumstances. In the 1970s, the debate about public transit versus private automobiles is mainly relevant to metropolitan areas in the middle-size range of one to four million people. Large metropolitan areas such as New York, Los Angeles, Chicago, and Philadelphia can hardly make major changes in their basic systems. Small metropolitan areas cannot justify any public transit other than buses that share city streets with cars. But there is room for honest disagreement about the mix of public transit and automobile transportation appropriate in medium-size metropolitan areas. Not all such metropolitan areas should have the same mix of modes, but some general comments are applicable to many of them.

Time is an important component of commuting cost. Line-haul travel on a subway or on an express bus in an uncongested expressway lane is considerably faster than urban automobile travel, in most circumstances. Subways attain average speeds of 30–40 miles per hour, provided stations are a mile or so apart. An express bus has comparable speed, provided it travels in an uncongested expressway lane. Automobile commuting averages only about 15–25 miles per hour in urban areas. In residential collection and downtown distribution, however, the advantage is with cars. They have the important advantages that they are self-scheduling, they avoid changes of vehicle, and downtown parking places are usually closer to workplaces than are downtown transit stations.

To overcome these disadvantages, transit systems must have frequent rush-hour service if they are to be economical. Common specifications are a subway or express bus arriving at each suburban station every two minutes during a two-hour peak period. If commuters are to walk to the suburban station, they must live within a few blocks of the station, since a half-mile walk may more than offset the time advantage of a transit vehicle over auto travel on the line haul. If buses take commuters to suburban stations, they must stop close to residences and must provide almost as frequent service as the line-haul vehicle. "Park and ride" systems cannot be economical for many commuters because they have most of the disadvantages of automobile commuting in that they require a car exclusively for that purpose, but they lack the advantages of self-scheduling and absence of mode change that automobile commuting has. The virtues of the "kiss and ride" system depend on the extent to which the spouse is inconvenienced, which may be substantial if there are children in the home who require organization.

There can be little doubt that subway or express-bus systems are viable if there is a high density of passengers at particular origin-destination pairs. In that case, enough passengers to support the system can be collected from within a short distance of suburban stations, and can be distributed to downtown workplaces without long walks or changes of vehicle. But most medium-size U.S. metropolitan areas do not have high origin-destination densities, and suburbanization of residences and employment is increasing the diversity of work trips. In these circumstances, it is by no means clear that public transit systems are viable for most work trips.

The problem can be clarified by some data that are typical of medium-size metropolitan areas—although the data are not precisely correct for any particular metropolitan area. Consider a metropolitan area with a population of two million. Baltimore, Houston, Minneapolis, Pittsburgh, San Francisco, and Washington, D.C., are fairly close to that size. Assume that the metropolitan area has a typical labor-force participation rate of about one third, or about 650,000 workers. Consistent with Table 11-2, suppose that a little more than 60 percent of the work force, or about 400,000 workers, work in the central city, about 150,000 of whom work in the central business district. Suppose the metropolitan area to be semicircular in shape, with a pie slice of one fourth of the circle unavailable because of a harbor or some other topographical feature. The metropolitan area is assumed to have a radius of 12 miles, which implies an area of about 340 square miles and a population density of about 6000 people per square mile. It is assumed that the population density is approximately uniform in the suburbs, but not necessarily in the central city.

Now suppose that a subway or express-bus system is proposed, and that it will consists of several radial lines between the suburbs and the central business district. If a large number of commuters use the transit system, many lines and frequent service can be supported. Thus, most commuters will live close to a suburban transit station, and the transit system will be viable. But if only a few commuters use the system, only a few lines and little service can be supported. Thus, most commuters will live some distance from a suburban transit station, and the transit system will be unattractive in comparison with automobile commuting.

It is unlikely that a substantial number of those who work in the suburbs will use the transit system, because their origins and destinations are too diverse. Thus, the main issue is what fraction of those who work in the central city will use the transit system. As has been indicated, this is a difficult question, and the answer depends in part on the detailed characteristics of the existing transportation system and the proposed transit facility. The following two possibilities probably bracket the realistic situation in many metropolitan areas.

First, consider an optimistic case. Suppose that one half of the central-city workers, about 200,000 people, use the transit system. About 20,000 passengers each way per day, roughly 10,000 per hour during a two-hour peak period, are required to support a transit line at acceptably frequent service. Thus, the 200,000 passengers could support ten lines from the suburbs to the central business district. If the lines were spaced evenly around the semicircular city, no suburbanite would live more than three miles from a transit line, and most would live within two miles of a stop, even if stops were spaced at one-mile intervals along the lines. But relatively few suburbanites would live within walking distance of a stop. In this situation, it should not be difficult to design a residential collection system that would make the transit system competitive with automobile commuting for many central-city workers.

Second, consider a pessimistic case. Suppose the only users of the transit system are one half of the workers in the central business district, about 75,000 passengers per day. They could hardly support four transit lines. In this situation, some suburbanites would live several miles from a transit line, and many would live almost as far from the nearest transit station as from their place of work. It would not be possible to design a residential collection system that would make the transit system competitive with automobile commuting, and the transit system could probably not retain even its 75,000 passengers without heavy subsidy.

Which of these two situations is more realistic? The answer is that we do not know, because we do not know what combination of fares and service would make transit systems competitive with automobile commuting for enough commuters to make a transit system viable. The second situation has been more realistic than the first for many urban transit systems since World War II. But it is possible that transit systems that provide much better service than has been typical in the postwar period might be viable.

Two criteria must be satisfied if a metropolitan transit system is to be viable. First, the metropolitan area must be large in order to generate the requisite traffic. Second, it must have a large concentration of employment in the central city, and especially in the central business district, in order to generate the requisite traffic on particular lines. New York, Chicago, and Philadelphia clearly satisfy both criteria. Los Angeles satisfies the first but not the second. It is at least doubtful whether many middle-size metropolitan areas satisfy both criteria. Chapter 6 showed that suburbanization of population and employment has proceeded rapidly since World War II. If those trends continue, it is doubtful that, in a few decades, transit systems will be viable in middle-size metropolitan areas.

THE EFFECTS OF TRANSPORTATION ON URBAN STRUCTURE

The foregoing analysis has taken as given the origins and destinations of work trips. In other words, it has assumed that the locations of residences and workplaces are unaffected by the urban transportation system. The assumption cannot be literally true. Indeed, the analysis in Chapters 4 and 5 showed that the residential density pattern is affected by the relationship between housing prices and transportation costs. Thus, it is inevitable that a major transportation investment such as the construction of a transit system would have at least some effect on the locations of residences and workplaces. Some writers take the view that the effect of transit systems on urban structure is profound. It is frequently maintained that a modern transit system would stop or reverse the alleged decay of downtown business areas, eliminate urban sprawl, and solve the unemployment problem among blacks in urban ghettos.

Remarkably little is known about the effects of transportation systems on urban structure. The appropriate tool of analysis would be a general equilibrium model that shows how locations of employment and residences are related to transportation patterns. The general characteristics of such models were discussed in Chapter 4, and a specific model is presented in Mills. But such model building is in its infancy.

The qualitative effects of transit system are not too hard to perceive. The purpose of a radial transit system is to make radial travel economical. People already employed in the central business district would find it advantageous to live farther out (on the average) to take advantage of lower land prices and therefore housing prices. Indeed, it was shown in the mathematical model in Chapter 5 that a decrease in transportation cost would flatten the residential density function of a fixed group of central business district workers.

The transit system would make the central business district a more attractive location for firms, since it would be more accessible for their employees. Thus, central business district employment would increase at the expense of suburban employment, making the employment density function steeper. The increased centralization of employment would induce some employees to live closer to the central business district than before, since their suburban residence would have been far from their places of work.

Thus, it seems clear that the effect of an urban transit system must be to centralize employment to some extent. But there are offsetting effects on residence. Employees already working in the central business district decentralize their residence, whereas employees formerly working in the suburbs centralize theirs. It is not possible to know the magnitudes of the offsetting effects on residential suburbanization without knowing the magnitude of the effect of the transit system on central business district employment.

It is, however, a reasonable guess that transit systems would not have major effects on central business district employment in most urban areas. It was shown in Chapter 6 that employment suburbanization has been rapid and persistent for many decades. During that period, there have been many improvements in urban transportation, and they seem to have had little tendency to slow down the suburbanization of employment. Furthermore, as was indicated in Chapter 6, the important causes of employment suburbanization seem to have been the growth of metropolitan areas, the suburbanization of populations because of rising incomes, and rapid improvement in the intercity road movement of freight. None of these causes would be affected by the construction of urban transit systems.

TRANSPORTATION AND URBAN POVERTY

There are two ways in which urban poverty enters into a consideration of urban transportation. First, low-income housing is sometimes displaced by the construction of urban transportation facilities, especially expressways. In some ways, the problem is similar to the displacement of low-income housing by urban renewal (discussed in Chapter 10). Unlike urban renewal, however, urban expressways are not restricted to the poor parts of central cities. In fact, much of the postwar construction of urban highways has been of circumferencial roads, which affect only suburbs, and radial expressways, which pass through both low and high-income areas.

The problem is similar to that of urban renewal in that low-income people are affected differently than are high-income people by conventional compensation procedures. High-income residents tend to be owner-occupiers, and compensation of the property owner is therefore equivalent to compensation of the resident. Low-income residents, however, tend to be renters, and therefore do not benefit when property owners are compensated under condemnation proceedings. Moreover, renters may suffer, whether they are displaced by urban renewal or by highway construction, if their homes and neighborhoods are destroyed. It seems indisputable that renters should be compensated for such losses, be they financial or psychic. Determination of psychic losses is not easy, but it is done in other equity proceedings. The cost of such compensation is a cost of the facility being constructed, and should be borne by those who benefit from the facility.

Second, and more complex: an automobile-based urban transportation system has an income bias, in that the poorest people cannot afford cars. The problem is especially acute among blacks confined to central-city ghettos because of racial discrimination in housing markets. Some people advocate construction of public transit systems in order to improve the access of ghetto residents to suburban employment centers.

It can hardly be doubted that the problem is real. Many labor specialists believe that ghetto unemployment rates are high partly because blacks who live there lack access to suburban jobs. Even if there were no effect of housing segregation on ghetto unemployment, segregation would nevertheless impose costs on blacks in the form of excessive commuting to suburban jobs.

The first thing to be said is that the problem is not basically one of transportation. If ghetto residents are deprived of access to suburban jobs because of housing segregation, the obvious answer is to open up suburban housing to blacks on the terms on which it is available to others. One might realistically view special provisions for transportation of ghetto residents to suburban jobs as a way of maintaining all-white suburbs. Furthermore, it is not obvious that there is greater resistance of whites to racial integration of suburban housing than there is to integration of suburban employment.

The third point to be made is that little is known about what transportation system would be best for ghetto residents. It is clear that the mass transit systems now being planned are designed to bring suburban residents to central cities rather than to bring central-city residents to the suburbs. This is at least suggested by the proposed locations of radial rights of way and of suburban line-haul stations. It is also clear that suburban bus systems are planned to bring suburban residents to line-haul stations and not to bring central-city residents from suburban line-haul stations to suburban employment centers.

It is quite possible that the diversity of origins and destinations of ghetto residents who would commute to suburban jobs is such that an automobile-based system would be better for them than a transit system. If so, that the poor cannot afford automobiles implies that they are even less able to afford transit transportation. But the foregoing comments are meant to raise questions rather than to provide answers. The special transportation needs of the urban poor are simply not known.

The final issue to be considered is the claim that ghetto residents would benefit from transit systems because more jobs would be created in the central business district, to which ghetto residents have easy access. It has been claimed that transit systems probably would increase central business district employment, although there is doubt that the numbers would be large. But the main effect of a transit system is to increase the access of suburbanites to the central business district. Therefore, central business district jobs created by the transit system would presumably be held mainly by suburbanites. Undoubtedly, there would be some creation of complementary jobs for ghetto residents, but it is hard to imagine that the effect would be large. The claim here is rather like the argument for urban renewal, that it will make central cities more attractive to middle-class whites, and black ghetto residents will benefit thereby. That may be, but increasing the attractiveness of central cities or central business districts to middle-class whites is hardly the best way to help poor blacks.

SUMMARY

The purpose of an urban transportation system is to facilitate the exchange of goods and services in the urban area. The optimum transportation system for an urban area depends on the area's size and structure as well as on the historical development in the area.

Since 1940, the volume of urban transportation has grown rapidly, and there has been a massive shift from public to private automobile transportation. Total commuting in an urban area depends on locations of employment and residences. Choice of mode depends on prices, time, comfort, and convenience of alternative modes. Among realistic alternatives in U.S. urban areas, time is likely to be the dominant consideration. Any mode becomes congested if used by enough passengers. Congestion costs are an important element in planning and pricing urban transportation systems. It is likely that both public and private automobile transportation are underpriced in U.S. metropolitan areas.

The major policy debate in urban transportation is the benefits and costs of public transit and automobile travel in medium-size metropolitan areas. The decision depends mainly on whether a combination of fares and conditions of service can be offered by public transit that will be attractive to enough commuters to make public transit economical. There is serious doubt whether subway systems can be economical for a large number of medium-size metropolitan areas.

There is considerable doubt about the effects of urban transportation systems on the structure of urban areas. Public transit systems would probably increase central business district employment, but it is unlikely that the effect would be large. Very little is known about the urban transportation needs of the poor, but it is unlikely that public transit systems being designed for many metropolitan areas will be valuable for low-income residents.

DISCUSSION QUESTIONS

1. It is frequently proposed that New York's subways and buses be free to all passengers. Evaluate the proposal on the grounds of efficiency and equity.
2. Suppose technical improvements made it possible for helicopter buses to carry 50 commuters each at 60 miles per hour and a fare of 20 cents per mile. What would be the effect on location of employment and housing in metropolitan areas during the remainder of the century?
3. Do you think it might be desirable to have one or more circumferential subway lines in large metropolitan areas at some future date?
4. Do you think that low-income workers spend more or less time commuting than do high-income workers in metropolitan areas? Which group do you think commutes longer distances? Can you reconcile your answers with the theoretical analysis in Chapters 4 and 5?

REFERENCES AND FURTHER READING

Thomas Lisco, "Mass Transportation: Cinderella in Our Cities," *Public Interest*, No. 18 (Winter 1970), 52–74.

John Meyer, John Kain, and Martin Wohl, *The Urban Transportation Problem*, 1965.

Edwin S. Mills, *Studies in the Structure of the Urban Economy*, 1972.

Herbert Mohring and Mitchell Harwitz, *Highway Benefits: An Analytical Framework*, 1962.

Dick Netzer, *Economics and Urban Problems*, 1970.

Richard Quandt (editor), *The Demand for Travel: Theory and Measurement*, 1970.

Alan Walters, "The Theory and Measurement of Private and Social Cost of Highway Congestion," *Econometrica*, Vol. 29 (October 1961), 676–699.

Chapter 12
Financing
Local Government

In the United States, state and local governments provide most of the public services that have a direct and immediate impact on people's lives and welfare. Most of the federal government's budget is devoted to national security and other activities that affect the country's relationships with the rest of the world. Another part of the federal budget finances programs, such as research and space explorations, that affect the public only indirectly. A third use of federal funds is to help finance programs that are the direct responsibility of state and local governments. But state and local governments administer almost all public services provided directly to the people

Important examples are public education, public health and welfare programs, police and fire protection, public transportation, and water supply and sanitation. Most of these public services have not only direct, but also important, effects on people's lives. Few things are more important determinants of standard and style of living than the quantity and quality of education received. Likewise, police protection involves the safeguarding of life, property, and civil rights.

Practically no one is satisfied with the provision and financing of public services by state and local governments. Critics accuse these governments of timidity in responding to social problems, of inadequate and burdensome methods of finance, of squandering taxpayers' money, of permitting the quality of public services to deteriorate, and of many other deficiencies. In fact, it is striking how often complaints about the quality of urban life turn out, on analysis, to be complaints about the provision of public services. Many of these problems are beyond the economist's skills and tools. But economics can shed light on important issues related to the financing of public services.

THE SYSTEM OF STATE AND LOCAL GOVERNMENTS

Under the U.S. Constitution, sovereignty is shared between federal and state governments. Local governments, however, are the creations of state governments. A salient characteristic of our federal system is that state governments have created a bewildering variety of local governments. Although the subject is mainly the concern of political science rather than of economics, some understanding of the system of local government is prerequisite to an understanding of problems of local government finance.

In 1967, there were about 81,000 local governments in the United States, each with limited power to levy taxes and spend the revenues collected. The best-known of these governments are the 3000 counties that nearly blanket the country, and the 18,000 municipal governments. In addition, there are about 17,000 townships, 22,000 school districts, and 21,000 special districts. School districts are ordinarily empowered to levy property taxes to support public education. Special districts are established for specific purposes, most commonly water supply and waste disposal, and levy taxes to finance their activities.

The functions assigned to particular governments vary greatly from state to state. Some state governments perform functions that are performed by county or municipal governments in other states. In some states, municipal governments provide public education, whereas school districts provide it in other states. Furthermore, there is little coincidence among boundaries of jurisdictions. School and special-district jurisdictions may overlap municipal and county boundaries. Thus, it is very difficult to obtain comparable data on state and local public finance. For example, the fact that one state government has a much smaller budget than another may simply mean that municipalities in the first state finance services financed by the state government in the other. Likewise, the central-city government in a particular SMSA may have an unusually small budget simply because it is in a state in which education is provided by county governments or by education districts.

As a result of the complexity of the system, many citizens are within the jurisdiction and taxing power not only of federal and state governments, but also of several local governments. Furthermore, an integrated economic area, such as an SMSA, may contain an extraordinarily large number of local governments. The Chicago SMSA has more than 1100 local governments, and the New York, Philadelphia, and Pittsburgh SMSAs have more than 500 local governments in each.

Political scientists tend to be critical of our complex system of local governments from the point of view of governmental operations. Although the issues go beyond the scope of economics, it is difficult not to conclude that the system is cumbersome and unwieldy. Some of the implications of this for public resource allocation are explored later in the chapter.

There has been a tendency to reduce the number of local governments during recent decades, although the reduction results entirely from school-district consolidation. In 1952, there were almost 117,000 local governments in the country. In 1952, there were 67,000 school districts, of which two thirds had been eliminated by 1967. But the number of special districts has nearly doubled since the early 1950s.

TRENDS IN STATE AND LOCAL GOVERNMENT FINANCE

Whatever disagreements there may be about the role of government, it must be agreed that it has been a growth sector in the U.S. economy during the twentieth century. Table 12-1 shows the trend of government general expenditure per capita since 1902. In 1902, governments spent only about $20 per capita. By 1966–1967, 65 years later, it had risen to $1000. Since most government expenditure is financed by current taxes, taxes have risen at about the same rate. Of course, the private sector of the economy has also grown rapidly during the present century, and government expenditure has therefore risen less rapidly in relation to income or output than in relation to population. Between 1902 and 1942, per capita government expenditure approximately doubled each decade. This implies a 7 percent annual growth rate, considerably faster than the growth of the private sector. But since the adjustment following World War II, government expenditure has inched up only slightly in relation to total income. Government general expenditure was 26.5 percent of gross national product in 1952, and 28.1 percent in 1966–1967.

There have been two major trends in the relative sizes of federal and state and local governments during the twentieth century. Until after World War II, the federal government grew much more rapidly than did state and local governments. Although the trend was apparent during earlier years, it clearly resulted mainly from the depression of the 1930s and from World War II. But for most of the period since World War II the trend has been reversed, and state and local government expenditures have grown more rapidly than federal government expenditures. By 1970, state and local government expenditures were nearly as large as those of the federal government. In part, the rapid growth of state and local government expenditure since World War II has been financed through federal taxes. The federal government has always made grants to state and local governments to help finance specific programs. Since World II, such grants have been a major source of increased state and local government revenue. Federal grants to state and local governments were $7.15 per capita in 1940 and $16.39 in 1950. By 1966–1967, they had grown to $77.68. Since the early 1950s, more than 20 percent of the growth of state and local government expenditure has been financed by increased federal government grants. Adoption of federal revenue sharing would of course continue the trend.

It is sometimes claimed that state and local governments are inadequately financed because of the need to compete with each other for high-income population and employment, which makes it almost impossible for them to raise taxes. This claim is analyzed later in the chapter, but it should be noted here that the data in Table 12-1 do not lend it any support. Of course, no one knows how much state and local government expenditures would have grown if their taxation had not been affected by competition. However, the data in Table 12-1 make it clear that it is an exaggregation to say that state and local taxes are practically impossible to raise. Most state and local tax revenues grow less rapidly than personal incomes if rates are held constant. Yet state and local government expenditures grew from 11.6 percent of personal incomes in 1957 to 16.1 percent in 1966–1967. That growth has necessitated frequent introduction of new taxes and increases in the rates of existing taxes.

Revenue

Table 12-2 presents a detailed picture of the sources of state and local government revenue. The percentages refer to amounts that the governments raise from their own sources. Intergovernmental transfers appear at the bottoms of the columns. Transfers to state governments are from the federal

Table 12-1 Per Capita Government General Expenditures, 1902–1967

Years	Federal	State and Local	Total
1902	7.14	12.80	19.93
1922	33.04	47.41	80.45
1942	254.29	68.14	322.43
1952	415.38	166.29	581.67
1962–1963	487.90	339.19	827.09
1966–1967	624.36	471.79	1096.15

Source: *United States Census of Governments*, Vol. 6, 1967.

Table 12-2   State and Local Government Revenue, 1966–1967 (millions of dollars)

Source	State		Local		State and Local	
Property taxes	862	2.3%	25,186	66.2%	26,048	34.4%
Sales and gross receipts taxes	18,575	49.2	1,956	5.1	20,531	27.1
Personal income taxes	4,909	13.0	916	2.4	5,825	7.7
Corporate income taxes	2,227	5.9	—	—	2,227	2.9
Other taxes	5,354	14.2	1,016	2.7	6,370	8.4
Charges	4,197	11.1	6,285	16.5	10,482	13.8
Miscellaneous	1,659	4.4	2,686	7.1	4,345	5.7
Totals	37,782	100.0%	38,045	100.0%	75,827	100.0%
Intergovernmental transfers	14,289	—	20,188	—	—	—

Source: *United States Census of Governments*, Vol. 4, 1967.

government. Transfers to local governments may come directly from the federal government or indirectly through state governments, or they may come from funds raised by the state governments.

State governments raise almost one half of their revenues from sales taxes. Almost all states levy sales taxes, although the rates and the transactions to which they apply vary greatly among states. Personal income taxes are the second largest source of state government revenue, but they yield only 13 percent of total revenues. Of state government revenue, 11 percent comes from charges such as tuition at state universities, sales in state liquor stores, and license fees. The category "other taxes," which accounts for 14.2 percent of state government revenues, includes motor vehicle taxes, death and gift taxes, severance taxes, and several others.

Local governments receive almost two thirds of their revenue from property taxes. Many are also permitted to levy sales taxes, and a few have income or payroll taxes. But dependence of local governments on property taxes is great and of long duration. No other tax yields more than 5 percent of their total revenues. Local governments also raise substantial amounts of revenue from such charges as water bills, tuition at community colleges, parking fees, transit fares, and license fees. Table 12-2 shows that just over one half of all taxes and charges collected by state and local governments are collected by local governments.

Expenditure

What do state and local governments do with the money they collect? Some comprehensive data appear in Table 12-3. Expenditures in the table refer to direct expenditures for the purposes indicated. For example, state govern-

Table 12-3 State and Local Government Expenditures, 1966–1967 (millions of dollars)

Function	State		Local		State and Local	
Education	9,384	23.6%	28,534	43.1%	37,918	35.8%
Transportation	9,609	24.2	5,108	7.7	14,717	13.9
Public welfare	4,291	10.8	3,927	5.9	8,218	7.8
Health and hospitals	3,358	8.5	3,283	5.0	6,641	6.3
Police, fire and correction	1,188	3.0	4,500	6.8	5,688	5.4
Parks and natural resources	1,801	4.5	1,833	2.8	3,634	3.4
Housing and urban renewal	28	0.1	1,441	2.2	1,469	1.4
Sewerage and sanitation	—	—	2,523	3.8	2,523	2.4
Government administration	1,175	3.0	2,139	3.2	3,314	3.1
Utilities	—	—	6,006	9.1	6,006	5.7
Other	8,872	22.3	6,980	10.5	15,852	15.0
Totals	39,704	100.0	66,274	100.0	105,978	100.0
Intergovernmental transfers	19,056	—	374	—	—	—

Source: *United States Census of Governments*, Vol. 4, 1967.

ments finance substantial parts of local government expenditures on public welfare. Such expenditures show up as a direct expenditure of local governments in the table, and as an intergovernmental grant of state governments at the bottom of the table.

Education takes nearly one fourth of state government expenditures. The figure is mostly expenditure on higher education in state colleges and universities, which has grown rapidly in recent years. Many state governments also finance substantial parts of the cost of local elementary and secondary education, but this is included in intergovernmental transfers in the state government column. Transportation occupies another one fourth of state government budgets; it is mainly construction and maintenance of state highway systems. Public welfare and health expenditures each account for roughly 10 percent of state budgets, and grew very rapidly during the 1960s.

Local governments spend more than 40 percent of their budgets on education. The 7.7 percent of expenditures for transportation is mostly for streets and highways. Although health and welfare expenditures are rising rapidly, they still occupy only relatively small portions of local government budgets. Expenditures on utilities include publicly owned or subsidized water supply, gas, electricity, and transit systems.

Table 12-2 shows that state and local governments collect roughly equal amounts of taxes from their residents. But Table 12-3 shows that local governments spend almost two thirds more than state governments. The disparity between local government expenditures and tax collections is mainly financed by grants from federal and state governments.

Although total expenditures of state and local governments have grown rapidly since World War II, the proportions spent on important categories have changed relatively little. Contrary to much popular opinion, the proportion of state and local government expenditures used for health and welfare has changed little since the war. Among major expenditure categories, only education has increased substantially as a fraction of total state and local government expenditure since the war.

THE PLIGHT OF SMSA CENTRAL-CITY GOVERNMENTS

Much recent concern with local government finance has focused on the problems of central-city governments in metropolitan areas. Data presented in Chapter 9 showed that central cities contain a disproportionate share of the poor in metropolitan areas, and even the most cursory reading of daily newspapers indicates that central-city governments are financially pressed. But are they in worse financial straits than other local governments? If so, why? Is it because the central-city poor need more public services than do people elsewhere? Or is it because the poor are less able than others to pay taxes to finance local public services? And how do patterns of local government expenditures and tax receipts differ in central cities from those elsewhere?

Unfortunately, comprehensive data on local governments in central cities are not available. Many local governments provide services and levy taxes in central cities, and many of their boundaries do not coincide with those of central cities. For example, most central cities are in counties that provide some public services to residents of the city. In a few cases, the county's boundaries coincide with those of the central city, but in most cases the county also includes some suburban areas. In such cases, it is difficult to estimate the services provided to central-city residents by the county government. It is also difficult to estimate the taxes paid by central-city residents to the county government. Similar problems arise concerning school districts and special districts. Fortunately, the Advisory Commission on Intergovernmental Relations compiled data on finance of local governments in central cities for the 37 largest SMSAs for 1964–1965. The data are summarized in Table 12-4. The government tax and expenditure data in the table refer to local governments only.

The most striking data in Table 12-4 are the income data in the bottom row. They show that income per capita in the central cities of the 37 largest SMSAs is only about 5 percent less than in the suburbs. Both central-city

Table 12-4   Local Government Finance Inside and Outside Central Cities in the 37 Largest SMSAs, 1964–1965

Item	In Central City	Outside Central City	Remainder of Nation
Per capita total general expenditures	$ 332	$ 278	$ 203
Per capita educational expenditures	100	146	107
Per capita general noneducational expenditures	232	132	96
Per capita total general revenues	340	268	212
Per capita taxes	200	152	103
Per capita federal and state aid	88	80	76
Percent of general expenditures	26.5%	28.8%	37.4%
Percent of taxes	44.0	52.6	73.8
Per capita income	$2607	$2732	$1789

Source: Advisory Commission on Intergovernmental Relations, *Fiscal Balance in the American Federal System*, A-31, Vol. 2, October 1967.

and suburban incomes are much higher than elsewhere in the country. The small disparity between central-city and suburban incomes is striking, because the 37 SMSAs include all of the large SMSAs along the eastern seaboard whose central cities are usually thought to have the most serious fiscal problems. However, disparities between incomes in central cities and suburbs are greater in smaller SMSAs. In most parts of the country, per capita incomes in SMSA suburbs exceed those in central cities by between 10 and 25 percent.

The government revenue and expenditure data in Table 12-4 show clearly the problems of public finance in central cities. Per capita expenditures by local governments in central cities exceeded those of suburban governments by almost 20 percent. However, educational expenditures were considerably less in central cities than in suburbs. (It is shown in Table 12-5 that governments in central cities spend more than suburban governments on practically everything but education.) Table 12-4 also shows that per capita local government taxes are more than 30 percent greater in central cities than in suburbs. Finally, although intergovernmental grants to local governments in central cities are 10 percent more per capita than those to suburban governments, the disparity is less than that in local government expenditures.

Table 12-5 shows more detailed data, for a more recent year, for three large SMSAs on the eastern seaboard. They were chosen partly because they are representative of conditions in older, eastern SMSAs, but mainly because their local government structures are sufficiently simple to permit easy tabulation of the data.

Table 12-5   Local Government Finance in Three SMSAs, 1966–1967
(dollars per capita)

| | Baltimore | | Philadelphia | | Richmond | |
	Central City	SMSA	Central City	SMSA	Central City	SMSA
Revenues						
Intergovernmental	173.95	135.69	67.64	64.97	100.95	79.42
From own sources	265.49	216.36	235.00	208.39	277.75	192.43
Totals	439.45	352.05	304.64	273.35	378.70	271.85
Expenditures						
Education	120.92	147.36	118.73	133.69	121.67	122.21
Transportation	30.30	26.46	14.54	17.85	31.68	24.19
Public welfare	62.71	33.25	7.34	9.16	51.40	25.16
Health and hospitals	26.11	13.70	15.05	8.33	.67	.66
Police, fire, and correction	53.90	36.31	42.53	26.24	34.82	21.27
Parks and natural resources	11.39	7.63	9.43	5.98	13.80	6.78
Housing and urban renewal	13.10	6.29	22.50	11.28	5.57	2.49
Sewerage and sanitation	18.05	13.66	17.09	15.13	23.30	16.63
Government administration	12.69	10.73	14.47	11.35	16.08	11.03
Utilities	12.26	10.73	11.83	9.81	49.23	33.28
Other	45.86	45.37	55.76	39.98	38.89	24.19
Totals	407.29	351.49	329.27	288.80	387.11	287.89

Source: *United States Census of Governments*, Vol. 5, 1967.

The top rows of Table 12-5 show roughly the same pattern as shown in Table 12-4 for the larger set of SMSAs. Local government expenditures per capita are much greater in central cities than in the SMSAs as a whole, and therefore greater than in suburbs. Governments in central cities receive more per capita in grants from state and federal governments, but not enough more to make up for their much higher expenditures. Therefore, governments in central cities also impose substantially higher taxes on their residents than do the suburbs.

On what public services are expenditures greater in central cities than in suburbs? The answer is practically all of them, except education. In all three central cities, educational expenditures per capita were less than in the entire SMSA, and thus less than in the suburbs. An unweighted average of the data in Table 12-5 indicates that suburban governments in the three SMSAs spent about 11 percent more per capita on education than did governments in central cities. In every expenditure category other than education, per capita expenditures in central cities were greater than in suburbs. The only exceptions to this generalization are transportation and public-welfare expenditures in Philadelphia, and both exceptions are small.

It is also noteworthy that no single category accounts for a large part of the disparity between central-city and suburban expenditures. Public welfare, for example, is often claimed to be a major reason for the financial difficulties of governments in central cities. Although considerably more is spent on welfare in the three central cities than in the SMSAs as a whole, it accounts for little more than one fourth of the excess of central-city over SMSA expenditures per capita. And in Philadelphia, per capita SMSA expenditures on welfare exceed those in the central city.

REASONS FOR FINANCIAL PROBLEMS IN STATE AND LOCAL GOVERNMENTS

It has been shown that state and local government tax rates, receipts, and expenditures have risen much more rapidly than taxpayers' incomes since World War II, and that central-city taxes and expenditures are greater than those in suburbs of SMSAs, although taxpayers' incomes in central cities are lower. Why? Why should state and local government expenditures absorb increasing percentages of taxpayers' incomes, and why should governments in central cities be in especially dire straits?

During recent years, economists have undertaken dozens of studies of the determinants of government expenditures in order to answer these questions.[1] Most such studies are unsatisfactory, partly because of the difficulty of separating demand from cost or supply determinants of expenditures, and partly because the demand for public services does not register on markets and is hence difficult to estimate. Although it is difficult to attribute specific amounts of expenditure increase to each cause, the important factors are both few in number and easy to identify.

Rising Relative Prices of Services

Most government expenditures are on services, and prices of services inevitably rise faster than prices of commodities. The phenomenon is present in the private sector as well as in the public. During the two decades between 1950 and 1969, the service component of the consumer price index rose 92 percent, whereas the commodity component rose only 37 percent. The reason is of course that productivity rises much faster in commodity than in service production, mainly as a result of faster technological progress.

---

1. An informative survey is Ginsburg et al.

Increases in service prices relative to those of commodities are an inevitable characteristic of an economy in which wages are high and grow rapidly. It is extremely unlikely that the trend will be reversed, either in the public or the private sector. In the private sector, the response has been both to increase somewhat the fraction of incomes spent on services and to substitute commodities for services. Between 1950 and 1969, the part of total consumption expenditure on services increased from 32 to 42 percent. As an example of the substitution of commodities for services, household appliances were substituted for domestic help during that period because of rising relative prices of the latter. Undoubtedly, both responses will occur in the public sector during coming years.

Rapidly Rising Demand for Public Services

The demand for public services has undoubtedly risen. One reason is that many public services, such as education and transportation, are highly superior goods whose demands increase rapidly as incomes rise. As incomes rise, people want longer and higher quality educations for their children, and they are willing to increase the fraction of their incomes devoted to the purpose. Likewise, passenger miles of transportation have increased more rapidly than incomes in the postwar period, and governments have been asked to devote increasing resources to transportation facilities. The foregoing can be summarized as a high income elasticity of demand for education and travel.

Another reason for the increase in demand for public expenditures is that the entire society has become more aware of the plight of the poor, and increasingly willing to devote resources to their needs. That disarming statement summarizes the outcome of years of political turmoil, and the process has by no means been easy or peaceful. But the fact is that the rapid growth of intergovernmental grants to central cities has been mainly motivated by a desire to redistribute income by the provision of services or transfer payments to the low-income residents of central cities. There is of course little agreement on whether the process has gone far enough.

Regressiveness of State and Local Taxes

The financial problems of state and local governments have been emphasized by repeated tax increases. It would be hard to design a tax system whose yield rose as fast as state and local government expenditures have during the 1950s and 1960s. But most state and local taxes are either regressive or much less progressive than the federal income tax. The result is that the elasticity of the yield of state and local taxes with respect to income increases is rather small. Thus, as the expenditures of state and local governments rise, frequent increases in tax rates are necessary. Property tax yields are generally less responsive to income than are the yields of sales and income taxes. Thus, since local governments raise most of their revenues through property taxes, they are forced to raise their rates even more frequently than are state governments.

Special Problems of Central Cities

The three reasons just discussed apply at least as much to governments in SMSA central cities as to state and other local governments. But central cities have additional sources of financial difficulties. First, property tax yields are particularly unresponsive to economic growth in central cities. Neither the amount nor the value of property in central cities increases very fast. The amount does not because central cities are almost completely built up, and most construction for both housing and employment occurs in suburbs. The value of central-city property rises slowly because the flattening of rent-distance functions (discussed in Chapters 4 and 5) means that most increases in land values occur in suburbs.

Second, incomes are lower in central cities than in suburbs. Therefore, a given per capita tax burden is a larger percentage of incomes in central cities than in suburbs. Furthermore, central cities contain a disproportionate share of very low-income people to whom society is committed to provide special services or transfer payments.

Waste and Corruption

The foregoing are easily understood and rather prosaic reasons for the financial difficulties of state, local, and especially central-city governments. No mention has been made of corruption, bureaucracy, and waste, factors that play a large role in newspaper and magazine accounts of the financial crises of state and local governments. Undoubtedly, the attention paid to these matters results more from their dramatic appeal than from their true importance, and relevant data are almost impossible to obtain.

Take the subject of corruption, for example. There can be no doubt that crime is a serious problem in our society. Despite the inadequacies of the statistics, it is clear that crime became much worse during the 1960s. Crime became more serious in the streets, in homes, and in businesses. It would indeed be surprising if government officials were exempt from the trend. But there is no evidence that government is more corrupt than other aspects of our society. In fact, familiarity with big city government in the nineteenth and early twentieth centuries persuades most observers that the long-term trend has been improvement in the integrity of public life.

Much the same is true of claims about bureaucracy and waste. The safe generalization is that all large bureaucracies become inflexible and unresponsive to change, whether they are in government, business, foundations, or universities. Beyond a doubt, state and local governments spend considerable sums of money on programs that have outlived their usefulness. It is also beyond doubt that governors, mayors, citizen study commissions and others should devote more effort to modernizing government programs. But there is no evidence that bureaucratic waste and inefficiencies are now more serious and costly than in the past.

SOME BASIC ISSUES IN THE PROVISION OF LOCAL PUBLIC SERVICES

Before discussing ways to improve the financing of local public services, it is desirable to step back from the immediate view and ask some basic questions about the optimum provision of public services. It has been seen that our system of local government is complex and cumbersome, with many layers of government, and with overlapping jurisdictions. But how should a system of local government be designed if it could be done from scratch? The question of optimum jurisdiction of local government is one that public finance specialists have only recently begun to subject to systematic analysis. Although there is certainly no consensus on the subject, it is at least possible to identify the basic issues.[2]

Scale Economies

In Chapter 1, it was claimed that scale economies are important, not only in manufacturing, but also in service sectors of the economy. The claim applies as much to the provision of public services as to that of private ser-

---

2. Among the best discussions of the subject are the papers by Rothenberg and by Buchanan and Wagner in Margolis.

vices. Many public services can be produced at lower cost if they are produced on a large scale than if they are produced on a small scale. On a theoretical level, the statement must be correct. If it were not, every child could be educated economically with a private tutor and every house could provide its own fire protection.

In applied studies it is very difficult to measure scale economies in the public sector. One reason may be that many local governments for which data are available may be larger than the scale at which economies are exhausted. A second reason may be that, given the difficulties of measuring the quality of services, local governments may appear to have high costs because they provide a high quality of service. A third reason is that scale economies may be masked by the fact that large local governments may pay high prices for inputs. A fourth reason is that there are two crucial dimensions to the output of public services, number of people served and geographical area covered. Although unit costs may decrease with the number of people served, they tend to increase with the size of the area covered.

Most of these difficulties are illustrated by municipal sewage collection and treatment. It is chosen as an example because it is almost the only local public service for which good data about scale economies are available. Government data show clearly that the cost per gallon of sewage treated decreases with the number of gallons treated, at least up to the amount of sewage produced by a community of about a million people. However, collection costs are a large part of total costs, and they increase rapidly with the area over which wastes are collected. If two communities have the same population, the one with the lower population density is likely to have higher sewage collection and treatment costs. Furthermore, many large cities have high waste treatment costs simply because they treat their wastes more adequately than small cities, that is, the quality of the service is higher. A large city may have high treatment costs because wages are high, or because the treatment plant is built on expensive land.

If the provision of local public services is subject to scale economies, this is a justification for local governments with relatively large jurisdictions. But if only a few public services are subject to scale economies, special districts can be established with jurisdictions large enough to exhaust the economies. Scale economies have been among the reasons for the establishment of the many special districts in the country. If special districts become too numerous and their jurisdictions too complex, however, they may become unresponsive to democratic processes.

Another possible solution to the problems raised by scale economies in a particular public service is for one government to produce the service and sell it to residents of other jurisdictions. For example, in some metropolitan areas, the central-city government owns the water-supply and waste-disposal systems, and provides the services to suburban residents for a fee. There might be some concern on the part of suburban residents at having an important public service supplied by a government over which they have no control. After all, one reason for providing a service through the public sector is to subject its provision to the democratic process. In practice this does not seem to be a problem. Some central-city governments actually sell water to suburban residents at lower prices than they charge their own residents.

It is often claimed that central-city governments subsidize suburban residents by providing them many services that are paid for by taxes on central-city residents. Use of libraries, museums, zoos, and parks, as well as water-supply and waste-treatment services, are examples. But the examples are all services with easily identified beneficiaries, and it would be easy to charge for the services. In some cases, it would be clumsy to charge non-residents and not residents, but the use of scarce resources would be improved if many of these services were financed, at least in part, by fees charged to all users.

Consensus

The demand for public services depends on taste, family status, and income.[3] Some kinds of public services, usually referred to as "public goods" in the public finance literature, either must or should be provided in the same amount and quality to all people within a single local-government jurisdiction. Elementary and secondary education and police and fire protection are reasonably good examples. Efficiency in the provision of public goods can be achieved by collecting together in a single local-government jurisdiction the people who want to receive, and pay for, a particular quantity and quality of public goods. This result surprises many people, but is easily verified.

Suppose for simplicity that there are two groups of people. Group A wants local public goods that cost $300 per capita per year and group B wants public goods that cost $200. Group A might consist of high-income people and group B of low-income people. If each group is brought together in a separate local-government jurisdiction, each local government can provide just the amount of public goods wanted by its citizens. If people

---

3. Some of the ideas in this section are taken from the paper by Rothenberg in Margolis, and from an unpublished paper by Hamilton.

from groups A and B are mixed together in a single jurisdiction, some people will inevitably get more public goods than they want and are willing to pay for, and some will get less. If a person of type A is in a community in which public goods and taxes are suitable for people of type B, and a person of type B is in a community in which they are suitable for a person of type A, both people can gain by exchanging communities. Only when members of the two groups are in separate jurisdictions can the provision of public goods satisfy the conditions for efficient resource allocation.

No one should think that the foregoing is a complete justification for residential segregation by income or the related demand for public services. It would be a justification only if consensus were the only criterion for choosing local-government jurisdictions. But the ideas do help us understand some of the most controversial phenomena related to suburbanization in metropolitan areas. As groups of relatively high income residents have moved to the suburbs of central cities, they have formed local governments to provide public services consistent with their demands. The public services are, as has been seen, mainly financed by property taxes on residents. Lot-size zoning and other public policies are used to exclude from the suburban jurisdiction those whose incomes or tastes do not permit enough housing consumption to pay the taxes necessary to support the public services. Zoning of course has other purposes, but one purpose is to prevent local governments from redistributing income by taxing high-income residents to pay for services or transfers for low-income residents.

The pattern of local public finance is certainly not the only, and probably not the main, determinant of residential location. It was shown in Chapter 4 that income levels and the interaction between housing prices and commuting costs tend to result in housing segregation by income class. But if local government jurisdictions in a metropolitan area are sufficiently fragmented, and if people can choose among residences in several jurisdictions without great effect on commuting costs, local governments have only limited ability to redistribute incomes through their tax-expenditure policies. The corollary is that central-city mayors are wrong when they say they cannot raise taxes to pay for needed public services because people will move to the suburbs. Intuitively, it should be clear that residents will support taxes to pay for public services they want. Available evidence supports this contention (see Oates). The fact is that central cities have only very limited ability to raise taxes for unwanted services or for redistributive purposes.

Scale economies indicate the desirability of relatively large local government jurisdictions, whereas the consensus criterion points in the opposite direction. Consensus suggests the desirability of small and homogeneous jurisdictions.

Spillovers

It is costly or impossible to confine the benefits from expenditures on some public goods to the residents whose taxes finance the expenditures. For example, if a community paves, lights, cleans, and protects its streets, it cannot easily prevent nonresidents from using them. People in one jurisdiction benefiting from public expenditures in another is called a "spillover effect." As used here, the term refers to externalities from services produced in the public sector. They may cause misallocations of resources in the public sector just as do externalities in the private sector. Residents of a jurisdiction lack incentive to devote sufficient public resources to services that benefit residents of other jurisdictions to any great extent.

Many people believe that central-city governments provide important services for the benefit of suburban residents, and that the central cities' inability to collect taxes from suburbanites in payment for the services is a major reason for the financial problems of central-city governments. Among the services claimed to have spillover effects are transportation, education, water supply and waste treatment, public museums, libraries, zoos, parks, and other services.

Part of the problem results simply from the refusal of central-city governments to charge adequate fees for services to nonresidents. It was suggested earlier that central-city governments should charge adequate prices for any service whose beneficiaries are easily identified and whose use of the service can be easily measured. Users of libraries, museums, zoos, and other public facilities are certainly in this category.

Transportation is a little more complicated. Insofar as it is public transit, there is no reason for not charging adequate fares, although that is rarely done. It was mentioned in Chapter 11 that there is dispute over the feasibility of metering the use of central-city streets and highways. It was also mentioned that user fees, in the form of gasoline taxes, are high enough to cover the cost of constructing and maintaining city streets, but they do not cover congestion costs, which are more important in central cities than elsewhere. It was also suggested that a metropolitan area-wide gasoline tax would be at least an approximation of a congestion fee. In any case, it is clear that central-city governments should not be made to bear the full cost of roads that largely benefit suburban commuters.

Education is the most complex of all spillover issues. It is sometimes claimed that the mere fact that people move residences frequently means that local governments cannot collect taxes from the people they educate to pay for it. People frequently move out of the jurisdiction in which they were educated before they become taxpayers. It is therefore concluded that local governments lack incentive to provide sufficient educational services for their residents. But the argument is false. To the extent that parents recognize the benefits their children will receive from education, wherever they live, they will be willing to pay for each year's education in taxes leivied that year. And public education is in fact financed on that pay-as-you-learn basis. Thus, local governments are reimbursed each year for the education they provide that year, and parents do not lack incentive to vote for educational expenditures.

A more sophisticated argument is that there are benefits from education that do not accrue to the educated individual at all, wherever he lives. It has long been claimed, and is surely true, that the entire democratic process works better if voters are well educated than if they are poorly educated. To the extent that education improves the functioning of local government, local governments fail to take the benefits into account if people move elsewhere after completing their educations. The argument is correct, although it may be questioned whether the resulting underinvestment in education is substantial.

A variant of the argument is that there is a social cost to poor educations, in that poorly educated people are more likely than others to appear on unemployment and welfare rolls. To the extent that poorly educated people collect their transfers elsewhere, local governments may be induced to underinvest in education. Again, the argument is hard to evaluate quantitatively. Is it possible that one reason southern communities provide poor educations for blacks is that the rapid migration of blacks to northern cities imposes the costs of supporting poorly educated people on other communities?

Spillover effects that cannot be corrected by appropriate fees distort resource allocation by local governments, in that local governments lack incentive to spend on services whose benefits will be realized by those who do not share the costs. One possible solution to the problem is to enlarge local-government jurisdictions to include the areas within which benefits occur. A second solution is to transfer responsibility for provision of the public service in question to a level of government, presumably state or federal, which has jurisdiction over the entire benefit area. A third solution is to retain responsibility for the provision of the public service at the local level, but to finance part of the cost by transfers from state or federal governments. Such transfers are usually referred to as "functional grants," meaning that they are intended to finance specific functions. Such grants are usually allocated by more or less complicated formulas. As mentioned earlier in the chapter, intergovernmental grants have grown rapidly since World War II.

Income Redistribution

It has been shown that there are severe limits on the ability of local governments to redistribute income in the United States. For that reason, redistribution programs such as welfare, unemployment compensation, and Medicare are mostly financed by state and federal governments. Some programs are directly administered by state and federal governments, and some are administered by local governments but financed at least in part by functional grants from state or federal governments.

In recent years there has been widespread discussion of a different kind of grant scheme. It has been proposed that the federal government give unconditional grants to state and local governments to use as they see fit. The most widely discussed proposal is the Heller-Pechman scheme (Heller), put forward in the mid-1960s. More recently, the Nixon administration proposed a revenue-sharing program to Congress. Although these and other proposals differ in important ways, each would take a part of each year's federal tax receipts and distribute it to state and local governments according to a formula, but with almost no restrictions on the use of the money.

Revenue-sharing proposals are controversial, and many of the issues go beyond the scope of this discussion. But their basic purpose is income redistribution. They would redistribute income even if the grants to governments in each state were proportional to federal taxes paid by the state's residents. Such grants would partially substitute progressive federal taxes for regressive state and local taxes in financing state and local government expenditures. If the formula provided grants that were a larger proportion of federal taxes paid in low-income than in high-income states, the federal revenue-sharing scheme would be even more redistributional.

Income redistribution is always controversial, but revenue sharing is especially so because the redistribution is entirely within the public sector. The point can be clarified by contrasting it with the negative income-tax proposal discussed in Chapter 9. Suppose a negative income-tax program that produced an equitable distribution of income. Residents of each state and local government could decide through the democratic process the part of their incomes they wanted to devote to public services, and how they should be financed. Under a revenue sharing program, these decisions would be made largely by the federal government.

Some people prefer that the federal government redistribute incomes among income groups, and that state and local government fiscal decisions be made at the state and local levels. Others, however, prefer that the federal government play at least a small role in state and local government fiscal affairs. To complicate matters, some people advocate both revenue sharing and a negative income tax, whereas others oppose both measures.

LOCAL GOVERNMENT TAX REFORMS

Property Taxes

As mentioned earlier, local governments raise about two thirds of the revenue they obtain from their residents by property taxation. In most jurisdictions, local property-tax liability is between 2 and 4 percent of the market value of the taxed property. Almost no one has a good word to say for property taxes. Some objections concern its administration, and some its economic effects. There are two major problems with property tax administration, which will be discussed before the more important economic problems are taken up.

The first problem has to do with assessment procedures. The relevant measure of the property tax is the annual tax liability in relation to the market value of the taxed property. The relationship depends on two parameters of the property tax, namely the tax rate per dollar of assessed value and the ratio between assessed and market value, or the assessment ratio. A taxpayer who owns a $20,000 home is in the same economic position if his home is assessed at $10,000 and the tax rate is 4 percent of assessed value, as he is if his home is assessed at $20,000 and the tax rate is 2 percent. In both cases his property-tax liability is $400 per year.

Tax rates are set by local legislatures and are normally uniform within a jurisdiction. An important exception is that in many areas elderly homeowners are excused from all or part of their property tax. It is an example of a well-meant provision that has undesirable effects. First, it benefits only those elderly who own homes. Although many elderly homeowners have low incomes, the poorest elderly people tend to be renters and therefore ineligible for the provision. Second, it provides the rebate regardless of need, which means that a large part of the reduced tax collection benefits those who are in a position to pay taxes. A much better provision would provide relief regardless of ownership, and would use income as the criterion for eligibility.

Property assessment for tax purposes is an administrative matter. Most states have laws that direct assessments to be made at fair market value. But the nationwide assessment ratio is less than one third, and is at about one third in metropolitan areas. If all property in a jurisdiction were assessed at the same fraction of market value, it would not matter what fraction was chosen. The tax rate could be adjusted to produce needed revenue, and all property owners would pay property taxes at the same percentage of market value.

However, it is notorious that assessment ratios vary enormously within jurisdictions. The reasons for variability in assessment ratios are numerous, including incompetence by assessors, corruption, a desire to favor particular groups of property owners, and the difficulty of ascertaining market value of a property that has not been sold for many years. In many communities the property owner is almost helpless in obtaining justice. The law says that assessments are to be at fair market value, and the property owner has no recourse to the courts unless his assessment ratio exceeds 100 percent, although he may be discriminated against if his assessment ratio is 60 percent in a community where the average is 40 percent. The situation is an invitation at best to sloppy assessment, and at worst to corruption.

The most commonly proposed reform is for more professional assessment personnel, which would doubtless help. But assessors have a vested interest in the status quo, since it prevents taxpayers from appealing their decisions. Another suggestion is for local governments to compute and publish the average assessment ratios of all properties sold during the year within the jurisdiction, and to permit taxpayers who believe their assessment ratios to exceed the average to use the published average as grounds for appeal.

A far more radical proposal is self-assessment. Under this proposal, each property owner would assess his property at its value to him and pay taxes accordingly, but the assessed value would be a legal offer for sale at the assessed price. The taxpayer would have an incentive to assess his property at least as high as its market value, since otherwise he would have to sell it. Of course, assessments would be much higher than at present, and tax rates would have to be correspondingly lower. An incidental benefit would be to reduce racial discrimination in the sale of housing. A common procedure is for white home owners to offer houses for sale at prices above market value and to refuse to lower prices to nonwhite bidders. Under the self-assessment proposal, the homeowner would have to sell at the assessed valuation.

The second administrative defect of the property tax is that large amounts of real estate are exempt from it. Religious, educational, and governmental institutions are invariably exempt. In many communities, a variety of other nonprofit institutions are also exempted, often on an ad hoc basis by acts of the local legislature. Some communities have used property-tax exemption as a lure for industry and commerce. It has been estimated that in some communities as much as one third of the real estate is exempt from property taxes. Many of the exempt uses are for worthy purposes, but it is doubtful whether many such exemptions are good social policy for hard-pressed local governments which are thereby forced to levy high real estate taxes on low-income housing.

The adverse economic effects of real estate taxation stem from the fact that real estate taxes are very large levies on housing services, whose cost and quality are matters of great public and private concern. In Chapter 10 it was shown that a real estate tax of 3 percent of a property's market value is approximately equivalent to a 25 percent sales tax on the value of housing services. Such a tax treats housing much as cigarettes are treated, as an imminent danger to health. But of course the practical issue is what alternatives there might be to the present heavy reliance on real estate taxes.

At the end of Chapter 3 the theoretical merits of Henry George's proposal for a single tax on land rents were discussed. The conclusion was that a 100 percent tax on land rents is probably not justifiable because it would be confiscatory, and because it would remove the incentive to search for the most valuable use of land. But it is unlikely that a large fraction of land rent is needed to provide that incentive, and a much higher tax rate on land than on improvements may therefore be justified. Some communities have long taxed land at higher rates than structures.

How much money could be raised by high taxes on land rent? A rough guess is that structures are worth about five times as much as the land on which they sit in large cities. Suppose that both are now taxed at 25 percent of their annual rent. If the land tax were raised to 75 percent of rent, the tax on structures could be lowered to 15 percent (i.e., by 40 percent) without decreasing the total revenues from the property tax. If the decreased tax rate on structures caused an increase in the capital land ratio, taxes on structures could be reduced even more.

Local Income Taxes

An alternative to high property taxes is increased reliance on income taxes by local governments. Table 12-1 showed that local governments now obtain little more than 2 percent of their revenues from income taxes. As was stated in Chapter 8, economists have a predisposition toward income taxes because they are almost inevitably less regressive or more progressive than other taxes, and because they are thought to be less distorting. Why do local governments make so little use of them? There are two important arguments entered against local income taxes.

First, it is claimed that income taxes are or should be reserved for state and federal governments. Some states explicitly prohibit local income taxes. But why should the fact that state and federal governments tax income deter local governments from doing so? Of course, high taxes are more painful than low taxes, but that is not the issue here. The issue is whether, given a taxpayer's state and federal income-tax liability, $100 of local income tax is more painful than $100 of local property or state sales tax. The advantages of an income tax over a sale or property tax do not seem to be less applicable just because other jurisdictions also tax income.

The second argument is more serious. It is claimed that income is more mobile than property, and therefore more likely to avoid the tax by leaving a local jurisdiction. It was claimed earlier that fragmented local governments have relatively little ability to levy any kind of tax that exceeds the value of public services taxpayers receive for their taxes. That argument applies as much to property taxes as to income taxes. Real estate is immobile only in the short run; in the long run, structures can be undermaintained and abandoned, and construction can be concentrated in other jurisdictions, Central cities have seen that massive movements of real estate investment to suburbs can occur in a few years, although it is unlikely that real estate tax differences have been a major factor in postwar suburbanization. The point is that the extent to which local income taxes would cause people to leave the taxing jurisdiction depends on the tax policies of alternative jurisdictions, the kinds of services provided by the jurisdiction, and the progressiveness of the income tax. The issue is a quantitative one.

Few localities in the United States have income taxes, and most that do exist are flat-rate payroll taxes. But Maryland has a local income tax that provides insight into the issues raised here. The state income-tax base is almost the same as the federal income-tax base and is moderately progressive. Since the late 1960s the state has required local governments to levy an income tax on their residents of not less than 20 percent and not more than 50 percent of the resident's state income-tax liability. Local legislatures choose the percentage within that range and the state government collects the tax (along with its own tax) and distributes it to the local governments to which it is owed. Within about three years almost all local governments had levied the maximum income tax permitted by the state law.

The tax could hardly have induced many high-income residents to leave Baltimore city, since all the suburban localities shortly had almost the same income tax rates as the central city. Furthermore, the data clearly imply that the local income tax was mainly used to avoid increases in property taxes. The Maryland experiment suggests that local governments will use income taxes if state governments encourage them and assume responsibility for collection. Within the limits set by the state government, tax rates differed negligibly between central city and suburb in the state's one large metropolitan area, and could hardly have caused much migration.

SUMMARY

The United States has a complex and cumbersome system of local government, consisting of counties, municipalities, townships, school districts, and special districts. Since World War II, state and local government tax receipts and expenditures have grown rapidly. Local governments raise about two thirds of their tax revenues from property taxes, and spend more than 40 percent of their revenues on education.

Local governments are in chronic financial difficulty. The costs of the services they provide rise more rapidly than the costs of commodities, their constituents have a high income elasticity of demand for public services, and their tax receipts increase slowly as their constituents' incomes rise. Central-city governments are especially in severe straits because their tax receipts increase very slowly and they have large concentrations of citizens with special needs for public services and transfers.

Economists have become interested in the problem of optimum jurisdiction for providing local public services. The appropriate jurisdiction is affected by the desire to achieve economies on a large scale in providing public services, by the desire for concensus, by spillovers, and by attempts to redistribute income through local government.

Local property taxes are badly administered and have many undesirable economic effects. Reforms are needed to increase their efficiency and equity. There are reasons to believe that local governments could rely much more on moderately progressive income taxes.

DISCUSSION QUESTIONS

1. What would be the effect on local government finance in central cities of a negative income tax? of President Nixon's revenue sharing plan?
2. What would be the effect of metropolitan area-wide local governments on each of the four criteria for optimum governmental jurisdiction?

3. Are local government expenditures likely to continue to increase faster than constituents' incomes for the foreseeable future?
4. What would be the effect on population suburbanization of a reduction in taxes on improvements, and an increase in taxes on land, throughout the metropolitan area?

REFERENCES AND FURTHER READING

William Baumol, "Macroeconomics of Unbalanced Growth: The Anatomy of Urban Crisis," *American Economic Review*, Vol. 57 (1967), 414–426.

Alan Campbell and Seymour Sacks, *Metropolitan America: Fiscal Patterns and Governmental Systems*, 1967.

Alan Ginsburg, Gunter Schramm, and Gail Wilensky, "The Problem with Government Expenditure Determinant Studies," forthcoming.

Bruce Hamilton, "Zoning and Governmental Decentralization in Urban Areas," unpublished.

Walter Heller, *New Dimensions of Political Economy*, 1966.

Julius Margolis (editor), *The Analysis of Public Output*, 1970.

Dick Netzer, *Economics of the Property Tax*, 1966.

Wallace Oates, "The Effects of Property Taxes and Local Public Spending on Property Values: An Empirical Study of Tax Capitalization and the Tiebout Hypothesis," *Journal of Political Economy*, Vol. 77 (1969), 957–971.

Charles Tiebout, "A Pure Theory of Local Expenditures," *Journal of Political Economy*, Vol. 64 (1956), 416–424.

Chapter 13
Pollution and Environmental Quality

Public and private concern with pollution has increased enormously since World War II. Before the war, concern with pollution was mostly restricted to small groups of conservationists, who sometimes appeared to be urging on society the irrational policy of not using depletable natural resources.

All that has now changed. Opinion polls show environmental problems to be high on the list of public concerns. Articles on the despoilation of the environment fill newspapers and magazines. Officials pollute the media with statements on pollution. Dozens of laws have been passed by federal, state, and local governments with the purpose of abating pollution.

The reasons for increased concern are not hard to find, although no one can work long with environmental problems and not realize the inadequacies of the data base. First, there can be no doubt that the volume of wastes discharged to the environment has increased in recent decades. At a given state of technology, and with a given mix of inputs and outputs, waste generation is about proportionate to the production of goods or to the level of real income. In 1970, real income and output were more than three times their 1940 levels. Improvements in technology and public policy undoubtedly mean that waste generation increased by less than output during the three decades, but it cannot be doubted that the increase was substantial. And modern technology produces some particularly persistent and harmful wastes that were unknown a few years ago. Atomic radiation and pesticides are good examples.

Second, pollution is more bothersome than it used to be. Popular writers refer to the revolution of rising expectations regarding the environment. It is a short step from that view to the position that worsening of pollution is partly a matter of perception. Widespread prosperity has provided the income and leisure necessary to enjoy the environment through boating camping, swimming, hiking, and skiing. Income elasticities of demand are high for such activities. Somewhat more subtle, but closely related, is the fact that people become much more concerned with effects of pollution on health and mortality when urgent problems of massive unemployment and poverty have been solved. Such concerns are neither irrational nor frivolous.

Third, rapid urbanization of the country makes pollution worse than it used to be. Despite some views to the contrary, waste discharges per capita are probably not greater in urban than in rural areas. The opposite is probably true, since some large waste-producing activities such as mining occur predominantly in rural areas, and more resources are devoted to waste disposal in urban than in rural areas. The environment has the capacity to assimilate wastes. If that capacity is not exceeded, environmental quality remains intact. But large concentrations of people and economic activity place great stress on the environment. Thus, the most serious deterioration in air and water quality has occurred in large metropolitan areas such as New York, Chicago, and Los Angeles.

It has been shown that poverty, poor housing, and inadequate finance of local public services are by no means exclusively urban problems. Pollution is no exception. Some of the worst open dumps and littering of landscapes are in rural areas. Rural lakes and streams are frequently polluted. Even though urban areas have more than their share of air and water pollution, rural pollution is of concern to urban residents.

WHAT IS POLLUTION?

Although illustrations have been given, no limits have yet been placed on the concept of pollution. As pollution abatement has become an accepted goal, the tendency has been to include a variety of odious activities under the rubic of pollution. Air and water pollution are familiar concepts. Most people are used to describing as pollution the littering of the landscape with solid wastes. Some people would include excessive noise under the pollution heading. Others would include a range of issues that relate to the beauty of urban and rural areas, social tensions, and other problems.

Here, the term will be used narrowly. Economic activity requires the withdrawal of materials from the environment. Most materials are eventually returned to the environment in ways more or less harmful to use of the environment. The term "pollution" will be used to describe the impairment of the environment by the return or discharge of materials to it. The definition includes the usual categories of air, water, and solid-waste pollution. But it excludes the problem of noise and the broad range of aesthetic and social issues. The reason for limiting the subject is not that the included problems are necessarily more important than the excluded ones, but that waste-disposal problems have many elements in common, not shared by the excluded issues, and can be analyzed in certain ways. Air, water, and solid-waste pollution result from waste disposal, and usually involve materials that have potential economic use—which is not true of noise, for example.

MATERIALS BALANCE

Recently, for the first time, the pollution problem has been placed in the context of a raw-materials balance for the national economy. Since this basic concept leads immediately to some of the most fundamental insights regarding pollution, it is important to understand it thoroughly.

All of the goods produced by the economy represent the application of productive processes to materials withdrawn from the environment. When goods lose their usefulness, the materials of which they are made must either be recycled into the productive process or returned to the environment. The materials balance is an identity that equates an exhaustive list of material sources to an exhaustive list of material dispositions. Formally, it can be stated as follows:

> During any time interval, materials placed into the productive process equal those that have been withdrawn from the environment, plus imports, plus materials recycled from waste or scrap. Materials placed into the productive process also equal those disposed of by returns to the environment, plus exports, plus capital accumulation, plus recycled waste and scrap.

The materials balance bears the same relationship to the national materials accounts as the identity between sources and dispositions of income bears to the national income accounts. Unfortunately, only fragmentary data are available concerning components of the materials accounts. Capital accumulation is roughly 10 to 15 percent of all output, and is probably about the same proportion of materials output. Materials imports and exports are not available separately in detail, but the United States, being the world's most industrialized nation, has net materials imports of about 4 or 5 percent of domestic production. The least complete data of all are those

concerned with recycling. About all that can be said is that in most industries, recycling is negligible.[1]

Data for total production plus net imports of materials in the United
States are reasonably complete and available in considerable detail as the
result of research carried out by a team of experts at Resources for the Future. Table 13-1 shows a breakdown for 1965. Roughly, the United States
withdrew about 4 billion tons of materials from the environment in its
mines, farms, forests, and wildlife areas, or about 20 tons per capita. Of the
4 billion tons, about 2.5 billion is classified as active materials. The figure
excludes inactive materials such as sand and gravel, used mainly in construction. Of the 2.5 billion tons, about 10 percent is food. Thus, feeding
the population requires the withdrawal of more than a ton of materials per
capita from the environment. Another 10 percent of active materials withdrawn is forest products. About half is mineral fuels, mostly coal and oil.
The remainder is a variety of other minerals.

Ways to Affect Discharges

The first insight provided by the materials balance is that, with a given input of materials into production, the only way to change the amount of materials returned to the environment is to change capital accumulation, imports, exports, or the amounts of materials recycled. The first possibility is
unpromising as a way of reducing pollution. Capital accumulation must be
governed by the needs of the economy, and unneeded capital should not be
accumulated to avoid pollution. In fact that might be regarded as a form of
pollution. Changing imports and exports is no more promising. Materials
imports and exports should be determined by an efficient pattern of world
materials production, not by pollution problems. The United States will
find it increasingly advantageous to import materials from abroad; but
solving our pollution problems by exporting them is hardly a way to make
friends abroad.

Increased recycling of materials offers enormous scope for pollution
abatement. Among available production methods in most industries, there
is great variability in waste produced per unit of output. Some industrial

---

1. Like all identities, the materials balance holds because the terms are defined so
that it must. If complete data were available, all the terms in the identity would have
to be defined carefully so that sources would equal dispositions. For example, capital
accumulation would have to include materials accumulated in people as a result of
population growth. But some materials incorporated in the human body are withdrawn
directly from the environment through respiration.

Table 13-1   Weight of Basic Materials Production in the United States
plus Net Imports, 1965 (millions of tons)

Food		
Crops	130	
Livestock	102	
Other products	6	
Fisheries	3	Subtotal 241
Forest products		
Saw logs	56	
Pulpwood	120	
Other	42	Subtotal 218
Mineral fuels		1448
Other minerals		
Iron and ferroalloys	245	
Other metals	191	
Construction materials	1763	
Other nonmetals	149	Subtotal 2348
Total materials		4255
Total active materials		(2492)

Source: Adapted from Ayres and Kneese (Table 1, p. 630).

processes utilize materials much more completely than others, some produce more usable by-products than others, and some produce goods much easier to recycle than others. Although the recycling of *all* materials is neither possible nor desirable, increases in recycling and efficiency in materials use are the major ways to reduce the discharge of waste to the environment. And the extent of recycling is an economic variable.

Form of Discharges

The form in which wastes are discharged is also an economic variable. Much of the roughly two billion tons of active waste returned to the environment per year can be discharged in solid, liquid, or gaseous form. In fact, most liquid waste is really solid waste which has been either dissolved or conveniently floated away in water. For example, kitchen garbage appears as solid waste if it is put in the garbage can, and as liquid waste if it is ground in a disposal. But other substitutions are possible. Particles from burning coal appear as air pollution if discharged from smokestacks, as solid waste if filtered out by a dry process, and as liquid wastes if filtered out by a wet process. The form in which wastes are returned to the environment depends on the kinds of production processes used and on the extent to which treatment processes, known for almost all forms of waste, are applied. The effects of wastes on man and his environment depend crucially on the form in which they are discharged. Treated sewage is much less harmful to a stream than raw sewage. And sulfur is much more harmful if discharged into the air over a populous area than if removed from the fuel or the smokestack and disposed of in some other way.

Absorptive Capacity of the Environment

Finally, every aspect of the environment has a considerable capacity to absorb waste and regenerate itself. A stream can dilute any waste and it can degrade and render innocuous organic wastes. But if a stream is overloaded with organic wastes, it loses its capacity to degrade organic material. The extreme form of overloading is when so much organic material is discharged into the stream that it becomes *anaerobic* (i.e., loses all its dissolved oxygen). Its regenerative capacity is then virtually destroyed and may take decades to return. An anaerobic stream cannot support fish life, and it stinks from the hydrogen sulfide gas it produces.

Chemical and other processes also take place in the atmosphere, which permit it to absorb limited amounts of waste without damage. For example, much of the sulfur discharged into the atmosphere is eventually converted to sulfuric acid and other compounds, and is returned to the earth by precipitation. Particles discharged into the air eventually settle back onto the earth's surface. But much less is known about the chemical and other processes by which air restores its quality than about those by which water restores its quality. Although hydrocarbons from automobile exhausts seem certainly to be a major factor, it is still not known, after many years of intensive study, just how smog is produced in Los Angeles and other cities. This is unfortunate since, as put by Allen Kneese, the leading economist who specializes in environmental problems, "We are in somewhat the same position in regard to polluted air as the fish are to polluted water. We live in it" (Wolozin, p. 33).

The environment can also degrade limited amounts of solid waste. Organic materials eventually rot, and ferrous metals rust. But problems arise when the environment is overloaded. And modern technology produces materials, such as glass and plastics, which do not degrade.

Pollution of all forms is most serious in urban areas because the overloading and subsequent impairment of the environment are most serious there. The concentration of people and affluence produces much more waste than the environment can absorb.

Unfortunately, we do not know how large parts of the two billion tons of active materials are returned to the environment each year. But we can now identify and quantify most of the harmful wastes that are discharged as air, water, and solid waste pollution.

AMOUNTS AND EFFECTS OF POLLUTANTS

Air Pollution

Large amounts of the materials discharged into the atmosphere are innocuous, at least in the short run. Most important, carbon dioxide is released in large volumes by combustion, and there is some evidence that man has measurably increased the atmosphere's carbon dioxide content during the twentieth century. Some experts believe this may have long-run effects on weather and vegetation, but there is no reason to believe that current or likely near-future levels are harmful. Of the materials discharged into the atmosphere, five are likely to have adverse effects on man, vegetation, and materials: carbon monoxide, sulfur oxides, hydrocarbons, nitrogen oxides, and particles. Table 13-2 shows U.S. government estimates of the amounts[2] and sources of these pollutants for 1965.

Americans discharge nearly a ton per capita of harmful pollutants into the atmosphere per year. About half is carbon monoxide, 20 percent is sul-

Table 13-2   National Air Pollution Emissions, 1965 (millions of tons per year)

Source	Carbon Monoxide	Sulfur Oxides	Hydro-carbons	Nitrogen Oxides	Particles	Sub-totals
Automobiles	66	1	12	6	1	86
Industry	2	9	4	2	6	23
Electric power plants	1	12	1	3	3	20
Space heating	2	3	1	1	1	8
Refuse disposal	1	1	1	1	1	5
Subtotals	72	26	19	13	12 Total	142

Source: Public Health Service "The Sources of Air Pollution and Their Control," Publication No. 1548, 1966.

---

2. The difficulty of estimating amounts of pollutants is illustrated by the fact that the best private estimate (Ayres and Kneese, p. 641) places the figure for automotive discharge of carbon monoxide at 135 million tons, more than twice the government figure.

fur oxides, and 10 percent each are hydrocarbons, nitrogen oxides, and particles. Almost all the carbon monoxide comes from automobile exhaust. Diesel engines, used by trucks and buses, do not produce substantial amounts of carbon monoxide. Almost all the 26 million tons of sulfur oxides comes from the burning of coal and oil, mainly in electric power plants, industry, and homes. Hydrocarbons are produced by a variety of combustion and industrial processes, but most come from burning gasoline in automobile engines. Nitrogen oxides are produced by all combustion processes, but again the automobile is the main culprit. Particles are small bits of solid matter, such as dust and ash, and are discharged mainly by the burning of coal.

What are the effects of these pollutants on materials, vegetation, and people? A good deal is known about the effects of various pollutants on materials and vegetation; such effects can usually be discovered by laboratory experiments. But knowledge of the effects of air pollution on people is much less adequate. Most of the substances in Table 13-2 are deadly to humans in high concentrations. A good deal is known about concentrations likely to be fatal or to produce permanent damage to the human body. It is also known that average concentrations produced by the discharges in Table 13-2 are far below these levels. But few people breathe average air. Most people breathe urban air, where concentrations are well above the average. It has long been known that spells of adverse weather in such places as London and New York produce crises in which pollutants, especially sulfur oxides, raise mortality and morbidity rates. But recent studies (see Lave and Seskin) have produced strong evidence that chronic exposure to existing air pollution levels in metropolitan areas adversely affects health and life expectancy. The best estimate is that reduction of sulfur oxide and particle concentrations by 50 percent over metropolitan areas might increase average life expectancy by three or more years in the affected areas.

Carbon monoxide appears to have no adverse effects on vegetation or materials at existing concentrations, but is of course a deadly poison to humans. There is no evidence that average exposures of urban residents are enough to produce more than occasional annoyance. But disturbingly high levels have been measured under adverse conditions. On one New York street corner during the period measured, levels continuously exceed 15 ppm between 9 a.m. and 7 p.m. (Am. Chem. Soc.). Eight hours of exposure to 30 ppm is regarded as serious enough to interfere with oxygen transport by blood. It is not known whether actual exposure levels produce chronic damage to policemen or toll-booth operators who work for long periods under adverse conditions.

Sulfur oxides are known to damage plants, building facades, and other materials at concentrations sometimes observed. More important, as was said, evidence indicates that they affect health and longevity at existing concentrations.

Hydrocarbons are complex substances. They are known to be culprits in producing smog, which irritates and annoys people. But no long-term health effects have been shown to result from observed exposure levels. Smog can also cause damage to certain plants and materials.

Nitrogen oxides can cause acute damage and death to plants and humans at high concentrations. Actual exposure levels appear to be far less, although little is known about the possible chronic effects of long-term exposure at observed levels.

Particles reduce visibility and sunlight penetration in the atmosphere. But eventually they settle, and soil or damage clothing, paint, and other materials. Particles are also implicated in health damage during severe pollution episodes and from chronic exposure.

Water Pollution

Humans have no feasible alternative to breathing air. Therefore all of it should be fit to breathe. But they drink only a small part of the available water, so by no means all of it needs to be fit to drink. When the layman thinks of water shortages and water pollution, he thinks of water for drinking and other domestic purposes. But domestic use is only a small part of the water story.

The most important distinction regarding water use is between instream and withdrawal uses. Instream uses are those for which the water remains in its natural channel. The most important examples are commercial and sport fishing, pleasure boating, navigation, swimming, hydroelectric generation, and aesthetic use. The last example refers to the fact that many recreational activities, especially hiking, picnicking and camping, are enhanced by proximity to bodies of water.

Withdrawal uses are those for which water must be withdrawn from its natural channel. The major purposes of withdrawal are municipal use, industrial processing, cooling, and irrigation. Water withdrawn by municipalities for public water supply is for domestic, commercial, and public (e.g. fire protection) uses. Industrial processing refers to a variety of industrial uses, many of which involve the washing away of wastes. Cooling means the use of water to dissipate heat, by far the most important example being thermal electricity generation. Irrigation refers to the withdrawal of water for farm animals and crops.

Water quality is a complex notion with many dimensions, and quality requirements vary enormously among the many uses of water. For pleasure boating and aesthetic uses, the major quality requirements are the absence of odors, discoloration, and floating solids. Quality requirements vary among industrial processing uses, but for many the major requirement is the absence of salts that will corrode pipes. Noncorrosive properties are also important for cooling uses, and so is temperature. Different kinds of fish can live in water of different qualities, and a good deal is known about the effects of water quality on many kinds of fish.

The highest quality requirements are for municipal water, since it must be fit to drink. Stringent quality standards are set by public health authorities in the United States, although there are many unanswered questions about the effects of relaxing one or more standards. But the United States has largely avoided many water-borne diseases endemic in countries that apply less strict standards for drinking water.

Swimming water is something of an enigma. Authorities tend to set the same requirements for swimming as for drinking water. But swimmers need not drink the water they swim in, and many people swim in water they should not drink. Various afflictions can result from swimming in poor quality water, but little is known about the likely incidence at different quality levels. The chlorine used to purify water in swimming pools may cause some ear and other afflictions. With swimming, as with other water quality requirements, there is an important subjective element in that people simply find it distasteful to swim in dirty water.

The subjective element in water quality standards causes much confusion. It is often claimed that people do not like to drink reused water, regardless of its quality. To the extent that the reason is a misunderstanding about its real quality, presumably people's feelings can be changed by education. But to the extent that subjective feelings represent genuine tastes, they should not be ignored. It is not proper to ignore the fact that some people will pay $100 more for color TV than for black and white, although the feeling is certainly subjective. But with water use, the wish is often for someone else to pay the cost. For example, New York City has long urged the federal government to build it a plant to desalt sea water, so that New Yorkers can avoid reusing Hudson River water. No New York mayor has yet seen fit to ask the city's residents whether they are willing to pay for high-cost desalted water. If they are, outsiders should not object.

Not only do the various water uses have quality requirements, they also have various effects on water quality. In the course of using water, humans discharge an enormous variety of wastes into streams and estuaries. The most important and best documented category of waste discharge is organic material. Although organic materials are of many kinds, most share the important characteristic that they use the dissolved oxygen in the water as they are degraded. The dissolved-oxygen content determines the kinds of fish and other life that can survive in the water, and affects virtually every use of water. An anaerobic stream is useless for almost all the purposes that have been discussed. Thus, the most significant measure of water pollution is the rate at which organic discharges use oxygen, referred to as biochemical oxygen demand (BOD). The quality of the water in a stream is determined by the BOD of wastes discharged into it and by the rate at which the stream can replenish its oxygen from the atmosphere, called its reaeration rate.

Table 13-3 shows estimates of BOD wastes produced in the United States in 1963. The figures in the table are waste production before treatment. Most of the domestic waste and some of the industrial waste was treated before discharge, which means that much less than 29 billion pounds of BOD was discharged to streams and estuaries. The table excludes wastes discharged elsewhere than in bodies of water. Most important, the domestic waste figure refers only to the two thirds of the population (120 million people) who were served by sewer systems. Most of the rest were served by septic tanks. The wastes represented in the table are heavily concentrated in urban areas. Most septic tanks are in rural areas, and some industrial waste

Table 13-3   Estimated Volumes of Industrial and Domestic Wastes Before Treatment, 1963 (millions of pounds)

Source	BOD	
Two-digit manufacturing industries		
Food processing	4300	
Textiles	890	
Paper	5900	
Chemicals	9700	
Petroleum	500	
Primary metals	480	
Transportation equipment	120	
All other manufacturing	110	
Total manufacturing		22,000
Domestic		7,300
Overall total		29,300

Source: Adapted from Am. Chem. Soc. (Table 1, p. 97).

is disposed of in rural areas without discharge to water bodies. But urban wastes are usually collected and discharged to water bodies, possibly after treatment.

Table 13-3 shows that industry produces about three times as much organic waste as do households. And about 90 percent of industrial waste is produced by three two-digit industries: food processing, paper, and chemicals.

Suspended solids such as salts and silt are the second important type of pollutant. Salts are corrosive, and affect fish life in streams. Irrigation leaches salts from the soil, and irrigation return flow is the major source of harmful salts in western rivers. Silt is mainly runoff from farmland and construction projects. Since slowly moving water allows silt to settle, it fills up navigational channels and water supply reservoirs. It also changes the color of water, affecting its aesthetic use. Most important, silt reduces light penetration in water, impairing its ability to degrade organic materials.

Heat is another major polluting waste. A large thermal electricity plant may withdraw most of the water in a moderate-size stream and raise its temperature 10 or more degrees. Atomic plants tend to be larger than the largest conventional plants, and they operate at lower efficiency levels. They therefore discharge enormous amounts of heat. Water temperature affects fish life. In winter, fish that have disappeared from other parts of streams can be caught near the outfalls of electric plants. But in summer, heat discharge may raise water temperature above the survival level. Most important, high temperature speeds the process of organic degradation, thus reducing the stream's ability to cope with organic pollutants.

Nutrients, such as phosphates and nitrates, are an increasingly serious source of water pollution. Nutrients are the major constituents of agricultural fertilizer, are an important part of detergents, and are produced by degradation of organic material whether it takes place in a body of water or in a sewage treatment plant. Nutrients thus enter bodies of water by degradation of discharged organic material, by the effluent from municipal treatment plants, and by runoff from fertilized farmland. Nutrients fertilize water as they do land. In water, fertilization causes algae growth, which affects the appearance, taste, and odor of the water. Fertilization, or eutrophication, of water from treatment plants is most common in estuaries or downstream from large cities. But eutrophication from agricultural runoff is of course most common in rural areas.

A large variety of long-lived chemicals is discharged into water bodies by the chemical and other industries. But chemicals also enter water bodies inadvertantly. DDT and other powerful pesticides enter water from agricultural runoff. A particularly perplexing problem is acid mine drainage. When coal mines are abandoned, they typically fill with water. As ground water passes through them, sulfuric and other acids are produced. Some of the acid eventually seeps into streams. The effects of chemical discharges vary from chemical to chemical. Some are poisonous to fish, wildlife, and humans. Others create odors and discoloration.

Solid Waste Pollution

The U.S. economy generates about 10 pounds of solid wastes per capita per day, or about 365 million tons per year. This figure excludes about 7 million motor vehicles that are junked annually.

About one half of our solid wastes, or 5 pounds per capita per day, is collected by public and private municipal refuse collection agencies. Roughly 80 percent of the municipally collected refuse is combustible, consisting of paper and cardboard products, garbage, wood, leaves, and grass. The rest is mostly glass, metal, and plastic.

Industrial solid wastes are known to be more variable than domestic wastes, although no inventory is available. Much is either noncumbustible or releases toxic substances when burned. Most mining operations generate enormous volumes of solid wastes.

Until recently, the town dump was the destination of most solid waste. There it would smolder, decay, or simply accumulate. And there is still great variability in the care taken with solid wastes.

About 10 percent of municipal solid waste is burned in closed incinerators. They vary in the efficiency of incineration, disposal of ashes, and use of air pollution control devices. Almost all the remaining 90 percent is disposed of on land sites. These range from the conventional town dump to modern scientifically controlled sanitary landfill.

At least some parts of most junk autos are eventually recycled in industry. But there is a large, and probably growing, inventory awaiting recycling or cannibalization.

A substantial, but unknown, part of industrial waste is recycled in industrial processes. The rest is disposed of in the same variety of ways as used by municipal agencies, except that some industries have private facilities. Mining wastes are mostly disposed of by storage in open land.

The most prominent effect of solid-waste disposal is aesthetic. Open dumps, slag heaps, and auto graveyards are a terrible eyesore. So are the bottles, cans, and papers wantonly discarded on streets, parks, and beaches.

In addition, poor incineration produces air pollution, mainly discharging particles into the atomosphere. Finally, dumps are breeding grounds for insects and rodents, but almost nothing is known about the health or other effects they may have.

ALTERNATIVE PUBLIC POLICIES

It is easy to understand the fundamental reason for the pollution problem. Polluting discharges to the environment are an external diseconomy as the term was defined in Chapter 8. As has been shown, many kinds of production can use combinations of inputs that generate a range of kinds and amounts of waste.

In many cases, productive techniques that generate large amounts of harmful wastes are cheaper than others. Furthermore, wastes can be discharged to the environment in many forms, depending on ways they are treated. But all forms of treatment require valuable resources. Finally, the extent to which used products are recycled or discharged to the environment depends on the relative costs of new and used materials. As has also been seen, people value a high-quality environment for health, aesthetic, and recreational reasons.

Producers can keep costs low by large and relatively harmful discharges to the environment. The cost of the resulting deterioration in environmental quality is borne by those whose use of the environment is impaired, but those who make the decisions regarding harmful discharges fail to take account of the costs that discharges impose. Although a high-quality environment is valuable, its value does not get counted in market transactions. Thus, too few resources are devoted to the reduction of waste discharges by recycling and to the treatment of wastes.

Why do producers and users of the environment not make private agreements to optimize discharges? Sometimes they do. Many agreements are made regarding waste disposal on private land. But air and flowing water are fugitive resources. Their movements are hard to predict, and it is extremely difficult for a user of the environment to compute the damage done to him by each discharger to the environment. Transaction costs of private agreements are so great for many environmental problems that private agreements are rare. The history of public policy toward the environment has been a history of search for policies that regulate discharges to the environment without large transaction costs to the public and private sectors.

It has never been true that wastes could be discharged freely into the public domain. The common law has long placed restrictions on activities that create nuisances. State water-rights laws have always provided some protection for the rights of downstream users. And public health laws have long imposed stringent restrictions on discharges into water used for domestic water supply. These laws have been important, especially in protecting public health. But from the point of view of optimum resource allocation, they are a patchwork created at different times and for many purposes, and they are extremely resistant to change. In the postwar period, the need for special laws aimed squarely at pollution has become clear.

Public Collection and Disposal

The most straightforward public policy is public construction and operation of facilities to collect, treat, and dispose of wastes. Public facilities are the predominant method of handling household and commercial sewage and solid wastes. Scale economies make it desirable for a single organization to perform these services for an entire metropolitan area. Such an organization should either be publicly owned, or privately owned and publicly regulated. Both methods are employed in the United States, but the former predominates.

Regulation and Enforcement

Aside from the construction and operation of public facilities, the most common antipollution policy in the United States is regulation and enforcement. A public agency is empowered to identify sources of harmful pollution and to force the abatement of discharges. Laws usually include elaborate procedural safeguards, such as hearings, conferences, court appeals, and other adversary proceedings.

There is no doubt that regulatory procedures can eliminate some of the most blatant and harmful discharges of pollutants. They have been most successful when public health was involved. But judicial procedures are generally poor ways to improve resource allocation beyond the removal of major public-health menaces because they entail high transaction costs. The use of coercive police powers makes it necessary to employ elaborate procedural safeguards. The procedures are thus drawn out and cumbersome.

Federal water-pollution cases frequently take a decade or more to settle, and usually result in conventional and unimaginative remedies. Enforcement must proceed case by case, and there is a danger that political favoritism will be shown in the choice and prosecution of cases. Once a firm or local government has complied with the outcome of the proceeding, it lacks further incentive to abate discharges even if there are inexpensive ways of doing so.

Finally, regulatory procedures require that government officials play a major role in choosing and executing abatement schemes. It is generally desirable that decisions as to most economical means of abatement be left to managers of firms in question.

Subsidization

Public officials frequently propose subsidies to firms that abate waste discharges. Specific proposals include a credit against corporate taxes for the construction of waste treatment facilities, the exclusion from sales and property taxes of such construction costs, and direct payments to firms in proportion to their abatement of discharges.

Economists usually oppose these proposals. They are inefficient in that they bias the response of firms in the direction of conventional treatment facilities, whereas process changes, which are difficult to include in subsidy schemes, are often more effective and economical. Also, tax forgiveness schemes hide the extent of the public subsidy. Direct subsidies are difficult to administer because it is impossible to know what the discharge would have been in the absence of the subsidy. Most important, tax subsidy schemes provide no real incentive to abate polluting discharges. Expenditures on pollution abatement normally do not result in a saleable product. They are therefore inherently unprofitable, even though tax subsidies make them less unprofitable. Although tax subsidies may reduce dischargers' resistance to public pressure for abatement, they do not provide positive incentive to reduce discharges.

Finally, many economists oppose subsidy schemes on equity grounds. Public subsidies impose the cost of pollution abatement on the taxpaying public. Instead, it is felt, polluters directly, and those who use products produced by pollution-generating processes indirectly, should bear the cost of abatement. Thus, although subsidies have lower transaction costs than the regulation of polluters, they rate badly on both the efficiency and the equity criteria.

Charges

Various kinds of charges have been proposed to deter harmful waste discharges. The most prominent, which has been used for decades in Europe is the effluent fee. The easiest kind of effluent fee to administer is a charge to liquid-waste dischargers that depends on the amount and strength of the discharge. An example would be a charge per pound of organic waste discharged to bodies of water. The charge should of course depend on the damage done to potential users of the receiving body of water.

Charges avoid many of the transaction costs associated with regulatory policies. They force the discharger to take account of the damage his discharges do to the environment, yet leave him free to make the kind and amount of adjustment that is in his interest. As long as he discharges any waste, he has incentive to seek economical ways of abatement.

It is hard for economists to understand the objections to effluent fees. The most frequent is that fees sell the right to pollute. But the materials balance makes it clear that it is neither desirable nor possible to avoid all waste discharges to the environment. Public policy should aim at an optimum amount of recycling of wastes and discharges in amounts and forms that are in keeping with the regenerative powers of the environment. Effluent fees would induce large abatement of discharges where abatement was relatively cheap. In a sense, it sells the right to pollute, but it is wholly desirable. If effluent fees resulted in excessive overall pollution, it would merely prove they were too low.

A second objection is that effluent fees would make it necessary to meter waste discharges. That is correct, but it merely says that effluent fees would not avoid all transaction costs. All abatement schemes require metering, at least on a sample basis, but effluent fees do not require more metering than do other policies.

A generalization of the effluent fee is a materials disposal tax. Every material would be subject to a tax, levied at first sale for administrative convenience, equal to the damage done by the most damaging form of disposal of the material. People who disposed of the material would be refunded a portion of the tax depending on the form of disposal: the more innocuous the disposal, the larger the refund. If the material was recycled, it would not be taxed again. Recycled materials would thus be cheaper than materials taken from the environment, providing appropriate incentive for recycling. Much of the tax would be refunded to municipal sewage and refuse collection agencies. It would put the entire municipal sewage and refuse business on a user fee basis, thus eliminating the activities as a drain on hard-pressed municipal tax sources. To be workable, the tax would have to be collected by the federal government and refunded to private groups and local governments for appropriate waste disposal.

Consider an example. One of the most harmful constituents of coal and oil is sulfur. Coal and oil vary as to sulfur content. Sulfur can be removed from oil, at a cost, in the refining process. It can also be removed, with unknown efficiency and cost, from smokestack gases. A major component of the materials-disposal tax on coal and oil would depend on their sulfur content. Thermal electricity companies and other fuel users would have an incentive to use low-sulfur-content coal and oil. Refiners would have an incentive to remove sulfur in the refining process, and users of coal and oil would have an incentive to remove sulfur from stack gases. Much more sulfur would be recycled than at present, much less sulfur would poison the atmosphere, and much of the sulfur now being removed from the ground for commercial purposes would be left there for future generations.

CURRENT PUBLIC POLICY: A BRIEF SUMMARY

Before World War II, pollution was regarded as a local problem, outside the province of the federal government. In the postwar period, the unresponsiveness of rurally dominated state legislatures to this and other urban problems led to increased pressure on the federal government to step in. The federal government's first major response to the pressure was in the area of water pollution in the mid-1950s. Since then, federal programs have increased and expanded. Prodded by the federal government and, presumably, affected by redistricting ordered by the Supreme Court, state governments have begun to take an active part in pollution abatement.

Water Pollution

The first major federal legislation in pollution control was the Water Pollution Control Act of 1956. Its provisions have been strengthened and expanded several times. Under this law, the federal government provides technical and financial assistance to communities to construct waste treatment facilities. In 1966, this financial assistance became a casualty of the Vietnam war. Congressional appropriations were far less than authorizations, and state governments had to foot the bill for the federal share of construction costs. Since 1970, appropriations have been larger than ever before, and are now about $1 billion per year.

The 1956 law also provides for planning, research, and data collection and analysis by the federal government. Most important, it set the basic regulatory pattern that the federal government has expanded and used as a model for intervention in other pollution problems. Under the law, the federal government is empowered to intervene and require abatement of discharges that result in harmful interstate pollution. It has been used against private firms, municipalities, and even federal facilities.

An important provision of the 1965 amendment was to urge the states to set water-quality standards for streams under their jurisdiction. If the states did not set standards acceptable to the federal government, the federal government was empowered to do so. The purpose of the standards is to make their violation a basis for intervention, without the requirement that the government prove damages in each case. Many states now have their own agencies for enforcement of water-quality standards.

Air Pollution

Federal legislation regarding air pollution has followed closely the pattern set by water-pollution legislation. The basic legislation is the Clean Air Act of 1963. It was significantly amended in 1965 and 1967. Under the act, the federal government collects and analyzes data, undertakes research, and provides grants and technical assistance to state and local governments for air-pollution control. It also has limited enforcement powers, involving conferences and hearings, but relying heavily on voluntary cooperation and on cooperation with state and local governments when prosecution is required. Since 1967, the federal government can intervene directly when there is an imminent hazard to public health. This provision is intended to help prevent future episodes of serious air pollution. It is not, however, clear what the government can usefully do when an episode is imminent, or whether they can be predicted. As in the case of water pollution, states are encouraged to set air standards in air quality-control regions under the supervision of the federal government.

Following the example set by California, the 1965 amendment provides for national emission standards for motor vehicles. Standards were first effective for 1968 model-year vehicles and have been gradually tightened since then. Standards already enacted will require that 1975 cars discharge less than 10 percent as much pollutants as were discharged by new 1967 cars. Thus, although emission standards for other sources are set locally, those for vehicles are set nationally. The reason is of course that vehicles are manufactured for a national market. Not only would a variety of local standards be burdensome to the industry, autos from areas with low standards would sometimes be driven in areas with high standards.

Solid Waste Pollution

The federal government has a much less extensive program regarding solid waste pollution than it has regarding water and air pollution. The first federal legislation that established a national policy for solid wastes was the Solid Waste Disposal Act of 1965. It provided federally financed research, development, and demonstration projects to improve the state of technology in solid waste disposal. There is no federal enforcement program involving the use of police power in the area of solid waste disposal.

DIRECTIONS FOR PUBLIC POLICY

Something resembling a national antipollution policy has emerged since the mid-1950s. Its major elements are a large program of research and data collection and analysis; provision of federal funds to state and local governments for pollution control activities; and the use of the police power to regulate disposal, especially when public health is threatened.

Much effort has gone into the development and execution of this program. The results have been substantial, but not dramatic. Although there are relatively few examples in which great improvement has been recorded in environmental quality, deterioration has decelerated or halted in many areas.

But the federal program has been lacking in imagination and dramatic departures. Police power and adversary proceedings are traditional tools of government policy. Although they are useful in removing the most blatant damages from pollution, judicial proceedings are generally a poor way to achieve a major improvement in resource allocation. Markets are man-made institutions, and they can be structured in many different ways, each with its own implications for resource allocation. There have been basic and applied studies, and practical experience abroad, of ways to structure markets by the use of fees and taxes so as to provide strong incentives to abate harmful polluting activities. Much more is known about appropriate magnitudes and likely effects than with many other social programs that have been adopted during recent decades. The federal government has been urged to experiment with economic incentives by many expert panels and commissions. But the economic input in programs adopted has been negligible.

SUMMARY

Pollution is defined as the deterioration of the environment resulting from the return of materials to the environment. The materials balance is an exhaustive list of sources and dispositions of materials used in economic activity. The practical ways to abate polluting discharges are to recycle more materials and to alter the form of discharges by process changes and by treatment of wastes.

Pollutants are discharged to the environment as gases, liquids, or solid wastes. There is now considerable evidence that air pollution affects mortality and morbidity as well as property. Water pollution affects a large variety of water uses. Inadequate methods of solid waste disposal mar the landscape and impair many uses of land.

Economic theory shows that excessive pollution results unless discharges are controlled by public policy, because costs of pollution are not borne by those who discharge wastes. Public policies to abate pollution may entail public collection and disposal of wastes, regulation of discharges, subsidies for waste treatment, or fees for the discharge of wastes. In the United States, an array of public treatment and regulatory policies has been instituted since the 1950s. But governments have been unwilling to employ economic incentives for pollution abatement.

DISCUSSION QUESTIONS

1. What would be the relative effects on rich and poor people of more stringent controls on air pollution? On water pollution?
2. What would be the effects on profits of detergent manufacturers, on prices of detergents, and on wages and employment in detergent production, if there were a tax on detergents to finance the cost of the waste treatment that detergents impose on municipal treatment systems?
3. How would the following firms be affected by a fee levied on discharge of

sulfur to the atmosphere: regulated electric utility? manufacturer of atomic reactors? sulfur mining company?
4. Evaluate the argument that polluters should be jailed on criminal charges rather than fined effluent fees.

REFERENCES AND FURTHER READING

American Chemical Society, *Cleaning Our Environment: The Chemical Basis for Action*, 1969.

Robert Ayres and Allen Kneese, "Environmental Pollution," pages 626–684 in *Federal Programs for the Development of Human Resources*, Vol. 2, Subcommittee on Economic Progress of the Joint Economic Committee, 90th Congress, 1968.

Allen Kneese and Blair Bower, *Managing Water Quality: Economics, Technology, Institutions*, 1968.

Lester Lave and Eugene Seskin, "Air Pollution and Human Health," *Science*, Vol. 169 (August 21, 1970), 723–733.

Harold Wolozin (editor), *The Economics of Air Pollution*, 1966.

Chapter 14
The Public Sector and Urban-Area Prospects

A wag has said that an urban economist has the same professional advantages as a dermatologist: his patients never die and never get well. That urban areas have serious ills, or problems, can hardly be disputed. But if the urban ills of the 1970s are serious and difficult to treat, they are far from fatal. Despite the protestations of big city mayors, neither urban areas in general nor central cities in particular are near death. In fact, rapid urbanization during recent decades has produced substantial improvement in the economic and noneconomic conditions of both the poor and others who are increasingly concentrated in urban areas.

This hint of optimism is likely to be such a shock to newspaper readers of the 1970s that it requires elaboration. Urban areas in the United States were crowded with desperately poor immigrants in the nineteenth century and the early decades of the twentieth century. Although immigrants were often oppressed and treated with callous indifference, nobody thinks that the cities caused their poverty and misery. On the contrary, immigrants came here to escape much worse poverty and oppression in Europe. Although they lived badly enough in U.S. urban slums, their migration was successful in that they achieved better lives for themselves and their children. The urban economy generated higher and more rapidly rising standards of living than were possible in their native lands. And the U.S. political system enabled them to organize to demand their rights.

In the middle decades of the twentieth, there has been a similar migration of poor, and in the case of blacks, oppressed people to the cities. But this time they have come from the rural south, Appalachia, and midwestern farms. They too have improved their lives by migration. The urban economy has generated higher standards of living than did the miserable areas they left, and blacks have been more successful in demanding political rights in the cities than they were in the rural south. Evidence for this was presented in Chapters 9 and 10, but the conclusion really requires little documentation.

The foregoing is not to say that urban migration of blacks from the rural south and of whites from Appalachia has ended poverty and oppression. To claim that a black resident of a northern city has equal economic opportunity or equal protection under the law is an insult to common observation. The strong reaction of the young against such notions is related more to the naive foolishness they were taught by their elders than to the facts of the situation. But recognition of the existence of urban misery and oppression should not hide the fact that post-World War II urbanization of the poor has been part of a historic and successful struggle for economic and political improvements. As in earlier periods, urban areas have had a remarkable capacity to absorb large numbers of poor and to enable them to improve their economic and political condition.

Each large influx of poor people into urban areas has generated social conflict, stress, and trauma. Undoubtedly, the recent influx of blacks has been the most traumatic of all. Racial prejudices are stronger than ethnic prejudices. Equally important, whereas earlier migrants had been oppressed by foreign despots, recent black migrants have been oppressed by their fellow American citizens.

The point is that most of the ills of urban areas are the ills of the society at large transferred to urban areas. But far from having made the ills worse, urbanization has contributed more to their solution than was previously possible. There is little reason to doubt that urbanization will continue, and that its continuation holds the greatest promise for solution of social problems.

Many proposals for specific improvements in urban public policies have been discussed. In this chapter, the book concludes with some general remarks about the role of public policy in improving urban life. Like skin diseases, many urban ills are not subject to cure in an absolute sense. But there are many improvements that public policy can help to bring about.

No one can survey the urban scene without being impressed with the role of racism as a cause of urban ills. Poverty, poor housing, crime, drug abuse, the fiscal problems of central cities, and other problems are caused or worsened by discrimination against black people in every aspect of life. What can public policy do to improve the situation? That subject extends far beyond the bounds of this book. But it is worth noting that almost all the measures adopted by governments to reduce the amount or effects of racial discrimination have been federal rather than state or local measures.

They include almost all of the present income-redistribution and income-maintenance programs and the important civil rights laws. There is little reason to doubt that in the foreseeable future the federal government will continue to be the main source of public policies to improve race relations.

A second observation is that there are many public policies, mostly the responsibility of state and local governments, that either worsen urban ills or do little to cure them. Excessive reliance on property taxes heads the list. It is a crushing burden on the poorest people, whose housing is a matter of national concern. Poorly designed and badly administered sales taxes must also be included. So must misconceived zoning laws. Many political scientists believe that the cumbersome structure of local government impairs the efficiency of local public services. Most economists who have studied it would include the urban renewal program on the list of misdirected public policies. Major reforms are needed in almost all of these areas. Among the most important things that state and local governments can do to improve urban conditions is to abandon or reform policies that are making conditions worse.

The final observation is concerned with the role of professionals in state and local government. In the federal government, an elaborate system exists for the provision of scientific, technical, economic, and other expert advice. In the president's executive offices, the Office of Management and Budget, the Office of Science and Technology, the Council of Economic Advisers, and the Council on Environmental Quality exist to advise the White House in their areas of expertise. Likewise, each cabinet department has organizations to provide professional advice in the department's areas of responsibility. In addition, the federal government has·a system of committees and panels on which experts from universities, industry, and elsewhere provide advice in their areas of expertise.

Such expertise is almost completely lacking in state and local governments. In many states, the governor's staff contains no scientists, technologists, or economists. In most states, the only professionals in operating departments are those responsible for administering the department's programs. And professional advisers are almost unheard-of in governments of even large cities. The sole important exception is that large cities have departments of city planning. But city planners provide advice on a narrow range of issues, and the average level of professionalism is not comparable with that available to the federal government.

In part, the reason is a lag in the adjustment of governmental structure to present realities. In an earlier day, governments of even large states and cities spent little money and provided few services. But all that has changed since World War II. Governments in large states and cities now spend hundreds of millions of dollars per year and are responsible for complex and technical programs in health, education, transportation, welfare, and other areas. Some state and local governments have annual budgets in excess of a billion dollars, yet seem to be run like the county court house in a Faulkner novel.

In part, however, the reason is the lack of a tradition of high-quality research in areas of importance to state and local governments. A good example is project evaluation, or cost-benefit, studies by economists. There is a long history of high-quality studies by economists of the social benefits and costs of water-resource projects undertaken by the federal government. And there are traditions of high-quality studies in defense and other areas of federal government responsibility. But there have been few high-quality cost-benefit studies of urban transportation systems, local water-supply systems, local health-care systems, or local education systems. It will be difficult for state and local governments to undertake good cost-benefit studies until more examples of good studies are available in the scholarly literature, and until there are universities where appropriate techniques are taught.

REFERENCES AND FURTHER READING

Samuel B. Chase (editor), *Problems in Public Expenditure Analysis*, 1968.
Robert Dorfman (editor), *Measuring Benefits of Government Investments*, 1965.

Index

Accelerated depreciation, effect on housing markets of, 181–182

Advisory Commission on Intergovernmental Relations (ACIR), 224

Agglomeration economies, 16–17

Agriculture, effect on industry of, 27 effect on land rent of, 40

Agriculture, Department of, and poverty income level, 142

Aitcheson, J., 113

Albuquerque, N.M., 194

Amenity resources, 19

American Chemical Society, 250

Appalachian Regional Development Act of 1965, 153

Area Redevelopment Act of 1961, 153

Asset price, 38

Automobile, as dominant mode of urban travel, 195

costs of, 205

See also Transportation, highway; Transportation, urban

Ayres, Robert, 247n, 249n

Baltimore, 101, 210

population of, in 1840, 25

Baumol, William, 199

Beckmann, Martin J., and model of location, 108–112, 115–116

Beesley, Michael, 201n

Berry, Brian, 105

Boston, population of central city relative to SMSA, 7

Brown, J. A. C., 113

Buchanan, James, 230n

Building codes, 183–185

Butler County, Kansas, population density of, 8

California, air pollution standards of, 261

Capital/land ratios, as function of distance from center city, 57

Census Bureau, United States, and definition of substandard housing, 166

and restrictions on disclosure of data, 92

SMSA data of, 27

urbanized area, defined by, 10

urban place, defined by, 10

SCA, defined by, 11

SMSA, defined by, 10

Central business district (CBD), 79

Central city. *See* City; Governments, central city

Central city/suburban ring, and suburbanization, 91–93, 97, 99

Central place theory, 14–16

See also Location theory

Chicago, as part of SCA, 11

population in 1840, 25

SMSA governments in, 219

and urban transportation, 209

Christaller, W., 108

City, defined, 7, 11

legal boundaries of, 7, 92
postwar congestion in, 197
See also Urban areas; Urbanized
areas; Urban place
City planning, 267
Clean Air Act of 1963, 261
Cobb-Douglas production function,
68, 79, 82
Community Action Program, 152–153
Commuting, 28, 195–197
costs of, 85, 209–212
and housing location model, 60–65
modes of, 207–209
See also Transportation, urban
Comparative advantage, 17–19
and urban size, 103
See also Location
Congestion, 21
costs of, 201–205
Consumer behavior theory, and
welfare economics, 119, 120
Cost-benefit studies, 268
Council of Economic Advisers, 267
on poverty, 141–142, 150–152, 158
Council on Environmental Quality,
267

Davis, Kingsley, 2
Des Moines, Iowa, 7

Economic efficiency, consumption
model of, 121–124
production-consumption model of,
124–127
variable input/output model of,
127–129
Economic performance, criteria for
evaluating, 120–121
Economic Opportunity Act of 1964,
152–153
Economies of scale. *See* Scale
economies

Economy, growth of, and poverty,
149–150
Education, and spillovers, 234–235
Efficiency criterion, 120
Employment, and agglomeration
economies, 16
agricultural, 26, 31
data on, 92–93
distribution of, by sector, 25, 28
exponential density functions for, 97
growth of, 30
and poverty, 150
rural non-farm, 27
shifts in, 30–31, 34
suburbanization of, 72, 93–95
See also Manufacturing employment
Employment decentralization. *See*
Employment; Suburbanization
Environmental quality, 243–263
Equilibrium analysis, and urban
studies, 75–76
Equity criterion, 120
Excess burden, of different taxes,
134–135
External diseconomy, defined, 131
and government intervention, 132
External economies, 130–132

Federal Housing Administration
(FHA), and mortgage guaran-
tees, 183
Filtering, 176
Food-stamp programs, 141
Fraser, B., 107n

Garrison, William, 105
Gaussian distribution, 104
George, Henry, 40, 48–49, 239
Ginsburg, Alan, 227
Government programs, transfer
payments through, 150
See also Economic Opportunity Act

of 1964; Food stamp programs; Medicaid; Medicare; Poverty, public policies against
Governments, central city, expenditures of, 226–227
  financial problems of, 224–227, 229
  state grants to, 225
  taxes of, 226
  See also Governments, local; Governments, state and local
Governments, local, financial problems of, 241
  and income taxes, 239–241
  inefficiency of, 267
  and property taxes, 237–239
  in SMSAs, 224–227
  tax systems of, 237–241
  See also Governments, central city; Governments, state and local
Governments, state and local, expenditures of, 222–224
  financial problems of, 227–230
  financing of, 218–241
  fiscal systems of, 219–220
  functions of, 218–220
  and public services, 227–228
  revenue sources of, 221–222
  and revenue sharing, 221, 236–237
  structure of, 267–268
  tax systems of, 228–229
  trends in, 210
  See also Governments, central city; Governments, local; Governments, suburban
Governments, suburban, expenditures of, 226
  state grants to, 225
  taxes of, 226
  See also Governments, local; Governments, state and local
"Gravity" model of transportation demand, 198–199
Grebler, Leo, 164

Hamilton, Bruce, 232n
Harberger, Arnold, 135
Headstart program, 152
Heller, Walter, 236
Herriot, Roger, 153–155
Housing, and construction industry, 59, 163–165
  costs of ownership and rental, 164–165
  and "filtering," 176–178
  and racial discrimination, 170–173
  supply and demand, 79, 81, 163–165, 168–176
  See also Substandard housing; Slums; Urban housing
Housing location, effects of income differences on, 71–85
  model of, 60–65
  theory of, 59
Houston, Texas, 210

Immigration, 265
Income, of nonwhites, 146
  percent distribution of families by, 147
Income distribution, and public policy, 120
  through tax transfers, 129–155
  See also Income redistribution
Income maintenance, defined, 150
  programs in 1969, 151
  and public policy, 150–158
Income redistribution, 236–237
Income taxes, and federal provision for owner-occupied housing, 180–181
  and local governments, 239–241
  in Maryland, 240–241
Indiana, 11
Industrial classification. *See* Standard industrial classification code

Industrialization, history of, 25–26
  and urbanization, 24
Industrial location, 73
  model of, 54–58
Industry, location of, 30, 73
  suburbanization of, 94–95
  urbanization of, 31–35
  See also Employment; Manufactur-
    ing employment; Manufactur-
    ing industries; Service industries

Jacobs, Jane, 17
Job Corps, 152

Kain, John, 93, 168
Keiper, Joseph, 49
Kneese, Allen, 247–248, 249n

Land, costs of, and urban growth, 14
  as a factor in production, 45
  markets, suburban, 90–91
  use, 37
  See also Land rent; Land values
Land rent, defined, 37–38
  ethical aspects of, 48
  and land values, 38
Land rent theory, 39–48
  Ricardian theory (classical), 40–43
  marginal productivity theory (neo-
    classical), 43–46
Land rent function, 41–42
  in urban model, 82
Land values, defined, 38–39
  effect of scale economies on, 14
  See also Land rent
Lave, Lester, 250
Lewis, Oscar, 139n
Lisco, Thomas, 209
Location, of suburban employment, 72
  two-industry model of, 66–68

See also Lösch, August; Central
    place theory; Housing location;
    Industrial location; Location
    theory; Urban areas
Location theory, economic, and
    urbanization, 12
  See also Central place theory
Los Angeles, 25, 194
  structure of, 19
  transportation in, 209
Lösch, August, 108, 112, 115
  and Beckmann model, 110
  and location theory, 15

Madden, Carl, 106
Malthusian population theory, and
    Ricardo/George theory, 48
  and Ricardo theory, 41
Manpower Development and Training
    Program, 153
Manufacturing employment, decrease
    in depression, 26
  and SIC code, 32
  in SMSAs, 30, 32–33
  and urbanization, 27, 34
Manufacturing industries, employment
    in SMSAs, 30, 32–33
  location of, 73–74
  urbanization of, 30, 33–35
  See also Industry; Manufacturing
    employment
Margolis, Julius, 230n, 232n
Maryland, and local income taxes,
    240–241
Mass transit, 209–212
  See also Public transit
Materials balance, defined, 245–246
  and pollution, 245–249
Meadows, Paul, 2
Medicaid, and definition of income
    level, 141

Medicare, and definition of income
    level, 141
effect of eligibility for, 157
Megalopolis, 11
Meyer, John, 205, 207, 208n
Miller, Herman, 153–155
Mills, Edwin S., 78n, 97n, 100n
Milwaukee, Wisconsin, 101
Minneapolis, Minnesota, 210
Mizruchi, Ephraim, 2
Monopoly, and resource misallocation, 130
Monopsony, and resource misallocation, 130
Mortgage guarantees, effect on suburbanization of, 183
Muth, Richard, 71n, 78n, 164, 167n, 169n, 173
Myrdal, Gunnar, 146

National Bureau of Economic Research (NBER), on rise in housing prices, 164
Negative income tax, 158–160, 236–237
Neighborhood effect, 169, 173–174
Netzer, Dick, 206
New Jersey, northeastern, as part of SCA, 11
New Orleans, population of in 1840, 25
New York City, air pollution in, 250
    as part of SCA, 11
    population of, 8, 25
    rent control in, 185
    and SMSA governments, 219
    transportation in, 209
Niedercorn, John, 93

Office of Management and Budget, 267
Office of Science and Technology, 267

Pareto efficiency criterion, 120
Pareto distribution, 108, 113–116
    and distribution of urban areas by size, 104–105
    as test of rank-size rule, 107
Pechman, Joseph A., 236
Perloff, Harvey, 19
Philadelphia, 101, 194
    expenditures of, 227
    population in 1790, 25
    SMSA governments of, 219
    transportation in, 209
Pittsburgh, 210
    and SMSA governments, 219
Pollution, abatement of, 246–247
    defined, 244–245
    and materials balance, 245–249
    and recycling, 246–247
    types of, 247–249
    as urban problem, 243–263
    and urban size, 114–115
Pollution, air, and auto emission standards, 261–262
    effects of, 249–251
    in New York, 250
    and public policy, 261–262
    types of, 250–251
Pollution, solid waste, 255–256, 262
Pollution, water, and biodegradation, 253–254
    cause of, 253–255
    effects of, 251–255
    and public policy, 260–261
    and urban health, 252
Pollution and public policy, 256–263
    and collection and disposal, 257
    and current practices, 260–262
    and effluent charges, 259–260
    evaluation of, 262–263
    regulation of, 257–258
    and subsidies, 258
Population, exponential density functions for, 97

growth of, 24
in Ricardo's theory, 41
rural, 24, 26
urban, 24–25, 28
urbanization of, 35
suburbanization of, 93–95
See also Urbanization; Suburbanization
Population decentralization. *See* Suburbanization
Population density, defined, 8
effect of scale economies on, 14
in model of urban structure, 84, 88
Poverty, 139–160
the culture of, 140
and housing, 167, 177
incidence of, 142–149
measures of, 140–142
public policies against, 141–142,
149–155, 157–158
and transportation, 213–215
Price theory and land rent, 37
Production theory and land rent
theory, 37
Proportionate effect, law of, 112–114
Public housing, 186
See also Housing; Urban housing
Public sector, scale economies in, 16
Public services, demand for, 228
economic analysis of, 230–237
and income redistribution, 236–237
and legal boundaries, 8
price increases in, 227–228
and scale economies, 230–232
and spillovers, 234–236
Public transit, demand for, 193
postwar shift from, 195–197
pricing of, 206–207
urban, 209–212
See also Mass transit; Transportation, urban
Public Works and Economic Development Act, 153

Quandt, Richard, 198n, 201n

Racial discrimination, and civil rights
legislation, 157
and housing, 59, 170–172
models of, 169–173
and poverty, 145–149
public policies against, 266–267
and slums, 169–173
and urban problems, 266–267
and zoning, 183
Rank-size rule, in Beckmann model,
111
defined, 105–108
Rashevsky, N., 108
Redistribution of assets, and "single
tax," 50
Redistribution of land, and "single
tax," 49
Reid, Margaret, 164
Rent control, 185
Rent-distance functions, flattening of,
and slums, 169, 175–176
See also Land rent function
Rent functions, 65
Rent-offer function, defined, 66
of households, 69–72, 94
of industries, 94
in model of urban structure, 86–88
Rent supplements, 186
Rent theory, 37–51
See also Land rent, theory of
Residential sector of urban area, and
model of urban structure, 78
Resource misallocation, 130–135
Resources, natural, and regional com-
parative advantage, 17
Revenue sharing, 236–237
See also Governments, state and
local
Ricardo, David, 46, 51
and theory of land rent, 37, 40–43, 48

Ricardo/von Thünen model, and
    theory of land rent, 42
Rochester, N.Y., 101
Rothenberg, Jerome, 173n, 179, 186n,
    230n, 232n
Rothman, Jack, 168
Rural-urban migration, and law of
    proportionate effect, 114
    See also Urbanization

San Bernardino, California, 10
Scale economies, and agglomeration
    economies, 16
    defined, 13
    and local public services, 230–232
    in public sector, 16
    in service industries, 73
    and urbanization, 13–14
Scitovsky, Tibor, 118
Services, public. *See* Public services
Service industries, scale economies of,
    73
    urban incidence of, 15
    urbanization of, 30–31
Seskin, Eugene, 250
Shopping center, as suburban sub-
    center, 74
Simon, Herbert, 108, 112–116
"Single tax," 49–50
    See also George, Henry
Slums, consequences of, 178–179
    postwar improvement of, 177–178
    rural, 165
    and urban renewal, 186–190
    See also Housing; Substandard
        housing; Urban housing
Slums, causes of, 167–186
    flattening of rent-distance functions
        as, 175–176
    malfunctioning housing market as,
        169
    neighborhood effect as, 173–174

poor maintenance as, 177
poverty as, 168–169, 177
racial discrimination as, 169–173
Social welfare, defined by utilitarian
    economists, 120
Solid Waste Disposal Act of 1965, 262
Special districts, defined, 219
Spillovers, 234–236
Standard consolidated area (SCA), de-
    fined, 11
    reasons for defining, 28
Standard Industrial Classification code
    (SIC), 31–32
Standard metropolitan statistical area
    (SMSA), defined, 10–11
    governments of, 219
    incomes of residents of, 225–226
    postwar suburbanization in, 93–99
    and United States population, 10–11
    and work trip data, 196–197
    See also Urban areas
Stigler, George, 37n
Substandard housing, defined, 166
    incidence of, 166–167
    See also Housing; Slums; Urban
        housing
Suburbanization, 90–102
    before World War II, 99–101
    expressed by exponential density
        functions, 95–99
    emotional attitudes toward, 90–91
    of employment, postwar, 93–95
    measures of, 91–93
    and mortgage guarantees, 183
    of population, postwar, 93–95
    postwar, 74, 95, 97–98
    and urban transportation, 213
Subways, 204–205, 208
Sussex County, New Jersey, popula-
    tion density of, 8

Taxes, and equity criteria, 135

excess burden of, 134–135
federal income, 155
income effects of, 133–135
on income from land, 49–51
property, 237–239, 267
real estate, 59, 179–180
and resource misallocation, 133–135
sales, 22, 267
state and local, 154–155, 228–229
substitution effects of, 133–135
See also Governments, central city;
    Governments, local; Govern-
    ments, state and local; Govern-
    ments, suburban
Tax-transfer system, 153–155
Technical progress and urbanization,
    34, 103
Transfer payments, through govern-
    ment programs, 150–155
Transportation, highway, costs of,
    205–206
and suburbanization of manufactur-
    ing, 74
Transportation, urban, 190–216
by automobile, 201–205
and commuting, 195–197
and comparative advantage, 18–19
costs of, 14, 200–209
demand for, 193, 198–212
evaluation of, 198–201, 215–216
of freight, 192
and mass transit, 209–212
modes of, 193–195
and poverty, 214–215
pricing of, 198–212
and public policy, 193, 204
and spillovers, 234
and subsidies, 206–207
and suburbanization, 213
subways, 204–205
supply of, 192–193
time costs of, 200–201
trends in, 194–197

and urban structure, 212–213
and user fees, 205
See also Mass transit; Public transit

Urban areas, defined, 7–12
location of activities in, by sector, 74
problems of, in larger society, 266
prospects for, 268
public policies toward, 266–267
racial composition of, 148
single-industry model for, 54–58
sizes of, 15, 20, 103–116
and specialized services, 15
See also Location; Urbanization;
    Urbanized areas; Urban place;
    Urban renewal; Urban struc-
    ture
Urban economics, defined, 1–2
historical data on, 25
sources of United States data for, 10
Urban growth, limits to, 14
Urban housing, 162–190
and building codes, 183–185
and federal income tax, 180–181
public policies toward, 179–190
and real estate taxes, 59, 179–180
and slums, 165–167, 176–178
and urban renewal, 186–190
and zoning, 182–183
See also Housing; Substandard
    housing; Slums
Urbanization, 2
of blacks, 149, 177–178, 265–266
deceleration of, 25, 28
factors in, 12–13
and industrialization, 24
of poor, 265–266
and scale economies, 13
and social ills, 266
See also Rural-urban migration
Urbanized areas, 10–11
See also Urban areas

Urban place, 10–11, 23
  and SMSAs, 28
  See also Urban areas
Urban renewal, 186–190, 267
Urban structure, model of, 78–89
  effect of transportation system on,
    212–213
Urban subcenters, postwar growth of,
  74

Valentine, Charles, 139n
Veteran's Administration, and educa-
    tional benefits, 156
  and mortgage guarantees, 183
Volunteers in Service to America
    (VISTA), 152
von Thünen, Johann, 41

Wagner, Richard, 230
Walters, Alan, 201
Washington, D.C., 210
Water Pollution Control Act of 1956,
    260

Welfare in urban areas, 145
Welfare economics, and consumer
    behavior, 119–120
  defined, 118
  value judgments in, 119–120
White House, advisory system of, 267
Wichita, Kansas, 8
Wicksell, Knut, 46–48
Wicksteed, Philip, theory of land rent,
    40, 46–48
Wicksteed-Wicksell theorem, 46–48,
    56, 76, 80
Wolozin, Harold, 248
Work-study program, 152
Work-training program, 152
Work trips, 195–197

Zipf, George, 105–108
Zoning, effect of, on housing markets,
    182–183
  influence of, on suburban population
    density, 91
  and racial integration, 183